OUTSIDE LITERARY STUDIES

OUTSIDE LITERARY STUDIES

Black Criticism and the University

Andy Hines

The University of Chicago Press   Chicago and London

The University of Chicago Press, Chicago 60637
The University of Chicago Press, Ltd., London
© 2022 by The University of Chicago
Published 2022
Printed in the United States of America

31 30 29 28 27 26 25 24 23 22   1 2 3 4 5

ISBN-13: 978-0-226-81856-6 (cloth)
ISBN-13: 978-0-226-81858-0 (paper)
ISBN-13: 978-0-226-81857-3 (e-book)
DOI: https://doi.org/10.7208/chicago/9780226818573.001.0001

Library of Congress Cataloging-in-Publication Data

Names: Hines, Andy, author.
Title: Outside literary studies : Black criticism and the university / Andy Hines.
Description: Chicago : University of Chicago Press, 2022. | Includes
bibliographical references and index.
Identifiers: LCCN 2021046119 | ISBN 9780226818566 (cloth) | ISBN
9780226818580 (paperback) | ISBN 9780226818573 (ebook)
Subjects: LCSH: African American critics. | American literature—
African American authors—20th century—History and criticism. | New
Criticism—United States. | Criticism—Political aspects—United States—
History—20th century. | African Americans—Study and teaching—
United States—History—20th century.
Classification: LCC PS78.H56 2022 | DDC 801/.9508996073—dc23
LC record available at https://lccn.loc.gov/2021046119

For Keegan

Contents

Introduction

In the early 1950s in New York, the faculty of instruction of the arts at the Jefferson School of Social Science organized their critical and pedagogical activities around the idea that "the arts have always been partisan." They argued that universities clipped the political capacity of literature via a "Southern clique . . . who represent the approach to literature . . . saturated with racialisms, apologetics for slavery, deliberate distortions of American history, explanations of the most bestial violence as being 'human nature.'"[1] This clique privileged literary form as a means to absorb "racialisms," and the Jefferson School faculty listed among its members the progenitors of the American New Criticism, including Allen Tate, John Crowe Ransom, and Robert Penn Warren. To challenge this critical practice with "roots in the reactionary political and economic forces of our time," the assembled Jefferson School faculty members pledged to pursue a criticism that "place[s] works of art directly in the context of the political, social, and philosophical struggles which they reflect in clear or distorted fashion."[2] Against those they opposed, the faculty refused to present their critical work as objective and separate from the world in which it emerged. They also invoked a different genealogy for their critical formation. The always partisan arts echoed with W. E. B. Du Bois's 1926 claim that "all Art is propaganda."[3] For Du Bois, the propaganda character of art makes possible "a vision of what the world could be if it were really a beautiful world."[4] With this intertext, criticism for the Jefferson School faculty offered a crucial tool in a struggle against the political economy of American liberal capitalism: a means for conditionally enacting and imagining a future "beautiful world" in the present.

From its opening in 1944 to its closure in 1956, the arts and culture faculty at the Jefferson School included many important Black writers on the left (Lorraine Hansberry, Shirley Graham, Claudia Jones, Alice Childress, Yvonne Gregory, Augusta Strong, and Lloyd Brown), artists (Elizabeth Catlett and Charles White), and political leaders (Alphaeus Hunton, Ben Davis, Claudia Jones, and W. E. B. Du Bois). They were assembled and supported by Doxey A. Wilkerson, an expert in Black education who left Howard University to join the Communist Party, and who served as the Jefferson School's director of curriculum. Black radicals on this faculty, with the support of labor activists, challenged the terms of academic literary criticism that buoyed the racialized political economy of the United States.

The faculty of the Jefferson School was not the only entity to suggest that New Critical formalism was a reflection and instrument of the political, economic, and ideological expansion of the United States in the years after World War II. Attacks on New Critical assumptions abounded in Black literary circles on the left, and were lobbed publicly and privately by writers as well known as Langston Hughes, Lorraine Hansberry, and Ann Petry, and those lesser known, like Melvin B. Tolson, Arna Bontemps, and Doxey A. Wilkerson. These writers shared affiliations—explicit or tangential—to the communist-led left in the mid-twentieth century. During the era of red-baiting, they faced the constant threat of condemnation from most public institutions for their political views, not to mention the scrutiny of the surveillance and investigatory arms of the federal government.[5] While their particular approaches varied to the New Criticism's role in the imperial expansion of US-backed capitalism abroad and continued racial oppression at home, one thing is clear from a careful archival study: they agreed that the New Criticism and the university system were part of the racialized red-baiting that suppressed Black people who challenged the inequities of US liberal capitalism.

Midcentury Black writers on the left envisioned literary-critical methods and institutions that were opposed to the solidifying interpretive practices of the university and the state. Black left practices for reading, writing, and institution making foregrounded literature as a crucial instrument in articulating the multifaceted dimensions of anti-Black racism and a vision of a future world that could sustain Black life and Black culture. For these writers, literature engages, reveals, and imaginatively portrays the material reality of the Black past, the present struggle, and the future to build. This was not the definition of literature espoused by the era's white critics, nor was this mode of reading and writing valued in university classrooms. The dominant literary criticism of the era—the New Criticism—was defined by the objectification and isolation of the literary object from the circumstances of its creation. Many literary studies scholars still describe this critical movement as an effort to eliminate history or contemporaneous political concerns from its methodological emphasis on the text above all else. The effect of the New Criticism's enclosure of literature and its ways of reading and evaluating literature was a large-scale exclusion of Black writing—or, as the Jefferson School cultural faculty put it, an absorption of "racialisms" and an overrepresentation of white norms in their definition of human nature.[6] The New Critics saw Black writing as too invested in the particulars of the present for it to be able to enter into the timeless, universal tradition they espoused. This midcentury clash between Black criticism and the New Criticism has largely been passed over in scholarly investigations, despite the essential contributions made by Black writers regarding literature's social and political function, not to mention their political economic analysis of how the university and the state work to value whiteness at the expense of Black people. The latter, which offered a critical view of the articulation of the university and the state, would anticipate a similar realization from student movements in the mid- to late 1960s; according to Melinda Cooper, those students "perfectly understood the connections between domestic race relations and anticommunism abroad and . . . refused the cozy relationship between the public research university and American imperialism."[7]

In this book I show how midcentury Black left critical practice was—and has remained—on the outside of literary studies as it has come to be established, historicized, and practiced in the American university. This outside position results from the methodological particularities of white critical practice and how the New Critics linked US anticommunist and anti-Black principles to the institutions of criticism. Put differently, the Black writers, critics, and thinkers I discuss here—Hughes, Hansberry, Tolson, Petry, Wilkerson and others—identify that what limits an understanding of Black literature are forces coalescing to devalue, attack, and suppress Black people and Black life.

The mode of study they propose requires an analysis of how racism works through the interpretation of literature and how the interpretation of literature gains authority and support through racist institutions. From this lens, it is difficult to separate New Criticism from the political plea of its founders for a return to an agrarian South against communism; to separate universities from a federal government that upheld segregation and a liberal capitalism rooted in slavery; and to separate the federal government from its policing agencies, which employ retooled versions of academic criticism to antagonize and dismantle Black freedom movements, as well as decolonial movements across the globe. As the varying scale and degree of the entanglements of criticism, the university, and the state indicate, Black left struggles against literary interpretation are not esoteric exercises conducted primarily for an integrated middle-class audience. Instead, they can be seen as part of what Jacquelyn Dowd Hall has termed the long civil rights movement that challenged racism, capitalism, and American militarism from the 1930s to the 1970s.[8] In the 1940s, Black literary critical activity foregrounded a struggle for an antiracist, anticapitalist, anticolonial world beyond literary studies along the intersecting lines of race, class, gender, ability, and even ecology. This is an often-submerged thread of Black thought that is neither nationalist nor integrationist, but deeply committed to an analysis of race and class.

This book supplies an account of a crucial precursor to the late 1960s demand for Black studies, and it contributes to discussions regarding the interdisciplinary praxis of Black studies scholarship. Specifically, I build on discussions about how the practice and imagination of Black social life generates a future world inside of the present, despite the fact that the present regime of white supremacy has attempted to render the existence or conception of such a world as impossible. Katherine McKittrick argues that "Black matters are spatial matters," an insight that informs the spatial metaphor of my title, *Outside Literary Studies*. McKittrick shows that Black people create space and place in spite of the fact that Black geographic activity is understood as "ungeographic and/or philosophically undeveloped."[9] Her work makes possible a comprehension of Black space on its own terms, and a recognition of how anti-Black discourse seeks to interrupt and delegitimize that understanding. Importantly, McKittrick makes clear that Black imaginings have material ramifications and instantiations. The production of

Black space is an imaginative activity, in addition to a practiced one; this is praxis, the directed creation of a Black world bringing together theory and practice. In this book, McKittrick's Black geographies draw our attention to a "terrain of struggle" unfolding through vectors of race, gender, and political economy.[10] When creating metaphorical and material space in territory deemed ungeographic, Black critical acts in this period necessarily invoke the need to dismantle institutionalized cultural spaces governed by whiteness and anticommunism. They thus challenge in their very practice and imaginings the forces that place Black criticism and Black life on the outside—such as Cleanth Brooks's insistence that "the principles of criticism define the *area* relevant to literary criticism"—and create another material, practiced world through liberatory acts in the zone of irrelevance.[11]

These limitations placed on the area of literary criticism occurred during the wider context of Jim Crow segregation and communist purges. In the 1940s and '50s, Black writers on the left were blocked from entering predominantly white colleges and universities, and their work was actively barred from classrooms and other publishing venues. Black writers with communist connections were even pushed out of institutions nominally devoted to Black people and Black culture. Gwendolyn Bennett, for instance, began her work teaching Black culture in people's schools after she had been forced out of her position as the director of the WPA-funded Harlem Community Art Center because of communist affiliations. The area or field of literary study—spatial metaphors commonly used to discuss scholarly activity—has an emplaced realization in universities, publishing, and classrooms. Put differently, literary studies must be maintained and fortified; they require labor and resources, and entail an inclusion of the few predicated on the exclusion of the many. As McKittrick has elaborated, academic practices and disciplinary thinking, including "the canon, the lists, the dictionaries, the key thinkers, the keywords," contribute to this regulation; or, simply put, "Discipline is empire."[12] In drawing attention to the spatial practice of literary study, I articulate the scholarly discipline of the university, the state, and the wider political economic order that establishes and reproduces forms of spatial segregation. This framing allows me to identify how these activities generate and support anti-Black violence both within the university and in the wider confines of the imperial nation-state.

Black critics recognized that the inside/outside structure was precisely that which the New Criticism and other liberal midcentury institutions endorsed for managing difference. This postwar template for the state's rhetorical engagement with racism while maintaining racist practice has been referred to by Jodi Melamed and others as "racial liberalism."[13] Black writers on the left argued that a path toward an antiracist future did not merely mean gaining access to the inside. It meant abolishing the terms of this division altogether by generating a different way of thinking about literature and culture. Put differently, midcentury Black left writers and critics develop another world against the one envisioned and maintained by white supremacy.

Primarily, this book offers a cultural history and analysis of the "Black matters" of midcentury Black critics, criticism, and institutions that have not been a mainline object of study in English and literature departments in American universities. This cultural history relies on extensive archival research, and ranges in scope from the imagined importance of an unpublished essay to the operations of a curriculum for the study of Black literature and culture at the Jefferson School. I also offer a multifaceted critique of the New Criticism in terms of the connections it establishes between the federal government and the university system to maintain an anti-Black and anticommunist US political economy. Because the New Criticism has often been seen as foundational for today's literary critical institutions and for the university, this has important implications for the current organization and practice of that academic discipline and higher education more widely. The criticism of Black left writers makes clear that academic critics must do more than reform definitions and methods alone to slake the discipline's historical anti-Blackness. Institutions, labor, and politics—or "the group competition over scarce resources," in Lester Spence's definition—stand as additional sites for reconfiguring the work and affiliations of literary studies.[14]

Throughout this book, I situate the work of midcentury Black left critics as part of what Cedric Robinson terms the Black radical tradition. Robinson suggests that the Black radical tradition can be characterized as "the continuing development of a collective consciousness informed by the historical struggles for liberation and motivated by the shared sense of obligation to preserve the collective being."[15] These struggles are material and epistemological. They move along the dialectical matrix of "capitalist slavery and imperialism," a dialectic the cultural faculty at the Jefferson School engage when situating their struggle against the "reactionary political and economic forces of our time."[16] Melvin B. Tolson explored a similar critique in his invocation of the sociological work of his friend and colleague Oliver Cromwell Cox in his *Libretto for the Republic of Liberia*. Black left critics sought a literary criticism that attends to how the New Criticism and the United States upheld a racialized division of labor, and which situates Black critical struggle as part of an international effort to dismantle colonialism. Beyond the fact that Du Bois stands as one of Robinson's three exemplary Black radicals, his term is relevant here because this book chronicles the development of a Black criticism that pushes toward an "actual discourse of revolutionary masses, the impulse to make history in their own terms."[17] I show how Black left writers generate this discourse and situate it within the longer history of the Black radical tradition in the first part of this introduction. Titled "Outside," this section explores how and where Black writers were making knowledge beyond the realm of literary studies as it had been imagined.

The second part of this introduction, "Inside," follows because I understand New Critical activity as a reactionary and counterrevolutionary response to the political and cultural activities of Black writers. Here I define racial liberalism, a particular form of nominal antiracism that the New Critics work to uphold and establish in the 1940s and 1950s. Attending to the construction of racial liberal discourse requires situating the development of academic literary criticism with respect to critical histories of the postwar racial state. This section chronicles how contextualizing the disciplinary work of literary studies in political and economic terms falls in line with recent accounts of the discipline and the university by scholars including Jodi Melamed, Roderick Ferguson, Stefano Harney, and Fred Moten. While the first part of the introduction contextualizes my project's contribution to Black studies and Black histories of the left, the second part outlines what I offer to contemporary critical investigations of the university, and how the project speaks to what Laura Heffernan has termed the "new disciplinary history" in literary studies. I explain why recounting a Black critique of the New Criticism remains necessary, and urge caution to those in literary studies who may see the mere incorporation of Black left critiques as a solution for moving through existing impasses within the discipline and the university. The introduction closes with a summary of the book's structure and a recapitulation of its interventions.

Broadly, this book suggests that the struggle over culture and the methods for interpreting it extend well beyond the university, especially in Black left movements. As I show, Black left struggle foregrounds that debates about interpretive methods in the university are partial unless they engage a political economic understanding of the university's operations, especially with regard to its management of difference, its place in imperial expansion, and its circulation and accumulation of capital. These insights decenter the university as an exclusive site of knowledge production, and expand the stakes for how scholars working within the university position and organize their work. In this book the criticism of Black left writers does not emerge without an organization of the terms and sites under which acts of interpretation unfold. This work provides a provocative reframing of present struggles in and beyond the university over method, but more presciently of the condition and structure of academic labor, the purpose of the institution, and the imaginings of what other universities and societies may be possible.

OUTSIDE

Black people have long pursued modes of knowledge production in forms often unrecognizable to academic spheres. Scholars in Black studies root some of these forms in the United States to the performance and making of spiritual songs by enslaved Black people, knowledge that W. E. B. Du Bois has famously termed the sorrow songs. Clyde Woods connects this mode of knowledge making to class, gender, and region in his analysis. What Woods terms blues epistemologies challenged and provoked the counterrevolutionary political economic development of the plantation bloc within the South and eventually, as the scene of struggle expanded, within the United States. These ways of knowing forge modes of collectivity and solidarity to challenge the social and political structure of racial capitalism as they create new aesthetic, social, and political possibilities.[18] Such knowledge making was not limited to creating, performing, listening to, and assembling around music; the multiple and myriad forms of this nearly limitless expansion is, if nothing else, the subject of an entire line of inter- and extradisciplinary inquiry.

By the mid-twentieth century, some Black writers saw the Communist Party and other left political affiliates as spaces that provided institutional and material support for Black cultural production and for Black interpretive practice. Nearly all of the Black writers I discuss in this book had some relationship to communism, whether it was through explicit membership in the Communist Party USA or general solidarity with movements to end racial capitalism and imperialism. Over the last two decades, scholars of the Black left have worked to complicate the idea that the CPUSA and the Communist International tokenized Black causes and Black art in order to grow their rolls with Black members in the United States and advance Soviet propaganda goals.[19] These accounts challenge the long-held common sense established by canonical Black writers, some of whom either were members or expressed deep sympathy with the party. Black writers disaffected with communism suggested that the white leaders of the Comintern and the CPUSA had a naive understanding of anti-Black racism. For instance, Richard Wright explains in his autobiographical *Black Boy* that "white Communists had idealized all Negroes to the extent that they did not see the same Negroes I saw. And the more I tried to explain my ideas the more they, too, began to suspect that I was somehow dreadfully wrong. . . . I began to feel an emotional isolation that I had not known in the depths of the hate-ridden South."[20] Wright's experience has been magnified, confirmed, and shared by a number of Black writers and intellectuals, including Ralph Ellison and Harold Cruse. In their view, to serve the orthodoxy of the Party line, the CPUSA minimized lived Black experience. This contradicted the intellectual liberty that was hard won while living Jim Crow. Cruse states clearly his feeling about Marxist influence on Black writing before the 1959 American Society of African Culture (AMSAC) conference of Black writers: "It is a foregone conclusion that the Marxists will make strong attempts to exert influence on this conference either through Negro writers who are Marxists or other Negro writers who are under the influence of Marxists. This is, of course, a personal question of one's own political views, but based on this member's own personal experiences with the

Marxist movement in art and theater, Marxists are too aggressive to be allowed to wield influence behind the scenes with no opposition."[21]

Cruse's and Wright's statements, however, do not represent the only ways Black people experienced the CP or communism. Black literary scholars and Black labor historians have shown that there were other ways to engage with the party, and that its grip over forms of expression and organizing may have been at times more susceptible to Black intervention than Wright or Cruse suggest. Robin D. G. Kelley has shown that Black working-class people both anticipated and shaped the organizing tactics and goals of the Communist Party in Alabama in the 1930s. Black party members were so integral that many former Klan members who had joined the CP quickly defected after learning of the party's practiced and theoretical commitment to interracial as well as class solidarity. Kelley's *Hammer and Hoe* and other works that follow from it challenge the prevailing sense that the CP merely appropriated Black labor and ideas for its own gain. Claude McKay, for instance, long thought that "his Russian work spawned a shaping influence over Communist policy toward Black Americans," particularly the adoption of the Black Belt thesis by the Comintern in 1928.[22] As adopted, the Black Belt thesis asserted that Black people constituted a nation within a nation in the United States—meaning that Black liberation was a distinctly national struggle, an important distinction in Leninism. McKay's ideas, however, also challenged the party's thinking, arguing that "the Negro question is inseparably connected with the question of woman's liberation."[23] Black party members made use of the party to advance an understanding of political struggle and culture, as much as the party sought to make use of the work of Black party members to cover over racism within entities like the CPUSA, or to cover over national difference in favor of race.[24]

Nevertheless, Black leftists found that the CP eventually accommodated and incubated analytical approaches that, like McKay's, considered interlocking forms of oppression. They developed intricate positions—some decades ahead of their time—on the intersections of race, gender, and class. Claudia Jones, the Black Trinidadian woman who headed the CPUSA's Committee on the Women Question, further elaborated Louise Thompson Patterson's idea that Black women were triply exploited: by class, by gender, and by race.[25] Jones and other Black radicals—"left of Karl Marx," as Carol Boyce Davies has so aptly put it, because of their progressive, or ultraleft, views on race and gender—were able to establish their thinking as the official line of the CPUSA. This shows that Black analytical approaches and forms of assembly in the United States and across the diaspora had agency within the organization's orthodoxy.

Even when Black leftists were not establishing party doctrine, they could mobilize the resources of the international organization for their own purpose. For Black writers in the United States, the party was often the greatest well of resources available to them. In summarizing the extensive and important work by James Smethurst, Alan Wald, William Maxwell, and others on Black writers on the left, Mary Helen Washington determines that "these left-wing clubs, schools, committees, camps, and publications 'constituted the principal venues' for the production of African American literary culture."[26] A number of these venues were partially or sometimes even entirely Black-run and Black-funded. Lloyd Brown edited the journal *Masses and Mainstream* from 1948 to 1952; in 1950 Paul Robeson and Louis Burnham founded and edited the newspaper *Freedom*, which published reporting by Lorraine Hansberry and Yvonne Gregory. Founded through the organizing efforts of the National Negro Congress, the George Washington Carver School at 57 West 125th Street in Harlem was led by Gwendolyn Bennett and financially supported by Robeson and Hubert Delany, an African American civil rights attorney and New York City judge, and by $1,120 in donations from Harlem residents. When the Carver School faced financial trouble, the better-funded Jefferson School downtown absorbed the Harlem school's mission of serving the expressed needs of the Black working class.[27] From a certain angle, this appears as a form of incorporation, but, as I will illustrate in chapter 4, the Jefferson School altered its operations in ways much different from the diversity regimes that would later take root in the American university system. The CP was an organization Black people could work through—certainly turbulently, on occasion—in an effort to create interpretive theory and practice that could meet the demands of the different political, economic, and social forms they imagined.

Robin D. G. Kelley identifies the Communist Party as one of several sites where the "freedom dreams" of Black radical imaginations could flourish. Freedom dreams are imaginative visions of an alternative world in which oppressed peoples are emancipated from the various forces that oppress them: race, gender, and capital, among others. For Kelley, these creative imaginings "erupt out of political engagement," and therefore "collective social movements are incubators of new knowledge."[28] A similar position is developed by a Black radical named Randy in the 1954 novel *Youngblood* by John O. Killens, a cultural leader of the Black left in the mid-1950s and a regular student at the Jefferson School in New York. Randy's Howard University roommate, Richie, displays an affinity for reading both Black and red texts, but when it comes time to protest, Richie is reluctant. To convince Richie otherwise, Randy turns not to Lenin, but to Frederick Douglass:

> "*If there is no struggle there is no progress. Those who profess to favor free-dom, and yet depreciate agitation, are men who want crops without plow-ing the ground. They want rain without thunder and lightning. They want the ocean without the awful roar of its many waters.*" "That's what I'm talking about," Randy said, and handed Richard the big book. "You intellectuals don't ever want to do anything but read."[29]

Convinced by Randy and his Douglass citation, Richie goes out the next day to support the New Negro Alliance–led "Don't Buy Where You Can't Work" campaign, and after another demonstration discovers that he is not afraid of a picket line. In fact, for Richie at least, the picket line comes to be a place of sociality and a foundry for knowledge mak-ing through assembly, hallmarks of the Black radical tradition.

New knowledge grows from the complex and often contradictory experiences of organizing—talking with friends, standing on the picket line, marching in protest—and from intellectual labors. This scene from *Youngblood* indexes how Black writers on the left employed the combination of writing and organizing as a way to express and en-gender a Black critical practice that manifested freedom dreams. This combination of study and assembly can be located in a catalog of Lor-raine Hansberry's self-reported New York activities: "See only foreign movies, no plays hardly, attend meetings almost every night, sing in a chorus, eat all the foreign foods in N.Y., go for long walks in Harlem and talk to my people about everything in the streets, usher at rallies, make street corner speeches in Harlem and sometimes make it up to the country on Sunday."[30] Further, as Killens's novel highlights, these activities might not be determined by an entity like the CPUSA, even if they were adjacent to it. Black cultural workers could develop their own terms, epistemologies, and institutions for a struggle against racial capitalism while intersecting with CP activities.[31]

The mutually constitutive roles of assembly and intellectual study to knowledge making animate the work of Black criticism I describe in this book. Black writers challenging New Critical fundamentals targeted the exclusionary tendencies of the institutions in which the New Criticism was situated. Most universities in the 1940s and 1950s, even elite ones, enrolled few Black students, if any at all. Policies of spatial segregation delegitimized the knowledge-making capacity of work associated with social and political organizing. In addition, uneven levels of federal and state support for Black colleges and universities created labor conditions for scholars that were not conducive to writing and research.[32] Black writers excluded from the academy, doing work in other types of spaces and incorporating different forms of reference, evidence, and experience were rendered as outside authorized flows of knowledge. Yet, as Kelley, Killens, Hansberry, and other historians and practitioners of the Black radical tradition suggest, these sites outside the mainstream circuits of knowledge proved to be a powerful force for the production of radical ideas.

Killens, Hansberry, and the other Black writers who are the central protagonists of this book's later chapters—Melvin B. Tolson in chapter 2; Langston Hughes, Arna Bontemps, Ann Petry, and Hansberry in chapter 3; and Gwendolyn Bennett, W. E. B. Du Bois, Elizabeth Catlett, Killens, and Doxey Wilkerson in chapter 4—participate in this tradition. Their visions of literary and cultural interpretation were necessarily entangled with social and political aims and modes of assembly. Nearly all of the Black cultural workers I discuss would likely consider themselves writers or artists above being organizers, but nevertheless, they all participated in some form of political work or organizing. Petry helped to found Negro Women Incorporated, a consumer rights organization, in addition to working for the Laundry Workers Joint Board and the Play School Association Project in Harlem; Tolson organized tenant farmers and later served three terms as the mayor of Langston, Oklahoma; and others, including Hughes, Bennett, and Wilkerson, offered their literary talents to forward Black and left causes in poetry, fiction, and newspaper write-ups.

Leftist political affiliations were dangerous for any American during the McCarthy years, though they were especially so for Black people. There was a prevailing sense within the intelligence divisions of the US government and among the public that to be Black was to be subversive and therefore in close proximity to communists. For Black writers on the left, fighting anti-Black racism, the class inequities of capitalism, and gender oppression could not be separated from their approach to literary interpretation. Their political organizing activities made clear that the borders formed around literary interpretation served a particular purpose. Buoyed by the growth of the American university system more broadly and by the New Critical institutionalization of literary studies more locally, these borders ensured the reproduction of an exploitable labor force and signaled a hierarchization of America's empire of capitalist influence. In short, it was clear to Black writers on the left that the New Criticism was an integral part of the expansion and retooling of political, economic, and social forms of material oppression. This critique was particularly urgent as the United States. adopted an antiracist facade to further disseminate, install, and support regimes friendly to US liberal capitalism while the Soviet Union attempted to exploit American racism for its own geopolitical gain.

Because the Black writers I discuss faced a simultaneously intellectual, institutional, and spatial repression, they developed their attacks against the New Criticism and the racial state it supported in venues understood by white audiences to be beyond the proper spheres of thought. Tolson attempted an elaborate exposure campaign of the unspoken racial codes of the New Criticism by asking Allen Tate to write the preface to his *Libretto for the Republic of Liberia*. The exposure would come with an essay composed by Tolson for publication in the *Sewanee Review*, one of the major New Critical organs. Langston Hughes offered a description of the complex network of associations between literary criticism, the state, and their mutual aversion to Blackness in a closed-door testimony before the Senate Permanent Subcommittee on Investigations. Lorraine Hansberry launched a project of a utopian "New Romanticism" set against the ills of the nuclear age, drug and alcohol addiction, racism, sexism, and ableism. All of these efforts have a textual component, which I draw out of the archive, but they also have a component rooted in action and protest. They make knowledge and critique of midcentury critical practice by doing, seeing, and creating. By contrast, they reveal that the New Criticism itself isn't merely an intellectual project, but a political project for excluding Blackness and Black people and for expanding a tenuous coalition between reactionary and liberal forms of anticommunism.

Given that the New Criticism frequently marks the starting point for the discipline of literary studies, many of these accounts of Black radical critique have been at most suppressed and at least on the margins of the disciplinary history of literary studies. Tolson's *Sewanee Review* essay was never published. The pressure of continued public ostracization—cancellation of his public talks, declining sales of his books, leaving the famous writer for broke—led Langston Hughes to soften his critical position in his public testimony. Meanwhile, his subversive testimony would remain under government seal for fifty years. Hansberry's remarks were excised from the widely-distributed publication of the AMSAC conference proceedings on the recommendation of Harold Cruse, not to mention the fact that AMSAC served as a CIA front at this time.[33] Like other cultural and political histories about organized or everyday forms of Black radicalism, much of what I describe here are ideas and actions that were seemingly impossible to imagine within mainstream institutions, and their realization was often thwarted accordingly. From a methodological standpoint, this also means that the records of these critical activities are partial, or refracted through the lens of intelligence agencies scrutinizing Black lives.[34] Tolson's drafts of his essay on Allen Tate are various and unfinished; the Jefferson School destroyed its student rolls and refused to accept information from students to protect them from government surveillance; and FBI surveillance documents inform a number of my arguments.

Even though the Black radical ideas I discuss are not widely known, there exists ample evidence that they circulated to other Black thinkers. As Dayo Gore and Erik McDuffie point out, many Black radical women from the 1950s—including those affiliated with the progressive people's schools, such as Alice Childress, Shirley Graham, Augusta Strong, Beulah Richardson, and Louise Thompson Patterson—played a crucial role in the organization of late-1960s struggles, including perhaps most prominently the formation of the National United Committee to Free Angela Davis.[35] In addition, their ideas about the triple exploitation of women, purveyed by Claudia Jones and groups like the Sojourners for Truth and Justice, would reappear in the work of 1970s feminist groups including the Combahee River Collective. Late-1960s Black nationalism could be read as the reemergence of notions of Black self-determination that stemmed from the CP's Black Belt thesis. Student movements calling for Black and ethnic studies would bring to the academy a retooled version of the 1940s and '50s critique of academia leveled by the Jefferson and Carver Schools. Like those in midcentury people's schools, students in the 1960s and '70s believed that academia should serve and be party to knowledges produced by people of color, women, and working-class people.[36] Even so, as I highlight in chapter 4, the institutional difference between people's schools and the late-1960s university system leads to notable distinctions in how the former approached the study and making of Black culture, particularly in terms of its practice and theorization of the impact of gender and class on race. The curriculum of people's schools anticipates that of the Freedom Schools formed by the Student Nonviolent Coordinating Committee in Mississippi. According to Robin D. G. Kelley, their "curriculum included traditional subjects that publicly funded black schools did not offer. . . . Students examined power along the axes of race and class."[37]

Another mark of the continued circulation of Black midcentury challenges to the New Critical hegemon is the legacy of Black critics targeting the New Criticism as reactionary and retrograde. In *The Black Situation* (1970), Addison Gayle suggests that the New Critics are but one instance of a line of Southern writers seeking to continue the plantation tradition in the United States. He does not mince words when he insists that the Agrarian manifesto, written by some of the most prominent New Critics in 1930, "is a racist, fascist document, equaled in the twentieth century only by Hitler's *Mein Kampf.*"[38] To support his polemic, Gayle highlights the New Criticism's ontological definition of literature that was supported by "the southern myth and gave authenticity to a society constructed along class lines."[39] For Gayle, what makes this particularly concerning is the ease with which the American university system and the state so quickly embraced the group's critical program.

Ishmael Reed, too, picks up on the connection of New Critical approaches and the development of official antiracisms some twenty years later. Reed's Professor Puttbutt, the Black protagonist of *Japanese by Spring* (1993), is an avid New Critic who hopes to earn tenure by reproducing the racist ideas stemming from color blindness, the official antiracism of the era.[40] Due to a shifting economy that has made stars of critical theorists, Puttbutt recognizes the profit possible for "even a New Critic like himself."[41] Though Puttbutt knows that his New Critical affinities are out of step with other literature and humanities faculty at the fictional Jack London College, he sees holding conservative credentials as the only path to tenure for a Black man. Reed's satirical novel affirms the sense that the seemingly depoliticized New Criticism is an appropriate shield for a person whose race makes him subversive by default. The wide-ranging canon of Black writers disparaging the New Criticism continues to this day.[42] This suggests that the literary, political, and economic conjuncture that midcentury Black critiques of the New Criticism addressed is alive in some form within current academic literary study and within the university. It also suggests that many of the midcentury critiques I describe in this book manage to circulate despite institutional and state suppression.

This circulation occurred in ways that remain difficult to track archivally or otherwise: in conversations, private letters, and rumors. Occasional traces of these networks make their way to the surface. For instance, the *Amsterdam News* reported some information on Langston Hughes's antagonistic closed-door testimony. As David Chinitz has suggested, the article printed there about his appearance before the Senate Permanent Subcommittee on Investigations includes details from the private hearing in addition to those from the public hearing, suggesting that Hughes leaked his less subservient performance to the press.[43] Beyond these whispered traces, the modes of pedagogy and literary interpretation promoted by Black writers challenging the New Criticism were modeled within midcentury Black literary texts. Black literature of this period frequently stages scenes of interpretation where the stakes are higher than in formal squabbles. These scenes suggest that interpreting Black literature, Black culture, and Black life can both challenge white supremacist ideas and activate white supremacist violence. They make plain the threat that a socially and politically situated interpretive practice can pose to a political, economic, and social order designed to protect whiteness. The fictionalized scenes of interpretation tend not to unfold in university spaces but in a public pageant, in an interrogation room, or around a dinner table. These sites spotlight that this mode of Black criticism is part of the grain of social and political life. Black criticism joins the struggle to reconfigure the racist regime supported by the US state, its global expansion of capital, and the New Criticism.

Many of the writers featured in this book pursue a definition of Black literature and of literary criticism that sees interracial unity as an opportunity, not a threat. These writers pursued this idea because they recognized how anti-Black racism was situated as a key piece in the oppression of not only Black people but other people of color and white people as well. Racism was one means of oppression that combined, intensified, and further developed with and through other modes of oppression, including those of class, gender, and sexuality. Despite the fact that positions on integration, segregation, and nationalism would rapidly shift on all sides of the political spectrum in the mid-twentieth century, Black writers on the left made calls for interracial unity precisely because solidarity across race, gender, and class posed the biggest potential threat to the extant order, which relied on the separation of and antagonism between these groups. By presenting an approach for interpretation attentive to those boundaries, Black left writers position the production of culture and its interpretation as central to social, political, and economic struggles of various stripes. For instance, Kate Baldwin argues that when Langston Hughes suggests in poetry of the 1930s that "Black and white can all be red," he takes "seriously the plausibility of new people under a rubric of 'red.'"[44] Baldwin shows that for Hughes the rise of the Soviet Union presented an opportunity to create, in Hughes's phrasing, a "new people." The "red" genre of humanity Hughes proposes is a new one altogether, something only made possible by political economic upheaval. Admittedly, these ideas of interracial unity often floundered, largely because of the failure of white leftists to commit to their radical demands. The lack of white commitment would further encourage exclusive Black radical organizing and ideas of Black self-determination in the closing years of the 1960s.

INSIDE

While the previous section focused on midcentury Black left modes of knowledge production based around literary and cultural interpretation, this section of the chapter contextualizes and emphasizes the counterrevolutionary forces that sought to contain and exclude those ideas in intellectual, institutional, and state forms. The antiracism that the midcentury liberal state established carried a different connotation than the calls for interracial unity within the CP. Rather than build a new people, the liberal state offered an assimilative model. A Black college student of the era attending a predominantly white university describes the model in stark terms: "We were being let into the university on the condition that we become white men with dark skins."[45] This state attitude toward race and gender has been referred to frequently as racial liberalism and, as this student intimates, universities, the state, and dominant methods for interpreting culture contributed to its establishment and circulation.

Racial liberalism became what Jodi Melamed deems the first official antiracism of the United States after the "racial break" of World War II. Official antiracisms are discourses by which the state can address claims of inequality, inferiority, and discrimination with rhetorical solutions rather than material ones. The US state developed an official antiracism after World War II because the nation sought to project ideals of freedom and democracy abroad after defeating the Nazis, despite ongoing white mob violence against Black people sanctioned by local police. In the geopolitical sphere, the mythic claims of American liberty were increasingly vulnerable to Soviet propaganda that targeted the racist limits on American freedom. At the same time, decolonial movements began abroad and Black Americans found new forums in which they could raise objections to Jim Crow.[46] Appeals to the newly established United Nations regarding US anti-Black racism were made in 1946, 1947, and perhaps most famously in 1951 with the Civil Rights Congress's submission of "We Charge Genocide."[47] In an attempt to address these wider ripostes to the US argument about freedom, democracy, and capitalism, the federal government, philanthropic foundations, and colleges and universities supported social science research on "the Negro problem." Gunnar Myrdal's *An American Dilemma* (1944) stands as the exemplar of this tendency. In it, amid the 242 "racial battles" in forty-seven cities that occurred in 1943, the Swedish-born researcher, who began work on the book in September 1938, positions the "American Negro problem in the heart of the American."[48] By drawing US racism as a moral problem, Myrdal left the large-scale structures of racism untouched even while they continued to shape all aspects of American life, including how research was conducted. Du Bois competed for funding from the same foundation as Myrdal to work on his "Encyclopedia of the Negro" project. The Carnegie Foundation selected Myrdal for their support because a European was deemed to be "wholly objective and dispassionate," something the academic community thought Du Bois could not be as a Black man.[49] The era's emphasis on objectivity would inevitably shape and frustrate Black writers and scholars. As Nick Mitchell has shown, the path toward funding and institutionalization necessitated making "Negro history" and later Black studies an object of study appealing to foundations and their embrace of academic and intellectual norms. This developed a separation between Black intellectuals and the "Black community" they would come to study.[50]

Midcentury studies of "the Negro problem" led to a liberal consensus that Black Americans could gain access to the privileges of citizenship by becoming "finally integrated into modern democracy."[51] The limitation of this view was that state entities put the onus on Black Americans to conform to white universalist understandings of democracy, rather than calling for a reconfiguration of a racist order. Myrdal figures this as "America's incomparably great opportunity for the future," meaning that there is capital to be gained by incorporating Black people into the US order rather than shifting that order itself.[52] Accordingly, racial liberalism hesitantly accepted some Black people into previously white spaces, but refused to significantly reconfigure those spaces and institutions that allowed racist practice, especially toward working-class Black people, to continue and to intensify. This intensification of racist practice occurred because entering into the American compact came to be figured as something Black people could choose to accept. As Keeanga-Yamahtta Taylor writes, "The premise of racial liberalism, and postwar liberalism in general, was that the systems of the institutions of the country were strong enough to bestow the political, economic, and social riches of American society onto all who were willing to work hard and commit themselves to a better future."[53] Even when this commitment was made, Black Americans still contended with systemic issues, including redlining, racist policing, and the continued underinvestment of federal, state, and local funds to Black communities.

Colleges and universities were crucial sites for the dissemination, development, and maintenance of racial liberalism. In addition to their limited matriculation of Black students, universities in this moment were part of a larger effort to develop a national culture that could incorporate large numbers of ethnically diverse working-class students into (white) Americans. As Michael Denning argues, "perhaps the most important federal intervention in culture was the building of the postwar university system, supported by government research and development funds and by the GI Bill of 1944, which financed higher education for 8 million veterans."[54] The GI Bill favored white Americans and predominantly white institutions for funding in its effort to shift the domain of universities from elite enclaves to sites of mass education.[55] Universities were enlisted in manufacturing consensus around liberal capitalism and American democracy, white ideals increasingly coded in the race-neutral language of objectivity and universality. Meanwhile, it was clear that objectivity and universality came to be measures that could be deployed to exclude Black people from the full privilege of citizenship—or, in a different context, to exclude Du Bois from foundation funding. Higher education became a means to assure domestic buy-in for the US-led expansion of liberal capitalism to the rest of the globe. This offered significant material benefits for white students, largely at the expense of Black working-class people, though to a lesser degree it also incorporated a small cohort of Black people.

Jane Bond, a Black student at Sarah Lawrence College, composed a letter to her friend Lorraine Hansberry in 1951 that shows this academic attempt to build consensus as a further means of exploiting Black people. It also shows how she perceived her inclusion to be a great opportunity for the college, not for her:

> I have also learned that most so called liberal colleges do not have Negro students because they are trying to fight for Negro rights or because they believe in Negro equality, but because they want one or two of us around as trophies, to prove how liberal they are. Once we are there, they don't care what happens to us and make no effort to deal with the special problems which Negroes are faced in a predominantly white institution. I will be very glad to get out of that rarified atmosphere and into a situation which is more down to earth.[56]

Bond's observations suggest that within institutions promoting racial liberalism, racism took the form of deliberate neglect. Those who fell outside the norms around race, gender, and sexuality that composed the universal or rejected the political terms of the US citizen-subject were vulnerable to additional violence, extraction, and exclusion.[57]

One finds resonance in Bond's remarks with contemporary critiques of academic diversity regimes by Sara Ahmed; accounts of how universities "work identity" by Devon Carbado and Mitu Gulati; and Roderick Ferguson's description of the strategic use of minority difference in higher education in the wake of Black, ethnic, and feminist studies movements.[58]

Recently scholars studying higher education from an abolitionist or critical ethnic studies perspective see the university as integral to—not distinct from—the machinations of racial capital and the state's interest, defense, and reproduction of the "possessive investment in whiteness."[59] George Lipsitz defines that investment as literal and figurative; whiteness has a material tendency to accumulate capital reliant upon the social and cultural reproduction of its supremacy. These scholars recognize the university as both a material and a symbolic node in this process of accumulation. Rather than redistributing material and symbolic resources, this process marshals significant amounts of capital for the university and the state to use. This understanding relies on a historical contextualization of the university system as part of the violence of US slavery and settler colonialism. As Craig Wilder argues, because its operations were financed with capital accumulated from the slave trade and because it developed racial science to justify servitude, "the academy never stood apart from American slavery—in fact, it stood beside church and state as the third pillar of a civilization built on bondage."[60] The adoption of a discourse of mass redistribution at midcentury suggests that the university changes its mode of racialization, but not its accumulative function. This discursive shift marks the incorporation of some into the accumulated American wealth, but largely sustains the same exploitative and extractive processes under revised racial terms. Abigail Boggs, Eli Meyerhoff, Nick Mitchell, and Zach Schwartz-Weinstein advise that a "more fulsome accounting [of the midcentury university] would necessarily include: absorption of surplus populations via institutional expansion, absorption of surpluses of land generated by taking land out of agricultural production and into suburbanization . . . and the consolidation of military-university financial and population flows."[61] In this analysis, higher education disseminated and designed the discourse of official antiracism while further developing new means to accumulate value for whiteness.

The New Criticism played a crucial role in supporting these activities of midcentury universities.[62] One of the most pivotal works of disciplinary history in literary studies—John Guillory's *Cultural Capital*—suggests that the New Criticism helped to establish, temporarily, a political and economic function for literary study in the years after World War II. To put this in his terms, the New Critics are responsible for "redefining the cultural capital produced by literary study in the university."[63] On the one hand, that new definition allowed for expanded access to that capital for new audiences. On the other hand, that expansion produced new terms by which to limit the same access for already devalued groups, particularly Black people, queer people, and women.

Midcentury observers both in the university and in the state recognized how New Critical aesthetic and interpretive practices could play an important role in melding the mixture of cultures bubbling within the United States into a unified entity. As Hershel Parker put it in commenting on the New Criticism's tendency toward unity, the New Critics "define their role as bringing order out of a chaos which they insist is only apparent, not real. The order *must* be there, awaiting the sufficiently attentive and unbiased reading which the present critic is always the first to supply."[64] Because of this ordering tendency, the New Critics came to be seen by the US state and by American universities as the appropriate means by which literature and its rhetorical tropes could be produced and parsed. For Guillory, this redefinition tasked literary studies with reproducing the distinction between mass and high culture. When read in terms of the long history of the accumulating university, however, this distinction mobilizes the further marginalization of Black people, especially, for the benefit of US capital expansion. Jane Bond, for instance, states that any benefits she accrued from being admitted to Sarah Lawrence paled in comparison to those that the college gained by trumpeting its acceptance of her. I show throughout this book how the New Criticism works to support the marginalization of Black people for the gain of predominantly white institutions.

The New Critics were particularly poised to update the discursive positioning toward race in the American university while maintaining the university's political economic function embedded in racial capitalism. A number of the most prominent New Critics, before they were known as such—including Robert Penn Warren, John Crowe Ransom, and Allen Tate—published a manifesto in 1930 that called for the return of an agrarian economy to the US South. Initially titled "Tracts against Communism," *I'll Take My Stand* "produced the South in the same way . . . social elites produce ideological realities: out of strategies for seizing and retaining power (cultural, political, sexual, economic, and so on) that are then reproduced as 'natural.'"[65] As Michael Kreyling suggests, the Agrarian manifesto sought to accumulate capital and power of various kinds for white Southerners by denying how slavery and racism was crucial to the region's—and nation's—political economy. Only one essay in *I'll Take My Stand* considers the role of Black people in the South at any length. In it, Robert Penn Warren endorses Booker T. Washington's program for vocational education as a means for "crime, genial irresponsibility, ignorance, and oppression [to be] replaced by an informed and productive negro community."[66] Warren coerces Black people to accept the terms white people have set out for them in an Agrarian society with the threat of criminalization, marginalization, and further racist violence if Black people refuse those terms.

Connecting the New Critics to their Agrarian past supplies a genealogy that links the racial liberalism the New Critics would eventually espouse to the foundational national defense of Black inferiority exercised through literary criticism. In his 1785 *Notes on the State of Virginia*, Thomas Jefferson establishes a connection between the US racial state and literary critical imaginations. Amid offering treatises on law, the subjects of commerce, and Black criminality, Jefferson deems Phillis Wheatley and her poetry to be "below the dignity of criticism."[67] Jefferson supports this claim by suggesting that Black people could not take raw emotion, whether misery or love, and submit it to the ordering faculties of poetry. For the Founding Father, this assessment was evidence enough that Black "inferiority is not the effect merely of their condition of life."[68] New Critical methodology perfected Jefferson's reasoned racism by capably obscuring racialized dimensions of literary interpretation. Importantly, this methodological development allowed for value to continue to accumulate to whiteness in the mid-twentieth century, in the "terms of an African American inclusion by exclusion, an African American *present absence*," in Lindon Barrett's phrasing.[69] To put this concretely, Warren's argument in *I'll Take My Stand* accepts a white vision of Blacks—I don't use "people" here, because Warren does not see Black people as such—as a means to exclude Black people and Black social life from their wider vision of society. This inclusion by exclusion becomes the objective logic by which cultural as well as political and economic judgments are made. It is, in effect, the very logic of racial liberalism.

The Agrarian imprint would remain in future forms of official antiracism in the United States, especially in how those forms impacted higher education. The Agrarian New Critics have been seen as playing an atmospheric role in the counterrevolutionary political economic developments of the 1970s that would shift the financing of public higher education from states to individuals in the form of increasingly predatory student loans. The neoliberal Virginia School economist James Buchanan would argue in the 1970s that the free mass access to higher education led directly to Black student uprisings in California. To address the "terror" he saw unfolding on public campuses—he had been working at UCLA when a bomb was planted in the office of the Department of Economics, and when Black Panther students Bunchy Carter and John Huggins were shot and killed in Campbell Hall—Buchanan effectively prescribed a privatization regime that would increase tuition and decrease state funding in an effort to deflate the system for the record number of students of color and poor students entering public universities.[70] I mention Buchanan and his alliance with Reagan's attack on public education in California in the late 1960s and early '70s, and later across the nation, because according to Nancy MacLean, as a young man in the 1930s Buchanan had taken inspiration from the Nashville Agrarians, particularly the Vanderbilt English professor Donald Davidson.[71] The case of Buchanan highlights how the Agrarian New Critics provided key intertexts and institutional strategies to preserve the accumulative capacities of higher education both in the midcentury and beyond. Though I focus here almost entirely on the 1940s and 1950s, the political economic ramifications of a New Critical university and state defense apparatus extend well into the present, and suggest a line of inquiry for future scholarly investigation.

I elaborate this history of racial liberalism, the university, and the New Criticism as part of my argument for two reasons. Primarily, midcentury Black left writers, including Hansberry's friend Jane Bond, understood the American university and the New Criticism within this political economic context. Chapters 2, 3, and 4 will show that the

Black radical visions of literary interpretation directly engage this articulation of the university, the state, and critical practice. This surfaces a Black political economic critique of the system of higher education in the 1940s and 1950s, decades before the bulk of Black studies movement activity in the late '60s and early '70s. Without this history of the state-university development and reproduction of racial liberalism, an account of the ongoing development of Black interpretive practice would be only partial.

Second, this political economic understanding of the New Criticism is distinct from the one typically circulated within disciplinary histories of literary studies. With a few notable exceptions, disciplinary histories have largely focused on the development of interpretive method and theory.[72] The New Criticism is frequently understood as that which sets the terms for those investigations. For example, Virginia Jackson argues that the New Critical "lyricization of poetry extended to a lyricization of literature tout court."[73] The New Critical interest in the ahistorical lyric genre came to cast an air of isolated ahistoricism on the methodology itself. The result is a general sense that the discipline's history can be summarized as merely a development of methodological approaches, like this diagram offered by Marjorie Levinson: "New Criticism → structuralism → deconstruction → new historicism → poststructuralism."[74] While Levinson only produces this chart to make an example of its limitations, its presumed legibility indexes how methodological developments of the discipline are kept separate from shifts in US political economy, changes in the structure of the university, and other factors impacting the labor and thinking of scholars and critics of literature. The persistence of this methodological emphasis in disciplinary history stands as one of several indices of the continuation of New Critical practice within literary studies, despite the widespread sense that the method is a practice of the past.[75] Nevertheless, there are several recent studies of the development of literary criticism that discuss forces perceived to be external to the discipline, including works by Evan Kindley, Merve Emre, Joseph North, Chris Findeisen, and Laura Heffernan and Rachel Sagner Buurma.[76] This work in what Heffernan deems the "new disciplinary history" expands for investigation the scope of institutions and the types and contexts of the practice of criticism.[77] Other scholars working primarily at the intersection of literary studies and Black and ethnic studies, like Dorothy Wang,

Sonya Posmentier, and the late Lindon Barrett, have explicitly defined the racism that New Criticism has thoroughly embedded in the discipline of literary studies and the university.[78] Meanwhile, Sarah Brouillette, Juliana Spahr, Andrew Rubin, and William Maxwell have investigated how literature and literary criticism have been embedded within various state functions including law enforcement and cultural diplomacy within the United States and the United Nations.[79] By adopting a political-economic understanding informed by critical race and ethnic studies approaches, this book develops an expansion of modes of disciplinary history by taking seriously literary-critical work that has long been made extradisciplinary or has figured as being outside the authorized spaces for making knowledge.

The danger of placing the Black radical critiques I discuss in terms of disciplinary history is that they can be read as offering a solution to the various methodological and disciplinary impasses that have preoccupied literary scholars during the era of the method wars. My aim in this book is not to offer a solution but, as la paperson has suggested in their analysis of the accumulative university, to make space for Black thought, as well as for Indigenous and queer visions of the world to come.[80] What midcentury Black left critics identified is the entanglement of interpretive practice with academic and state forces that together upheld the persistent though shifting forms of anti-Black racism. The incorporation of Black radical demands within academic spaces has allowed for those demands to be redrafted to serve new modes of official antiracisms. As Sylvia Wynter argues, Black studies "was inseparable from the parallel emergence of the Black Aesthetic and Black Arts Movements," but this academic connection to popular movements was later disarticulated once it had been firmly established within the academy.[81] The institutionalization of these popular movements has led to their professionalization and incorporation, and has paradoxically further yoked universities to anti-Black activities, including policing.[82] This is why Stefano Harney and Fred Moten end their pivotal essay "The University and the Undercommons" by clarifying that abolition is "not abolition as the elimination of anything but abolition as the founding of a new society."[83] Their argument "for the red and black abolition" states explicitly that the reform of professional disciplines or the university is not enough in the wider context of racial capitalism and conquest. In their perspective, that is, abolishing the university requires abolishing the entire society of which it is a part. It is with this aim in the present that the undercommons offers assembly for the development and practice of visions for a future world.

With their development and creation of spaces necessarily outside the confines of professionalized academic investigation, midcentury Black radicals identified universities as a particularly inhospitable place for Black thought. In recounting their history here, I offer an account of the development of Black undercommons thinking—always inter- and extradisciplinary—that necessarily frames professional academic study as contributing to and standing as an inextricable part of the broader social, political, and economic order. The undercommons and its emphasis on sociality is effectively outside of space—Harney and Moten call it a "non-space"—in that it is figured as illicit, despite the fact that it is often understood as being "in but not of" the institutions between which it coalesces. My book traces Black radicals who experiment with building institutions for a Black future under the pressure of an anti-Black world. These institutions were not at all "in" the institutions that Black critics sought to counter. The subtle difference amplifies and offers a clarifying argument to something often obscured in discussions of Harney and Moten's work. The university is not the horizon of the revolution, nor is it the only site for the development of Black imaginings. My book emphasizes that a history of thought, of politics, and assembly necessarily circuits outside and through academe. As a result, to understand the division of labor within the discipline, its methods, and its political economic functions requires a broader investigation of the university's connection to the state and its capacities to coerce and encourage consensus around forms of anti-racism acceptable to capital, the state, and white people.

ORGANIZATION

The material I discuss in this book unfolds in the years before and after 1950. This was a critical period for the development of racial liberalism, changes in the American university system, and for the imminence and repression of Black and/or communist freedom dreams. It was a time when the terms of the US state were especially in flux, albeit briefly and unevenly. By the late 1950s, the US state had concretized its approach to racism in the domestic and international spheres, the New Criticism had gained its capital letters as the premiere mode of literary study, and Black activists, thinkers, and artists widely sought new sources of support for developing their vision beyond the CPUSA. Because the terms and strategies developed at midcentury remain foundational to the function of anti-Black racism in the twenty-first century, the sometimes-forgotten postwar struggle against the racial liberal hegemony and racial capitalism remains illuminating.

This book's first chapter describes the connection between the New Criticism, the US state, and racial capitalism. I show how this connection figures Black literature, Black people, and blackness as outside the confines of literature, criticism, and professionalized spaces. The New Critics generate this figuration by their insistence on the fetishization of poetry, of literature, and of criticism itself. This operates as an enclosure and renders the outside illegible and irrelevant to an analysis of culture. Despite a widespread exhaustion around investigations of the New Criticism, my political economic contextualization of academic literary studies remains necessary. Without understanding the multidimensional scope of academic literary studies and its connections to anti-Black racism, it is difficult to register the simultaneously literary-critical, political, and social visions Black radicals unfurl when they target New Criticism. To illustrate the wide scope of Black radical literary-critical activity, I highlight an episode that the Jefferson School faculty and Langston Hughes identify as crucial for making plain the anti-Black logic operating in the connection between literary criticism and the state: the awarding of the Bollingen Prize to Ezra Pound in 1949 by the Fellows of the Library of Congress.

After establishing the means by which literary studies privileged whiteness at the expense of Black people in the midcentury, I turn to how Black left writers challenged the domestic and international conquest of US liberal capitalism by developing new modes of literary interpretation. Instead of moving chronologically, I organize these chapters in terms of the increasing scale and stakes of the critical imaginings Black writers developed against the New Criticism. The chapters also build with regard to the degree of CP intervention and affiliation with the otherwise Black-led attempts to form an antiracist literary criticism. This organization supports the book's argument by accumulating endeavors of increased size, scope, and material enactment to build a Black, communist world beyond the bounds of the liberal-capitalist US state.

This organization of the book also makes clear that Black visions for the future are not only imaginary. They are implemented and put into practice even if the state and academic apparatuses of the white world destroy these visions or seek to make their realization appear improbable. Despite the persistent violence of white supremacy, these visions are built, formed, and placed as much as they are imagined. Black matters, as McKittrick puts it, are both "real and discursive."[84] Black writers on the left animate their real, discursive, and critical as well as political institutional practices by figuring them in terms of space and what space might make possible. In chapter 2, I describe how Melvin Tolson imagines a unified Africa connected by multiform transportation technologies to create a context for his revolutionary criticism. In chapter 3, I show that Langston Hughes figures the New Criticism and his McCarthy Commission testimony in terms of a manure-filled lily pond to draw attention to the shared work academic criticism and state entities conduct in establishing anti-Black racism in criticism and in surveillance. These radical, spatial imaginings provide the terms for the material impact of these writers' discursive practice. In chapter 4, however, I show that the creation of an alternative material space (the progressive people's school) fosters the creation of a new epistemology to support literary critical practice. That space includes the Black-led classrooms and curricula at the progressive people's schools in New York and California. For W. E. B. Du Bois, these "were the only two schools who tried to teach the people about the Negro position in their relation to the nation and the world."[85]

The goal of my work is to further illuminate the long history of Black people generating new terms for investigating, imagining, abolishing, and liberating themselves and the world from white supremacy. Black writers in the mid-twentieth century approached the project of literary interpretation with a recognition that any critical practice must also require material circumstances that allow for Black thought and criticism. These writers teach that literature and literary critical practice impact and shape the world in which we live. Literature and its interpretation, as academic criticism has done and continues to do, can limit and police Black life.[86] But literature and criticism can also open up places of assembly, sociality, and liberation. This book is an investigation of this insight at a moment when this insight was, as it continues to be now, pushed outside.

⊙ 1 ⊙

New Criticism and the Object
of American Democracy

In the first sentence of *Understanding Poetry*, Cleanth Brooks and Robert Penn Warren identify their textbook's lodestar: "This book has been conceived on the assumption that if poetry is worth teaching at all it is worth teaching as poetry."[1] Or, as they put it several sentences later, "The poem in itself, if literature is to be studied as literature, remains finally the object for study." These simple statements set up both a taxonomical program and an interpretive method that would become known as the New Criticism, the foundation for literary studies in the academy since the middle of the twentieth century. Accordingly, this idea—"Literature is to be studied as literature"—has garnered ample scholarly attention. However, an essential question about the mid-century New Critical formulation has been pursued far less often: What political, economic and social formations does this tautological, even enigmatic principle lead its practitioners to establish and support? This chapter answers that question, suggests why it is asked so infrequently, and wagers that some fundamental but obscured aspects of the connection of academic literary study to the world beyond it are made visible in its answering.

Black writers on the left who were contemporaries of the New Critics in the 1940s and 1950s recognized the New Criticism as a literary program, a social and economic proposal, and a state-supported means to enforce anti-Black racism and, at times, anticommunism. As will become clear later in the book, Black writers' challenges to the New Criticism invoke a radical project that pushes against the intersecting exploitation of race, class, gender, and sexuality that the New Critical platform posits. When scholars see the New Criticism in only one of its dimensions, it becomes difficult to identify parlays against the movement from outside of the academy, particularly those leveled by Black writers.

Through its definitional and methodological insistence that literature is literature, the New Criticism modulated the actual and imagined differences between (white) citizens and Black others in terms that were on their surface devoid of race, but were fully racialized underneath. When the Harvard Redbook, a veritable guide for liberal arts education in the United States, cites the New Criticism as an answer to "a centrifugal culture in extreme need of unifying forces," it insists that the aesthetic principles can mold divergent subjects into the white citizen standard.[2] The separation of aesthetic and political activity the New Criticism promoted with its definition dovetailed with the US federal government's emphasis on culture as an instrument for forming a clear national identity domestically, and for advertising the liberty of the US political and economic system abroad. As has been well documented of Cold War cultural efforts, the US state sought to suppress the rampant inequalities of the country's social and political reality to project a liberal capitalist vision of freedom that was freer and more democratic than Soviet Communism.[3] At the same time, as John Thelin suggests, universities, where the New Criticism became firmly established, were newly figured as "integral to the national interest, including its international and social roles as well as national defense."[4] Managing and measuring people by the terms of US racial liberalism meant enacting and enforcing a program of anticommunism that marked Black people as potential subversives. The Agrarian New Critics carried a long history of pairing anticommunist and anti-Black sentiment—what David Caute describes as "the equation between the red and the black"—and thus proved well-suited to the American national interest at midcentury.[5]

The New Criticism formalized and institutionalized the separation of the literary from the historical, the social, and the political—a bracketing that has also been a hallmark of their scholarly reception. Aside from the method of close reading, the New Critical legacy lingering within literary studies is a myopia when it comes to joining interpretive method with its material ramifications. As well versed as they were readers of poetry, the New Critical group marshaled the full range of liberal-capitalist mystification strategies to ensure that what scholars and students exchanged at the marketplace (close reading) was kept far from the shop floor (the political-economic connection of the racial state, university, and literary criticism) necessary to produce it. Karl Marx's explanation of commodity fetishism offers a broad paradigm for understanding how the New Critical emphasis on the literary object obscures the process of its production, valuation, and exchange.[6] One way that Marx describes the exchange of commodities is that "the definite social relation between men themselves . . . assumes here, for them, the fantastic form of a relation between things."[7] That fantastic form, the fetishism of commodities, is at the heart of Marx's theory of value, pivotal for his understanding of capital more broadly. Thus, its interpretation is highly contested. As other critics have suggested, the commodity fetish is a way to invoke the illusion that social processes are objectified, a means for understanding an "epistemic problem," "a form of domination," or a site to examine the use and exchange value of "signifiers of raciality."[8] These readings of commodity fetishism operate simultaneously in my argument about how the New Critics imbue literature with supernatural qualities, seemingly from nowhere, that the critic merely discovers.

New Critics naturalize the literary object in a number of ways, but Brooks and Warren's frequent insistence that the poem ought to be compared to "something organic like a plant" highlights how social processes are evacuated from literary objects. They favor the organic explanation because they fear that a sense of a poem as made from "mechanically combined elements . . . as bricks are put together to make a wall"—a process of human production—is wrong because the relationship of the elements in a poem is "far more intimate and fundamental."[9] For Brooks and Warren, the intimate and fundamental relationship resides beyond the sphere of the poem's social production and, at the same time, comes to define poetry as unique.

In this chapter, I argue that the New Critics first separate literature, then criticism, and finally the New Criticism itself from the state-academic apparatus. This separation process requires the racialized exploitation of some to make possible the various political and economic freedoms of others. As Lisa Lowe argues, the condition of possibility of US liberalism is "the modern distinction between definitions of the human and those to whom such definitions do not extend," a condition that the New Critics extend in their objectification of the social pro-

cesses of reading, interpreting, and writing literature.[10] Investigating
the New Criticism through a frame that attends to its racialized fetishism provides a glimpse of how this literary-critical project supported
and established the supernatural idea of American liberal democracy
circulated by the US federal government in a number of spheres.

I begin this chapter by illustrating how the Agrarian program stated
its aesthetic principles by suppressing the racism inherent in its political economic aims, especially as argued in the group's manifesto, *I'll
Take My Stand*. In particular, I examine how the Agrarian insistence of
literature's status as an "organic" or natural object supports and masks
a racially ordered labor system in the Agrarian society for which they
advocate. The second part of the chapter examines how this fetishization process expands to criticism itself. It traces how New Critical
interpretive principles became entangled with various functions of the
US federal government as the United States turned to managing difference on the terms of racial liberalism. Building on historical accounts
of the political coalitions formed after World War II, I show how the
New Criticism offered a useful framework for modes of governance
while also supplying an argument for the so-called democratic function of literature and higher education. The final section considers
what has become known as the Bollingen controversy to show how
the Agrarian New Critics effectively cemented the movement as fully
literary, despite its ongoing social and political connections. It was only
after a group of New Critics who were affiliated with the Library of
Congress awarded Ezra Pound, a known fascist and anti-Semite, the
federally supported Bollingen Prize that the New Criticism became a
proper noun. It was this event that concretized the New Criticism's fetishization, which has been nearly impossible to sustainably demystify
in academic scholarly practice. I conclude briefly by suggesting that the
response of Black writers to Pound's award shows that the New Criticism remained for them an object by which they could critique the separation of art and politics, modes of America's imperial capitalism, and
anti-Black racism. That critique allowed for imagining new possibilities
for critical practice and the world that contained it, which I describe in
the book's next three chapters.

THE SOUTHERN AGRARIANS, AESTHETIC
REFLECTION, AND THE PLANTATION

In their 1930 manifesto *I'll Take My Stand*, the Nashville Agrarians sutured their aesthetic preferences to a set of material conditions required
to sustain aesthetic attention. Those material conditions were that of
an agrarian society. The Nashville group defines such a society as one
"in which agriculture is the leading vocation, whether for wealth, for
pleasure, or for prestige—a form of labor that is pursued with intelligence and leisure and that becomes the model to which the other forms
approach as well as they may."[11] This Agrarian vision of the world is set
against the rising tide of industrialism in the Southern United States
and, more implicitly, the fear that such industrialism would inevitably
lead to the spread of communism. The initially proposed title for the
Agrarian volume was not a line from the song "Dixie," but the more
clinical "Tracts against Communism."[12] The Agrarian concern is that
with industrialism, by insuring business "against fluctuation" the federal government would become an "economic super-organization,"
seemingly akin to the government of the Soviet Union.[13] At the same
time, there is a more quietly stated concern that "the militancy of labor"
fomented by industrial capitalism will seek to "bring about a fairer division of the spoils."[14] For the Agrarians, rampant industrialism either
leads to a continued incursion on the rights of Southern states by the
US federal government, or a coalition of class-united workers fighting
against the unequal accumulations of capital. While the anxiety about
big government and a racialized working class resonates with twenty-
first-century conservativism, it also reaches backward.[15] As W. E. B.
Du Bois stated plainly in his 1935 *Black Reconstruction*, in the Civil War
"the South was fighting for the protection and expansion of its agrarian
feudalism."[16]

With nostalgia for the plantocratic South animating their manifesto,
the Agrarians did not directly address at any length the exploitation of
labor that must take place in order for planters to accumulate wealth,
pleasure, and prestige. The primary mode of engaging the South's slave
past is through omission, though the volume does feature one essay by
Robert Penn Warren that discusses race at length. That essay calls for
the assimilation of Black people into a racialized hierarchy of labor in

the Agrarian South largely via an extended critique of W. E. B. Du Bois's arguments about education in *The Souls of Black Folk*, though Warren avoids mentioning Du Bois by name.[17] The omission of a discussion of slavery reflects the political economic logic of the Agrarian gambit; accumulations of capital are made possible through an invisible, racialized class of Black laborers. As a whole, *I'll Take My Stand* emblematizes a continued effort to suppress this essential and violent fact of the political economy of the United States.

Scholars like Michael Kreyling and Paul V. Murphy have pointed to *I'll Take My Stand* as crucial in establishing a Southern identity rooted in nostalgia for the South as it was imagined to have once been.[18] Such a retrenchment was necessary in the aftermath of the 1925 Scopes trial in Dayton, Tennessee. Thanks to the widely circulated writing of H. L. Mencken, *The State of Tennessee v. John Thomas Scopes* turned a Tennessee teacher's refusal to abide by the state's mandate to teach creationism into a nationwide debate about Southern identity. Mencken's assertion that the South was "plainly incompatible with civilized progress" ignited Robert Penn Warren, Allen Tate, John Crowe Ransom, and others to define the South otherwise.[19] The Agrarian definition valorized a white planter class with a detached aesthetic refinement rooted in tradition in labor and politics. This Agrarian defense came at the expense of poor whites, lambasted by Mencken for being the base of the resurgent Ku Klux Klan, and of the complete elision of the role of Black labor in the region.[20] In reaction to Mencken's challenge to a civilized South, the Agrarians, in Kreyling's phrasing, "invented"—and, I add, imposed a cultural understanding of—the South based simultaneously on a political-economic order (an agriculturally driven capitalism), a race-class hierarchy (genteel whiteness above poor whites above invisibilized Blackness), and aesthetic principles (the disinterested, metaphysical poetics that would come to define the New Criticism).

The aesthetic principles of the Agrarian project relied upon the racialized division of labor that otherwise subtended the Agrarian desire for the accumulation of wealth, pleasure, and prestige. One of *I'll Take My Stand*'s general principles, composed by John Crowe Ransom, reads: "Art depended, in general, like religion on a right attitude to nature; and in particular on a free and disinterested observation of nature that occurs only in leisure."[21] Art thus relies upon a "disinterested observation," and therefore requires free subjects who have a distinct capacity to separate themselves from the immediacy of the world around them.

In Ransom's phrase there echoes what Denise Ferreira da Silva defines as the "core statement of racial subjection." Ferreira da Silva suggests that "while the tools of universal reason (the 'laws of nature') produce and regulate human conditions, in each global region it establishes mentally (morally and intellectually) distinct kinds of human beings, namely, the self-determined subject and its outer-determined others, the ones whose minds are subjected to their *natural* (in the scientific sense) conditions."[22] She comes to this statement through a reading of Western Enlightenment philosophers like Kant who suggest that rationality or reason is the distinguishing characteristic of man. Put differently, if a subject is fully determined by nature—the world beyond the self—rather than being self-regulating or disinterested, then such a subject violates the natural law of man and is effectively excluded from humanity.[23] That subject is outer-determined, "affectable," and inescapably embodied, while the subject self-governed by reason becomes fully transparent. Ferreira da Silva argues that this becomes the basis for the social and political processes of modernity, thus linking a philosophical and aesthetic discourse to the racialized, material world. For the Agrarians, the creation and interpretation of art rely upon this "free and disinterested observation" made possible by the leisure generated by Black labor for an elite class in their formulation of an Agrarian society. While not philosophically novel, this simple statement about art from *I'll Take My Stand* highlights that the Agrarian position toward art relies both on racialization and on making invisible the labor of those racialized others.[24]

This aesthetic and political-economic nostalgia made the Agrarians excellent capitalists. They rhetorically mastered liberal capitalism's fundamental contradiction between freedom and violence, a contradiction naturalized by the racialized division between the self-determined subject and those who "react to" rather than control external forces, whom Ferreira da Silva terms outer-determined others.[25] For instance, the Agrarians proved themselves savants of print culture with *The Fugitive*, a little magazine of poetry that predated *I'll Take My Stand*. The success of *The Fugitive* relied on Black labor; the group selected a Black press to print the journal because they offered the cheapest rate in Nashville.[26] *The Fugitive*'s printing presents an explicit material instance of the Agrarian reliance upon Black labor, and it also stands as one of many efforts of the Agrarian group to circulate their political-economic platform by emphasizing their cultural contributions.

The university soon came to their attention as a crucial site to disseminate their ideas. Writing in 1935, the Agrarian Donald Davidson declared that college English teachers "will map out an orientation that will determine the culture of our generation."[27] Davidson saw the classroom reader as essential to this endeavor, and his Agrarian compatriot Robert Penn Warren, with Cleanth Brooks, fundamentally redefined the literature textbook in the years that followed. First published in 1938, Brooks and Warren's *Understanding Poetry* became "the most widely used college textbook in the university-level study of poetry."[28] When Brooks and Warren figure the poem as having an "organic nature," and as being "rooted very deep in human experience," they reiterate Agrarian claims about labor and leisure in aesthetic terms.[29] To see poetry as entangled within a nexus of organic nature and human nature is to insist that poetry must be observed disinterestedly because it is part of nature; this entanglement also means that poetry has a natural character because it emerges from man's rationality. Put differently, the orientation that Brooks and Warren use to, in Davidson's words, "determine the culture of our generation," grows from the Agrarian articulation of a political economy based on racial hierarchy.

The Agrarian interest in the university as a key hub of cultural circulation means that the New Critical attention to the peculiar organic nature of the text further led to a skewed vision of the institutions that support aesthetic inquiry. They claim the discipline itself as discrete, embedding their cultural belief within the routines of institutional practice and disseminating those beliefs to the future members of the professional and managerial class who encounter those ideas in the New Critical classroom. Lindon Barrett describes this expansion when he writes:

> The variety of critical programs joined under the title New Criticism hold in common the penchant to specify the literary text as an "autonomous" object in and of itself, having a peculiarly independent existence from industrial prosaic, disturbingly "democratic" modern society. The literary text, the valued form under the stewardship of New Criticism, provides a quintessential object for eliciting "anxiety about corruption, about containment, about penetration."[30]

Beyond circulating earlier Agrarian anxieties about the potential racial coalitions that may have emerged from federal "overreach" in the

South, the New Critical embrace of the organic or autonomous literary text generated value for itself at the expense of the racialized others on the other side of the boundary they reinforced. As Lisa Marie Cacho characterizes Barrett's idea, "value *needs* negativity," meaning that the "'object' of value needs an 'other' of value."[31] The world beyond the self-determined world of literature can then be seen as a suppressed but necessary repository for the import granted to academic literary study. Further, Barrett's claim suggests that the need to isolate purely literary inquiry from "penetration" relies on widely held and inherited white supremacist and patriarchal narratives about the necessary defense of vulnerable white women from hypersexualized Black men.

The false separation of literature and literary studies from paraliterary forms, as well as historical material realities of the production of those structures, disguises the violence against Barrett's "other of value" that is necessary for the existence of literary studies. The New Critics implicitly posit a tenuous analogy that underlies their definition of literature: just as Agrarian definitions of leisure required that one not glimpse the precincts of the South where Black people were violently forced to labor, so too do New Critical definitions of literary studies blaze the borders of literary activity against any material and symbolic incursions of blackness. Barrett chalks this up to a long history of "unthinkable logic rendering African Americans unthinkable" that can be traced across texts written by Thomas Jefferson, George Fitzhugh, the Agrarians, and even New Critics without a Nashville pedigree.[32] When the New Critics define the text as distinct, enclosing literary studies to make a material arrangement of institutional practice, they invoke and repeat the racialized violence of value precisely through their failure to attend to race. By fetishizing the bounds between the literary and the extraliterary, between the proper subject of value and its other, the New Critics effectively racialized inquiries into literature along the lines of their Agrarian program from the early part of the twentieth century. Or, as Michael Szalay has put it, the "commitment to poetic autonomy" masked a "commitment to obscuring the [professional and managerial class's] role in laundering black labor power" by midcentury.[33] The New Critical aesthetic bracketing animated by a defense against Blackness is yoked to political-economic logics that take advantage of a similar arrangement.

Examples abound of the tendency of academic critics to deploy the category of literature as a proxy for discussing the dynamics of race and racism in midcentury assessments of Black writers. When Stanley Kunitz reviewed Gwendolyn Brooks's Pulitzer Prize–winning poetry collection *Annie Allen* in 1950, he focused on the poem's "intrinsic value."[34] In the review, Kunitz posits that this intrinsic value relies not on Brooks's presentation of "a Negro urban milieu," but on the use of "these incendiary materials *naturally*" in the poems.[35] Kunitz unfurls his argument for his deracinated Brooks when he writes the following about "Pygmies Are Pygmies Still, Though Percht on Alps," his favorite Brooks poem: "Knowing its own limits, it is cleanly and truly separated from the jungle of conception and sensibility that constitutes the not-poem."[36] For Kunitz, Brooks's best work is that which is most controlled and which conforms most completely to a naturalized rationality; it is, in other words, the work furthest "from the jungle." Further, when Brooks is most regulated, her racialized and gendered body becomes invisible, allowing not-poems to become poems. Indeed, Ferreira da Silva reminds us that rationality ascribes the universalized European subject—what she refers to as the "transparent I"—with the capacity to own property and one's self. Kunitz fully encloses Brooks within this universal reason when he ends his review by cataloging some of Brooks's lines that are in his eyes the most right. He opines, "These are as many kinds of rightness, scattered though they be, as are tentatively possessed by a poet of her generation. To make the possession absolute and unique is the task that remains."[37] The transparent I becomes accessible to Brooks, implies Kunitz, when readers forget her body exists, and it is this condition that allows Kunitz to claim that modernity's full possession of her poetics is the horizon of Brooks's poetry.

The capacity to generate a natural object—the fact that allows Brooks's poetry to have intrinsic value as a literary object—and to possess it is remarked upon in another review of *Annie Allen*, by the poet William Jay Smith. He writes, "Much of her other work is marred by a use of jagged rhythms and an excessive striving for modernity. The reader feels at times also the burden of the author's attempt to come to terms with, and yet avoid, racial bias. But still, within their own convention, which is the convention of serious light verse, the poems make a just claim to our attention."[38] The attention sought here is that of the white reader, and a discussion of race is not how to garner it. Rather, the natural subject of poetry is modernist form, here denoted as "modernity," and Brooks's poetry pursues this form in spite of her subject.[39] For these critics, what makes Brooks's writing attention-worthy is its literary aspirations, not its subject matter. Commenting on a similar assessment of Brooks's work by Louis Simpson in a foundational Black Arts Movement text several decades on, Hoyt Fuller writes:

> "Certainly," the argument might proceed, "to be important, writing must have *universal values, universal implications*; it cannot deal exclusively with Negro problems." The plain but unstated assumption being, of course, that there are no "universal values" and no "universal implications" in Negro life.[40]

Indeed, both Kunitz and Smith address at some length how Brooks, a Black poet, can suppress an attention to Blackness, "the jungle of conception and sensibility that constitutes the not-poem"—a force they view as destabilizing to literature as such. In their eyes, this suppression is key to Brooks's literary achievement.

It is worth noting that neither Kunitz nor Smith was a member of the Nashville Agrarian movement. Yet their evaluations of Gwendolyn Brooks echo the fundamental critical principle stated in the first sentence of *Understanding Poetry*: "If poetry is worth teaching at all it is worth teaching as poetry."[41] When an aesthetic category is meant to make Blackness invisible, its encounter with Blackness requires a surfacing of the anti-Black logic it has internalized. The awkward acrobatics these writers undertake illustrates that the Blackness of Black writers had to be explained away by white critics to make literature a useful category for works written by Black people. What is remarkable about the reviews of Kunitz and Smith is how they explicitly explain away any possible sediments of race within the work of Gwendolyn Brooks. They preserve the literary object produced by Black writers by making invisible both Black labor and the material circumstances of Black people. This making invisible of Black labor and Black life is, in effect, an essential fetishization brought about by the New Critical definition of literature. Literature's status as a natural, organic object means that discussions and exchanges of it as literature obscure any discussion of the social relations that produce it.

NEW CRITICISM AND THE STATE

No Southerner ever dreams of heaven, or pictures his Utopia on earth,
without providing room for the Democratic party. Is it really possible that
the Democratic party can be held to a principle, and that the principle can
now be defined as agrarian, conservative, anti-industrial? It may not be
impossible, after all.

JOHN CROWE RANSOM, "Reconstructed but Unregenerate"[42]

In the middle of the twentieth century, racial discord within the United States increasingly became a geopolitical vulnerability. As Nikhil Pal Singh writes, "If New Deal economic reforms helped make the status of black [people] a national concern, World War II elevated U.S. racial division to a question of national security, international relations, and global justice."[43] Before and after World War II, the Soviet Union emphasized US racial inequality as a selling point for communism, even going so far as to recruit Black American artists like Langston Hughes and Gwendolyn Bennett to make propaganda art.[44] Such efforts were redoubled by the Communist Party USA and by Black activists within the United States. The tendency for global issues to be codified in terms of race led to the professionalization of race relations—what Howard Winant refers to as the "racial break." As Jodi Melamed puts it, "The liberal social sciences, now with the backing of the academy and the federal government, as well as philanthropies, envisioned social engineering on a national scale to create a racially inclusive US national culture and an unprejudiced citizenry."[45] Melamed defines this as the first "official anti-racism" of the United States. She emphasizes that official antiracisms sought to reframe American inequalities rather than significantly address them. These strategies, according to Melamed, "make structural inequality appear fair."[46] In other words, they generate a culture around a mode of inclusivity that still insisted upon the power and privilege that white people could and should continue to accumulate.

The postwar United States featured a significant fracturing of already tenuous political coalitions, particularly within the Democratic Party. The result was a reframing of American political discourse in terms of the emergent racial liberalism, the first form of official anti-

racism.[47] Within this shifting discursive landscape, the New Critics positioned themselves as objective and evaluative arbiters of culture and
its interpretation, a position that would make their methods particularly valuable to the state. New Criticism's aesthetic program bracketed
material inequalities along the lines of race and class in favor of a unified, organic society. This tension between what John Crowe Ransom
referred to as the "logical structure" and "local texture" of a work would
reflect the model of US federal and state governance in the postwar
years. By highlighting how parts of the federal government embraced
or mirrored New Critical principles on a number of fronts, I show that
the New Criticism played an important role in the establishment and
reproduction of US racial liberalism, particularly with regard to state
cultural activities and the American university system.

In the years after World War II, the fractious coalition Franklin Delano
Roosevelt had established between Southern Dixiecrats, labor advo-
cates, and corporate liberals in the Democratic Party finally cracked.
The breaking point was an effort to unionize industrial workers both
Black and white in the South. Center-right factions within the party
worked tirelessly to defeat interracial union campaigns because they
feared an end to segregation.[48] This type of interracial union campaign
sought to dismantle what Du Bois has famously called the "public and
psychological wage" afforded to white Southern workers.[49] That wage
of whiteness has long stood as the cornerstone not only of American
anti-Black racism, but for keeping actual wages low for the white working class and for disrupting interracial labor coalitions.[50] Beyond mar-
ginalizing the faction of social democrats, the consolidation of corporate elites and Dixiecrats preserved "access to exploitable labor and the
privileged political position of the underdeveloped and conservative
South."[51] President Harry Truman consolidated this fraying coalition
and became the standard bearer for racial liberalism, particularly after defeating challengers on the left and the right in his 1948 electoral
victory.[52]

It may not have been the utopian blueprint that Ransom laid for
the Democratic party in his contribution to *I'll Take My Stand*, but the
new Democratic coalition offered one path to maintain vestiges of the
Agrarian racial order. The cover for this political economic conceit of

the postwar Democratic coalition, and of Agrarianism, was a rhetorical collapse of anti-Blackness and anticommunism. To make the compromise tenable, a need arose to state plainly a disdain for communism (stigmatizing and criminalizing certain union activity) while blowing a whistle over the social and cultural ascendance of Black people (a play to the forceful hold on the wage of whiteness). In this frame, to know Paul Robeson made someone a communist, as demanding racial integration threatened the sanctity of the family. Uniting a disdain for "racial progress" and communism provided a key tool for racial liberalism, even when its contradictions jeopardized American Cold War efforts against Soviet Communism. As Mary Dudziak writes, "During the Cold War years, when international perceptions of American democracy were thought to affect the nation's ability to maintain its leadership role, and particularly to ensure that democracy would be appealing to newly independent nations in Asia and Africa, the diplomatic impact of race in America was especially stark."[53] The diplomatic pressure to address racism did not, however, lead to significant changes in policy at home. What resulted in most instances was, in Mary Helen Washington's description, "not action but pamphleteering"— that is, the misleading promotion of limited policy changes.[54]

The Democratic coalition positioned universities as crucial in defining, circulating, and animating the domestic and international visions of American empire during the Cold War. In 1946 Truman commissioned a study to evaluate the "objectives, methods, and facilities" of higher education. The seven-volume report, titled *Higher Education for American Democracy*, codifies racial liberalism for American universities by calling for curricula and institutions that "inspire in our young people a consuming enthusiasm for the democratic way of life and at the same time develop in them an active appreciation of different cultures and other people."[55] Universities were to train students to consume, to propagate American democracy, and to appreciate cultural difference. In sum, students were taught to live out postwar racial liberal values. These values may be so generally American that they appear to be politically neutral, but their enactment and practice belies how they would be used not only to reinforce American power globally, but to animate the uneven development along racial lines within the United States.

To their credit, the authors of *Higher Education for American Democ-*

racy register that their goals for higher education would ultimately not be realized until equal funding was granted to Black colleges, and until quotas on Jewish and Black students at predominantly white institutions were rescinded. Among scholars of the history of higher education, the Truman Commission report is seen as a progressive vision for colleges and universities in its call for a broad, equitable expansion of college access through federal aid, and its promotion of a general education curriculum that would undercut hierarchized divisions between institutions emphasizing the liberal arts and those focused on vocational education.[56] Yet, as the report's authors acknowledge, this advice could not be made compulsory without significant legislative and social change well beyond the limits of the report's purview. Because it was a nonbinding report, many of the commission's proposals were not adopted until the mid-1960s at the earliest, if they were adopted at all. As Nicholas Strohl has shown, the commission was most challenged to find consensus on issues where federal incursion into the business of states and private entities might have been necessary, especially with regards to segregation. Four members of the commission—including Frederick Douglass Patterson, the president of Tuskegee Institute and the Truman Commission's only Black participant—refused to sign on to the report's call to dismantle Jim Crow, because of concerns about gradualism.[57] In this respect, the report quietly registered that its progressive claims at the federal level presented only toothless challenges to segregation and the disinvestment in Black institutions.[58] The overall result was that the report, in Strohl's phrasing, "promoted an individualistic, rights-based vision of democratic freedom that would predominate in the postwar era."[59] That is, through its progressivism, *Higher Education for American Democracy* reproduces and endorses racial liberalism.

Just several years earlier, Dixiecrats had shaped the 1944 GI Bill to allow for segregation and disinvestment in Black institutions, highlighting the ways that policies that are seemingly liberal can further increase racial inequity. As Edward Humes has shown, "on its face, [the bill] was free of discrimination, promising equality of benefits and opportunity to all. Their genius, however, was in making certain the practical administration of those benefits and opportunities remained in "safe" hands—hands that wouldn't rock the boat of Jim Crow."[60] This meant that states could manage the distribution of benefits by making state-level decisions regarding which institutions should be expanded with state funding, a caveat that allowed for local control to maintain the racial status quo. The result was that Black veterans were denied home mortgages at staggering rates, and were refused admission to predominantly white institutions of higher education even as those institutions were nearly doubling their enrollments. Meanwhile, historically Black colleges had to turn away nearly seventy thousand benefit-seeking students, because those colleges could not secure the necessary funds to support the matriculation of those students from the governments of the states in which they operated.[61]

The Agrarian vision in *I'll Take My Stand* anticipated a model for enacting programs that would expand racial inequity through a deliberate turn away from the South's racist politics. Beyond memorializing its own dematerialized vision of the South, the Agrarian-cum-New-Critics' 1930s critique of communism required an approach that marginalized the role of Black labor in the South, effectively reinforcing the wage of whiteness by offering the promise of culture to white people alone. By couching this in the language of leisure, the Agrarians were able to make arguments explicitly devoid of race rhetoric but deeply rooted in maintaining racial hierarchies. The shape of this Agrarian approach persisted within New Critical aesthetic and political statements in the 1940s with the rise of a racial liberalism that carried a similar rhetorical structure.

The New Critical mode of interpretation came to be figured as distinctly democratic—a stroke against totalitarianism and communism—precisely because it allowed for the local elements of a poem to act independently of the poem's governing idea. John Crowe Ransom referred to this as poetry's capacity for the concrete universal, to be both specific and general. He figured the concrete universal as democratic in a set of lectures delivered in 1941, later published as "Criticism as Pure Speculation." There, Ransom articulated the poem and the state in a way that resembles the states' rights strategy of the Southern Democrats:

A poem is, so to speak, a democratic state, whereas a prose discourse—mathematical, scientific, ethical, or practical and vernacular—is a totalitarian state. The intention of a democratic state is to perform the work of state as effectively as it can perform it, subject to one reservation of conscience: that it will not despoil its members, the citizens, of the free exercise of their own private and independent characters. But the totalitarian state is interested solely in being effective, and regards the citizens as no citizens at all; that is, regards them as functional members whose existence is totally defined by their allotted contributions to its ends; it has no use for their private characters, and therefore no provision for them. I indicate of course the extreme of polar opposition between two polities, without denying that a polity may come to us rather mixed up.

In this trope the operation of the state as a whole represents of course the logical paraphrase or argument of the poem. The private character of the citizens represents the particularity asserted by the parts in the poem.... A poem is a *logical structure* having a *local texture.*[62]

Critics of this passage have seen it as reaching backward to Ransom's Agrarian ideal and forward toward establishing a "purer democracy [that] would defeat totalitarianism and bring an end to the cold war."[63] In this respect, this important statement about New Critical interpretation bridges the political-economic visions of Agrarianism with the racial liberalism of the United States at the outset of the Cold War. Ransom insists that the state, like a poem, offers a mere framework under which local actors can assert their own individuality, even if these individuals act against the wider aim of the logical structure of the democratic state. Aspects of Ransom's framework can be seen in legislation, like the GI Bill, that offers a nominally equitable framework which in certain local jurisdictions can be retooled to fit long-standing racist practice on the ground, counteracting and generating tension between that wider framework and the "free exercise of . . . private and independent characters." Ransom had suggested before that the concrete universal could be applied to political economic situations. In 1930 he wrote, "Slavery was a feature monstrous enough in theory, but, more often than not, humane in practice."[64] Ransom's theory of poetry is tied to his theory of liberal democracy and his questionable historiography of the plantocracy.

This New Critical argument about poetry as a state would soon stand as a platform for the state's mobilization of literature and culture. The Agrarian/New Critical state vision launched the New Critics to positions of prominence both within the university system and

in the emerging federal and federal-adjacent cultural apparatus, which
Evan Kindley has called "Big Criticism."[65] In 1943, Allen Tate became
the US consultant in poetry to the Library of Congress, and Robert
Penn Warren took the chair the following year. In 1947, Cleanth Brooks
joined the faculty at Yale, where Warren would join him three years
later. This rise to prominence has at times been attributed to close
reading's minimal requirements for prerequisite knowledge, making it
well-suited for the massive influx of mostly white students to the university system. As Gerald Graff has argued, putting emphasis on the
literary text "seemed a tactic ideally suited to a new, mass student body
that could not be depended on to bring to the university any common
cultural background."[66] In Graff's analysis, the New Critical method
filled a need that grew out of a democratizing program. Yet Graff concedes that the critical abstraction required in the New Criticism proved
more successful at elite institutions, such as Stanford, than at universities that later faced more acutely the problems of mass education, like
CUNY.[67] If the New Criticism did not serve the masses in practice, its
success at elite institutions and the frequency with which its rhetoric
about logical structure and local texture appeared in curricular recommendations offers a different read on its democratic credentials. What
Graff passes over in his otherwise astute observation regarding the
theoretical dimension of New Criticism's democratizing credentials is
that the poetic and political theory of New Criticism shaped the very
idea of what it meant to be democratic in the midcentury. The New
Criticism appeared to be suited for mass democratic education because its ideas critically shaped US racial liberalism in the context of
higher education and cultural production. Concisely, in certain contexts, the New Criticism defines the democratic state of racial liberalism, not merely capitalizing on it.

New Criticism conducts its definitional work by finding an explanation to otherwise unify the diverse elements within a work. The
conveners of influential public and private reports on higher education's function for an expanding populace wagered that if the harmo-
nizing of diverse strands within a logical structure could occur in a
poem, so too, could it shape the democratic state. In *Higher Education for American Democracy*, colleges and universities are positioned
as those which "embody the principle of *diversity in unity:* each institution, State, or other agency will continue to make its own contri-

bution in its own way. But educational leaders should try to agree on certain common objectives that can serve as a stimulus and guide to individual decision and action."[68] The principle of *diversity in unity* echoes, of course, the motto emblazoned on the seal of the United States, "E pluribus unum"—an echo that suggests a longer history of abstracted and limited notions of competing elements being resolved into an American ideal. The midcentury usage maps onto Ransom's reflection on the concrete universal while also recalling Ransom's definition of minority groups offered in *I'll Take My Stand*, suggesting the ways in which flexible and selective definitions of "diversity" can be marshaled to serve the wider interests of racial liberalism. In *I'll Take My Stand*, Ransom argues that the South is a "minority group" similar to "Western farmers" and "ancient New England townships." He insists that "the unifying effective bond between these geographically diverse elements of public opinion will be the clean-cut policy that the rural life of America must be defended."[69] In 1930 Ransom argued that a mode of diversity in unity was possible, when what constituted diversity to him were geographic differences in white rural circumstances. To phrase this in the terms of his 1941 essay, his counterrevolutionary coalition offered a check to the logical structure of the federal government. Where Ransom's democratic system has local texture and a logical structure, the American system of higher education has the "individual decision and action" of particular institutions shaped by "common objectives." Like Ransom, the report's authors contrast this democratic structure with what they call an "authoritarian" society; they insist that their common objectives bolster the "social role of education" in a democracy. Ransom's thinking highlights how progressive calls for ideas such as diversity in unity could be cast to describe counterrevolutionary crusades and be a model for the success of the political-economic goals of those movements. Ransom's Agrarian essays provide an important model for how beleaguered "Lost Cause" white Southerners could adopt a minoritarian rhetorical position to otherwise protect the power of white people through this managerial strategy.[70]

The perceived efficacy of the New Criticism's management of difference in the racial liberal scheme further lodged the movement within the US state and helped to spread the principles of American capitalism within and beyond its borders. A number of scholars have argued

that the New Criticism proved pivotal to the formation of the professional and managerial class, or, more simply, in Paul Bové's phrasing,
the development of "a strategy for management."[71] Describing the university's role in shaping this class formation and determining its managerial terms, Christopher Newfield writes that "mass culture was . . .
multiple culture" to be managed by "political, economic, and legal
means, such as ethnic as well as racial segregation, economic stratification, immigration restrictions, racial 'sciences,' and intellectual
admissions exams, but it also used cultural methods, enabling competing claims to be handled by subordinating their (sub)cultures of
origin to an Anglo-Saxon core."[72] The New Criticism proved central
toward establishing the cultural norms by which these material distri-
butions could be meted out racially. The growing importance of this
cultural project bridged political divides between different critical
schools (such as the New York Intellectuals and the New Critics), in
part because they all benefited from the influx of federal, academic, and
foundational dollars being devoted to the project of defining literature
and culture.[73] These coalitions and the broad literary principles they
espoused led to a wide array of critical orientations being folded under
the New Criticism.

When these critical modes were made part of this cultural project,
their particularity was lost to the logical structure of the racial liberalism offered by Ransom and the Agrarian group. For example, Joseph
North has suggested that misreadings of I. A. Richards's materialist
criticism are due to the New Critics "adopting Richards . . . to rescue
the aesthetic from the realm of practical, material, and instrumental
values."[74] One place we can see this redirection in action is in the connotation of the "diversity in unity" idea articulated in *Higher Education
for American Democracy*. Richards was a committee member on James
Bryant Conant's *General Education in a Free Society* (1945), the widely
influential text produced by Harvard with the goal to create and shape
a new curriculum. While the report largely failed at Harvard, Gregory Galt Harpham has argued that the volume, often referred to as the
Harvard Redbook, "became national policy" in proposal form as the
Truman Report.[75] There is much similarity to the Truman Report's insistence on finding "diversity in unity" in the Redbook's suggestion that
the United States is "a centrifugal culture in extreme need of unifying
forces."[76] In their account of the report, however, Mark Garrett Cooper

and John Marx suggest that the Redbook's authors "proposed John Crowe Ransom's 'scientific' reading practice as general intellectual equipment" and therefore particularly suited to establishing the norms necessary to unify American culture.[77] Cooper and Marx suggest that beyond Richards, other committee members had fluency in a generalized and abstracted version of the New Criticism's theory of communications; this assisted in institutionalizing an ideally rather than materially rooted version of Richards's thought. These curricular and higher education policy reports highlight how the shape of New Critical ideas and methods becomes a means to manage difference and to allow for local practice contra the national aim. Meanwhile, despite any practical and materialist investments, the fact that the many recommendations offered in these reports were never implemented leaves their recommendations in the realm of the rhetorical. As North suggests, the materialist aesthetic ideas Richards offers come to be appropriated by the racial liberal means that, like the Agrarian New Criticism, are idealist. This could be leveraged by the New Critics to argue most broadly for their plantocratic political economic organization, which at times was in direct opposition to the one proposed by the progressive Truman Commission, and to recast the aims of the report's recommendations with regard to literary and cultural education.

This appropriation was made possible by a reconfiguration in the rhetorical approach of some members of the Agrarian group. John Crowe Ransom eventually substituted some of his agrarian principles for American liberal capitalism's consumerism; he suggested that government support might be necessary for bringing white rural people more directly into the economy. In 1952 he argued, "You cannot have mass production unless you have mass consumption too; and that the cue for all future government in this country is by every possible indirect means to distribute purchase-money among the groups which have not had it."[78] Ransom's argument restates what the Truman Commission suggested was the role of higher education for the farmer: to teach that he was "a consumer, as well as a producer." This lesson in consumption would "come from general education," the very part of the curriculum that Ransom's scientific reading practice subtended.[79] In short, guided by Agrarian aesthetic and cultural principles, Ransom's imagined coalition of farmers from the West, South, and Northeast would finally be united under the banner of "consumer," all while further degrading Black access to capital's rewards through new modes of managing Black labor.

As the concrete universal shapes administrative power within the American system of higher education, New Critical literary study in colleges and universities helps to generate the individual, the privileged unit of American society. In *Higher Education for American Democracy*, the Truman Commission argues that literature "can do as much as any other single form of experience to broaden and deepen the perceptions and sympathies of the individual," and that this experience only occurs through the practice of close reading:[80]

> This consequence does not, however, follow from the study of details of literary history, literary biography, literary techniques, or any other of the accompaniments to literature that make up specialization in the subject. The contribution of literature to insight and emotional maturity will come from one's own reading of the world's literary treasures, and from reflection upon them.
>
> The world's literary treasures are not those of the West alone. They include the great intellectual statements of men everywhere and in all ages. There is probably no better way of promoting the intellectual and spiritual unity of mankind than through free trade in enduring literary expressions.[81]

Literature's capacity for making individuals, or individuation, emerges from a reflection on reading literature, not necessarily engaging with it on the terms of historical or philological study. If, as Paul Bové argues, "the effect of the institution of criticism . . . is to individualize persons by measuring them against a series of norms," then the norms established here relate to the universality of a definition of Western humanity and the insistence that "free trade" both exports and maintains that definition.[82] The Truman Commission's insistence on the universality of Western man and the protection of free trade positions New Critical literary education on the front lines to establish a US world order with universal aspirations against communism, a political-economic system that threatens free enterprise and the American brand of liberal education. This claim supports the report's larger argument that "America's strength at home and abroad in the years ahead will be determined in large measure by the quality and the effectiveness of the education it provides for its citizens."[83]

Higher Education for American Democracy unfurls the reasoning for the weaponization of a selective swath of New Critical practices within the Office of Strategic Services, and later the CIA and the FBI, for decoding the cultural work of subversives. These programs recruited students of literature to conduct intelligence gathering and counterintelligence operations against those identified as subversives for their communist affiliations, or for merely being Black. As William Maxwell argues, "the FBI is perhaps the most dedicated and influential forgotten critic of African American literature," based on the sheer scope of its observations on Black cultural production from 1919 to 1972.[84] The scope of the embeddedness of New Critical practice on US domestic and foreign intelligence agencies is certainly remarkable in its own right. Here, however, I point primarily to New Criticism's importance as a tool for exporting and maintaining the universalized American individual made possible by free trade, to highlight that the "series of norms" necessary for this process of individuation is both anti-Black and anticommunist. To recognize the anti-Black and anticommunist dimensions within the production of American individuals is to see that the call for "diversity in unity," which perhaps appears antiracist on its face, measures that unity on the basis of the unspoken standards of white universality. Indeed, these ideas helped to organize material and administrative apparatuses of the US state against Black and red "subversives."

In their explicitly political work of the 1930s and their implicitly political work of the 1940s and 1950s, the Agrarian New Critics develop a means for making anticommunist and anti-Black claims in relatively neutral terms, and for offering a path to enact a racially ordered political economy within, but against, emerging forms of federal antiracist discourse. Because this mode resonated deeply with the ruling political coalition formed after World War II, the New Critical ideas gained prominence both within the American system of higher education and within the cultural propaganda and intelligence operations of the Cold War. This critical mode became a way to acquire intelligence for the state, to enact racially and politically motivated surveillance, and to conduct counterintelligence operations against antiracist and decolonial writers and movements. Put differently, the Agrarian New

Criticism came to implicitly shape the ideas about and practice of the American democratic state.

THE BOLLINGEN CONTROVERSY

To this point I have established that the New Critical aesthetic vision of literature and its critical practice are both sutured to political economic models first of Southern Agrarianism, and then of US liberal capitalism. This suturing is made possible through an insistence on the separation of literature and criticism from the social and political world of which they are a part. The separation of literature foregrounds a literary object as the object of study by suppressing the social relations that go into producing literature. The isolation of criticism obscures the fact that the New Criticism is intimately entangled in the state project of racial liberalism, particularly in the development of a policy program for higher education and in the mobilization of state surveillance and intelligence operations during the Cold War. I refer to this process in terms of Marx's fetishism because the New Criticism tends to be remembered as solely an academic project about the autonomy of literature, not as a political economic project entangled with the US racial liberal state. What solidified the reception of the New Criticism as an aesthetic academic project rather than a state project associated with racial liberalism? The answer lies in the story of the first and last poetry award that was granted by the federal government.

When the Fellows of the Library of Congress awarded Ezra Pound's *Pisan Cantos* the inaugural Bollingen Prize for poetry, which included a one-thousand-dollar honorarium, a national controversy ignited over the question of politics in literary interpretation. To endure this controversy, many prominent New Critics—some of whom were among the Fellows who selected Pound—had to define publicly the function and purpose of their critical program. Their redefinition actively disavowed the political capacity of literary interpretation. Paradoxically, it was these disavowals that made New Criticism a recognizable object of investigation and a proper noun. Indeed, the late 1940s and early 1950s brought a new level of scrutiny to the growing New Critical claim that its methods were fundamentally democratic.

Among the most significant exercises in New Critical scrutiny is an essay by R. P. Blackmur titled "A Burden for Critics." Though it was published just before the Bollingen Prize was awarded, Blackmur anticipates the terms on which the New Criticism's public viability would be evaluated. He argues that "we must see how natural, and at bottom how facile, a thing [the New Criticism] has been."[85] Frustrated with the limits of New Critical formalism, Blackmur has decided that it is time "to make bridges between the society and the arts," meaning that critics must make explicit connections between poetry and the world in which poetry emerges.[86] Blackmur does not conclude that such bridges would crack the borders the New Critics had constructed around the literary, the borders that I earlier suggested gave occasion for reviewers to puzzle over whether Black writers could write a poem that was actually a poem. He does suggest, however, that his essay's titular burden is that "of knowledge and the division of labor" that has led to a loss of "the field of common reference," a melancholy of sorts that results from the simultaneous fracturing and expanse of knowledge (and ignorance) laid bare by World War II.[87] In asking for an account of criticism's relation to political economy, Blackmur touched the third rail powering the New Criticism's program. In response to Blackmur's argument, New Critical journals mobilized a number of essays and series to rearticulate their position, including the "My Credoes" series in the *Kenyon Review,* which literary historian Grant Webster has deemed the "climax" of the pivotal journal.[88]

As this series of essays began to unfold, the internal dissatisfaction with the disconnect between literature and society suddenly became news on the front page of the *New York Times* and the subject of a debate on the floor of Congress. The twelve Fellows of the Library of Congress—including T. S. Eliot, Robert Penn Warren, Allen Tate, Robert Lowell, and Katherine Anne Porter—gave a prize to a person being held at St. Elizabeth's Hospital in Washington, DC, because he was mentally unfit to stand trial for treason. Pound had been transferred to the asylum in 1945 after spending several weeks in a US Army compound in Italy, where he had turned himself in. Pound had been arrested on charges of treason stemming from his pro-Mussolini lectures delivered on Italian radio several years earlier. Predictably, granting a federally supported award to a prisoner of the state did not sit well for many.

Nevertheless, the ensuing firestorm eventually focused less on Pound himself and more on how a decision to honor Pound could be made by the US literary establishment on behalf of the federal government. Admittedly, Pound's poetics have often been placed in stark contrast with certain principles of New Critical formalism. However, contemporaneous commentators, such as Martha Millet, a CPUSA literary critic and instructor at the Jefferson School of Social Science, aligned Pound with the New Critical conservatism. As Sarah Ehlers's archival research reveals, Millet "dubbed the 'holy trinity' of Pound, T. S. Eliot, and Allen Tate as well as other devotees of what she described . . . as the 'malevolent rule' of New Criticism."[89] The Bollingen controversy would popularize a version of this alignment in liberal critical circles, and would thus shift attention away from Pound's politics and toward those perceived as New Critics. Karl Shapiro, one of the Fellows and later the editor of *Poetry*, told the *Baltimore Sun*:

> I disagree vehemently with the principle embodied in the Library press release that to judge a work of art on other than esthetic grounds is "to deny the objective perception of value on which any civilized society must rest." This is not a statement of principle but an apology; in no case is it a fact that can stand historical or logical inquiry. . . . I think it can be pointed out that such an interpretation of literature stems directly from a coterie of writers called the "new critics."[90]

In the *Saturday Review of Literature*, Robert Hillyer amplified the point that the Bollingen issue was about the New Critics when he claimed they were part of a conspiracy to install a totalitarian regime in the United States. Hillyer's polemic was largely panned for its invective, but more rhetorically measured accounts also saw the New Criticism's dogmatic commitment to aesthetic autonomy as a threat to American democracy. The editor of the *Partisan Review*, William Barrett, wondered why, when "making a public award and were therefore directly involved in public responsibilities," the Fellows couldn't put aside their "obsess[ion] with formal and technical questions."[91] The Bollingen controversy amplified Blackmur's concern about the public and political ramifications of the New Critical aesthetic orthodoxy at the same time as it widely circulated the notion that the New Criticism was not democratic but totalitarian.

The New Critical response to these dual fronts was to foreground the inherent value of the object that Ransom previously had claimed as democratic: poetry. Their defense of the selection of Pound deemphasized the process of determining what poetic value was, and instead argued that poetic value was simply to be found inside the poem; put differently, criticism became an act of discovery rather than a social process.[92] To look beyond the poem, they claimed, would not be objective or rational, and would be against certain principles that held together American democracy. This argument is laid out in the press release that announced Pound's selection for the Bollingen Prize:

> The fellows are aware that objections may be made to awarding a prize to a man situated as is Mr. Pound. In their view, however, the possibility of such objection did not alter the responsibility assumed by the Jury of Selection. This was to make a choice for the award among the eligible books, provided any one merited such recognition, according to the terms of the Bollingen Prize. To permit other considerations than that of poetic achievement to sway the decision would destroy the significance of the award and would in principle deny the validity of that objective perception of value on which any civilized society must rest.[93]

The press release foregrounds "poetic achievement" as that which determined the recipient of the award, rather than the Fellows themselves. According to this document, what the Fellows performed was not an evaluation but merely the observation of inherent value, a positioning that deemphasized interpretation's social labor. Indeed, with each sentence in the release the presence of humans in the process of aesthetic evaluation is progressively removed, so that the final clause is merely the statement of what was believed to be an empirical principle. This formal progression matches the argument the Fellows make: that neither the poet's background nor the political position of a narrator within a poem matter to evaluating poetry, because both disallow an "objective" evaluation of the poem. This brackets not only identity but also an attention to the social and political processes central to the evaluation of literature. Most important, this bracketing of social process stands as the foundation of "any civilized society." This means that identifying the value inherent in a democratic object—the poem—ultimately affirms the fundamental principles of American society, rather than dictating such principles in a totalitarian exercise. The

Fellows figured this process as objective, and in doing so, they asserted that this definition of literary value constituted what the Agrarians had earlier referred to as the "disinterested observation of nature," an aesthetic building block for "the political and racial order of modernity," according to David Lloyd.[94]

The Bollingen press release—and the New Critical response—deemphasized the work of the critic and thus seemed to "end" the New Criticism. No longer was the New Criticism a living entity; now it was something dead. William Cain writes, "The New Critics rapidly turned 'against' New Criticism itself at this time."[95] Even some of the most prominent New Critics denied knowledge of the movement as such. In 1949, Allen Tate wrote, "I do not know what the New Criticism is. . . . I merely acknowledge the presence of the myth." In the same year, Cleanth Brooks claimed in a letter that he could not "even claim to know certainly who they [the New Critics] are."[96] By 1951, in the wake of Bollingen, Austin Warren had come across the idea that "Anglo-American criticism has come to an end" so frequently that statements about criticism's demise had become "commonplace."[97] While these denials were being issued, editors at the *Kenyon Review*, the *Sewanee Review*, the *Southern Review*, and the *Partisan Review* began to capitalize the New Criticism as a proper noun. By declaring New Criticism a myth and disaffiliating with the movement, Brooks, Tate, and other New Critics ultimately generated something seemingly devoid of social activity and human labor: an American democratic object in its own right.

As I suggested at the outset of this chapter, the New Criticism's efforts to privilege literature and democracy apart from the social, political, and economic world has been a subject largely parsed piecemeal along disciplinary lines. One finds accounts, for instance, of the Agrarian New Critics and their rise to power in histories of American conservatism, the formations of Southern identity, and even the formation of the modern university.[98] Those historical accounts are distant from the investigations in literary studies that suspend these political-economic considerations for an analysis of the methodological and philosophical principles of New Critical aesthetics. On the one hand, the work of this chapter has been to highlight that despite the massive amount of work done on the New Criticism, more could be done to develop an account of how the political-economic considerations of the New Criticism inform and support its methodological tendencies, bridging more fully the disciplinary divide the movement itself seemed to engender. On the other hand, I have shown the New Criticism as an aesthetic, political-economic, and state program in order to highlight that when Black writers address this entity, their claims reach far beyond an esoteric literary project. Instead, critiques of the New Criticism by Black writers, especially those on the left, touch on the political-economic function of literary criticism, connections to the discourse of racial liberalism, and, more broadly, the state suppression of Black and communist movements.

The few mentions of the Bollingen controversy in the Black press suggest that Black writers identified the New Criticism as obscuring the social process of literature's interpretation and valuation, as well as the connection of New Critical practice to the state's racial liberalism. In a book review in the *Baltimore Afro-American,* J. Saunders Redding mentioned that Pound was one among several poets for whom a "new criticism" had been developed "to cope (and grope)" with white modernist poetry.[99] Redding suggested that this criticism was far removed from a direct address to the mind and the emotions, and that if anything, "you pore over the new criticism for hours only to discover in the end that you have come to an understanding of a critique of nothing."[100] Redding's assessment of the "new criticism" highlighted the interpretive movement's detachment from readers, and its admiration for its expansion of modernism's formal complexity.

Langston Hughes, however, took this a step further in a column in the *Chicago Defender.* Hughes identified that the vagaries of the New Critical project were directed toward the defense of a particular political-economic program grounded in white supremacy. The subject of this edition of Hughes's column was why Paul Robeson could and should express his political views as an artist, despite suggestions to the contrary. Hughes argued that Robeson's popularity stemmed from his "political and racial opinions" even if that meant he faced protests and violent threats from white Americans.[101] The white American reaction to Robeson came down to "the fashion in this American country of ours to keep Negroes from doing things that other citizens may do with impunity."[102]

For Hughes, Pound and his recent award provided an example of what those white Americans lauded in their impunity:

> Ezra Pound, who broadcast for Mussolini from Fascist Italy during the recent war, came home to win only a few months ago a Library of Congress poetry prize. I never heard the Klan or the American Legion utter a mumbling word against him at that time.[103]

The Fellows of the Library of Congress—and by extension the New Critics—were part of an institutional response that offered a particular type of political freedom to white Americans that was largely out of step with a communist coalition that called for the equality of the colored peoples of the world. It would not have been lost on Hughes or the readers of the *Chicago Defender* that a Black writer facing charges similar to those leveled at Pound would not be presumed "unfit" and sent to St. Elizabeth's. Just two years later, for instance, the federal government would indict W. E. B. Du Bois and put him on trial for treason because of his public and unapologetic opposition to nuclear war and his advocacy for peace. Robeson was tied to a similar strain of Black left politics. Hughes suggested that part of Robeson's appeal was the fact that his opinions "happen to be the opinions held by millions of people in the Soviet Union and China . . . where race prejudice, poverty, and Anglo-Saxon scorn are booked to go."[104] Hughes rightly suggested that Robeson stood as a great artist *and* pillar of Black decolonial and anticapitalist politics, something that white American institutions—of which the New Criticism was an integral part—were violently set against.[105]

Hughes identified the New Criticism as an institution that enforced an arbitrary separation between culture and politics, maintained practices of racial discrimination in a democratic nation, and rejected communism, which called for solidarity among people of color across the world. This observation evokes the wider sense of the New Criticism that Black writers on the left would target in their critiques. At the same time, Hughes's contrast of Pound with Paul Robeson highlights how Black left challenges to the New Critics did far more than identify the shortcomings of literary critical and state practice. These efforts proposed a different form and possibility for democracy, embodied perhaps most iconically by Robeson himself. As Shana Redmond has argued, "Robeson's sound-labor, which he launched from stages all over the world, was formative in the thought of progressive, radical, and Third World liberationist actors and organizations, the workers and the lovers, the thinkers as well as the musicians."[106] In other words, Robeson formed a clear-eyed vision of a world for the People, a world he pursued relentlessly and established in the present, despite the challenges of the Cold War state and its grip on culture. In drawing on Robeson as a counter to Pound, Hughes insinuated the wider stakes of a critique of the entanglement of literary criticism with the racial liberal state. Black radical challenges to the New Criticism expanded beyond, just as they circulated within, ideas of literary interpretation, the system of higher education, and the political economy of American democracy.

⊙ 2 ⊙

Melvin B. Tolson's Belated Bomb

A character in "The Curator," book 1 of Melvin B. Tolson's 1965 epic poem *Harlem Gallery*, finds himself reflecting on the dilemma of a Black artist: "the dialectic of / to be or not to be / a Negro."[1] This character is Hideho Heights, described by the poem's narrator as "The People's Poet," seemingly challenged by the "bifacial nature of his poetry."[2] When Hideho—named for the famous Cab Calloway song—enters Tolson's epic, he does so with an ode to Louis Armstrong performed before a crowd assembled at the Curator's Gallery. If one face in the "bifacial" nature of poetry is Hideho's tribute to Satchmo, emblematic of his embrace of jazz, a distinctly Black social art, then his other face chants the words of "the private poem in the modern vein."[3] The narrator glimpses Hideho's attempt at modern poetry strewn in his apartment, while Hideho himself remains passed out drunk. What the narrator discovers in those lines is "the eyesight proof / that the Color Line, as well as the Party Line, / splits an artist's identity."[4] *Harlem Gallery*'s narrator highlights the aesthetic repercussions brought about by the bifurcated political choice faced by Hideho. One option is the public poem that appeals to both Black and red, and the other is the private, modernist verse that ensures a degree of memorialization in the hallowed corridors of the institutions of literature. Tolson's literary legacy has been defined—and obscured—by this very bifurcation.

Though Tolson's positioning between the seemingly opposed private poem and Black social art is forcefully captured in *Harlem Gallery*, nothing exemplifies it more than the debate, the rumor, and the confoundment surrounding Tolson's solicitation of Allen Tate to write a preface for his 1953 poem *Libretto for the Republic of Liberia*. The poet

Dudley Randall writes of what Tolson told him about the decision in a 1966 issue of *Negro Digest*:

> After completing *Libretto for the Republic of Liberia* [Tolson] asked Allen Tate to write a preface for it, and Tate replied that he wasn't interested in the propaganda of Negro poets. Tolson spent a year studying modern poetic techniques and rewriting the poem so that it said the same things in a different way and then sent it to Tate. Tate wrote a preface in which he said, "For the first time, it seems to me, a Negro poet has assimilated the full poetic language of his time...."[5]

Tolson's story told to Randall only seemed to confirm the assimilationist critique that his notoriously difficult *Libretto* found from a number of contemporaneous Black critics, most prominently J. Saunders Redding, and to anticipate a similar criticism from some later scholarly observers, like Arnold Rampersad.[6] Nevertheless, this story illuminates why Tolson found pride in Tate's preface, which he once described as "our literary Emancipation Proclamation."[7] Tolson's account suggests that his trickster spirit earned this hard-won literary freedom, using the master's tools to celebrate the African nation for which the American Tolson had been named poet laureate. This reading is only bolstered by the fact that crucial details of the story told to Randall are fabricated, according to Tolson's biographer Robert Farnsworth.[8] Tate never rejected the poem, nor did he turn down Tolson's request for a preface. Tolson's rumor about his rejection and his refashioned modernist success is an effort to get in the last word on the politics of his poetics.

The characterization of Hideho marks another clear attempt to describe the institutional entanglement of aesthetics, racism, and political economy that Tolson saw as an index of both Western philosophical thought and the literary institutions of the American New Criticism. Hideho's "private poem in the modern idiom" plays with and challenges the historical reception of Tolson's encounter with Tate and with the major institutions of literary modernism. Through a lens that aligns the New Critical appreciation of modernist aesthetics to the supremacy of whiteness, such a poem potentially delegitimizes the Black, popular, and radical literary engagements and political commitments of Hideho and, by fiat, Tolson himself. While care must always be taken in collapsing a fictional poet with its creator, Tolson invites the comparison as a way to question the internal logic of the literary critical hegemony. The title of Hideho's private poem, "E. & O. E.," is the same as the title of Tolson's poem published in *Poetry* magazine in 1951, which earned Tolson the magazine's Bess Hokin Prize. The link Tolson offers between himself and Hideho provides a pathway to follow the ways in which literary critical practices and the wider figuration of the roots of the so-called "American Negro problem" are of pivotal importance to Tolson's poetic project.

Tolson's depiction of Hideho in *Harlem Gallery* highlights that Tolson's relationship to modernism, the New Criticism, and even US political economy has been both an important subject for his poetry and something that his work seeks to refigure. When composing his thesis for his master's degree in comparative literature at Columbia University in 1932, Tolson invoked the quarrel between Countee Cullen and Langston Hughes over the value of being a "poet" rather than a "Negro poet" as "antipodes of the Harlem Renaissance." "The former is a classicist and conservative," Tolson writes, "the latter, an experimentalist and a radical."[9] Indeed, the dilemma of the Black artist and its historical roots is central to Tolson's poetics, his criticism, and his politics. This dilemma has long shaped the scholarly understanding of Tolson in studies by Michael Berubé, Aldon Nielsen, Kathy Lou Schultz, and others.[10] Whether these scholars see Tolson's engagement with Tate as assimilatory or deterritorializing, they agree that Tolson is trapped between the implied racialization of literary modernism *and* the major canonized Black literary movements of the twentieth century (the New Negro Renaissance and the Black Arts Movement). Matthew Hart, for instance, concedes that "Tolson belongs fully to no literary movement."[11] Yet he registers that the "constant rearticulation" of Tolson's reception in terms of Blackness and modernism "risks perpetuating the very marginalization that critics have sought to redress."[12] Hart correctly identifies that studies of Tolson imply that the very terms scholars seek to undo in investigating his work still have a hold on how many literary studies scholars are trained to approach Black poetry.

In excavating Tolson's challenge to Tate, it becomes clear that the linked binaries embedded in literary modernism—literary or popular, white or Black, timeless or trendy, aesthetic or political, individual or social—are the very poles that Tolson sought to dismantle. Like the rumor Tolson passed to Dudley Randall, Hideho's bisected pursuit of the irreconcilable role of the people's poet and the canonical, private modernist obsessed with the unity of form and content shows that from Tolson's view, there was more to his solicitation of Allen Tate than a desire for white institutional acceptance. Tolson argues that Black poetry need neither be limited by modernist definitions of poetry nor defined by modernism's foil, the populist and historically determined forms promoted by American communists. Indeed, Tolson wagered that surfacing and destroying these submerged assumptions maintained by New Critical standard bearers would be a decolonial event of world-historical importance. Even Hart's account of Tolson's complex vision of Black revolution implies that it is precisely Tolson's engagement with modernism that still limits the radical ambit of his political imagination.

In this chapter I highlight how Tolson understood this differently. He targeted the New Criticism and Allen Tate because it was a literary emblem and a material check against his wider social and political visions which centered poetry's social and political import. Tolson invited Tate to a debate to challenge Tate's defense of the implicit knot the New Critics had tied between race, political economy, American empire, and literary form—a knot I have described in the previous chapter. Tolson hoped that Tate's preface would serve as an opening statement that he could counter, but the preface turned out to be the last public word on the matter until the story told to Dudley Randall. To disarticulate the racial, political, and aesthetic assumptions lingering beneath the authority of critical judgment, Tolson engaged Tate in a lengthy correspondence about the coherence of New Critical interpretation, a correspondence he sought to excerpt and publish as a rebuttal to Tate's assessment of *Libretto* in the *Sewanee Review*, a key New Critical journal once edited by Tate. Tolson's essay "Excerpts from a Letter to Allen Tate," drafted in 1950, was never published, but the typescript drafts located in Tolson's papers held at the Library of Congress show that Tolson hoped to illustrate that Tate's poetry and critical judgment were determined by the color line: what W. E. B. Du Bois characterized as "the problem of the Twentieth Century."[13]

As he does in *Harlem Gallery*, Tolson references Du Bois's color line throughout his discussion with Tate. For Du Bois, the color line simultaneously refers to the geopolitical order that has grown out of European colonialism and American slavery; the actual segregation and dispossession of Black people in the United States for the power, pleasure, and prestige channeled to white people; and the imagined and internalized consciousness of what Black and white worlds are to be. This concept is one of many that allows Du Bois—and Tolson—to challenge normative modes of thought and dominant historical narratives, and to imagine different forms for the articulation of what Du Bois calls "the strange meaning of being black."[14] When Tolson invokes Du Bois's color line in his writing, he identifies with Du Bois's challenge to extant epistemological and political configurations. As I will show, like Du Bois, Tolson identifies a bifurcated world not to insist on its inevitable resolution, but to highlight the vexed but revolutionary potential that lies in existing between those worlds. In Tolson's estimation, such an approach would bring the "dialectic of how to be or not to be a Negro" to a grinding halt, and thus radically reconfigure the literary, social, and political order.

This was no small goal. Tate develops his definition of criticism in opposition to those who in their study of literature "dissolve the literature into its history."[15] To suggest that the poet and the critic were invested in the particulars of the present and future world, as Tolson did, was to undermine the New Critical tenet of literature's transcendence: literature's status as, in Tate's phrasing, "*knowledge*, not historical documentation and information."[16] Among Tolson's fundamental disagreements with Tate was the relationship between literature and history, a cipher for discussing how poetry interacts with the world beyond its borders. Tate insisted that poetry was a distinct form of knowledge, separate from the mundane chronological unfolding of the material world. Unlike Tate, Tolson insists that poetry could impact the material world beyond its borders. When Tolson writes in a letter that his *Libretto* with Tate's preface would be "an atom bomb dropped on two worlds," we should take seriously that the arrival of this package could alter the world divided by the color line beyond the poem's bounds.[17] Put simply, Tolson argues that the material world outside the poem matters. Poetry's interpretation, therefore, must consider that supposedly external material. This interpretive method offers a direction for formulating poetry's social and political function, as well as reflecting on its transcendence.

Tolson sought to build a context around his *Libretto* to illustrate this point. Such efforts included the solicitation of Tate, Tolson's circulation of rumor and intrigue, and a creative elaboration on literature's potential to prompt new epistemological, political, and social configurations. Tolson's work raises important questions that prompt a destructive engagement with the terms and institutions that come together in New Critical interpretive practice: What if the dilemma of whether "to be or not to be a Negro" poet were not limited by the institutional assumptions regarding poetry? Could poetry be difficult *and* make a Black radical claim on the world?

I argue that Tolson's figuration of the dilemma of the Black poet suggests that the activities of criticism must imagine more broadly how literature functions. Rather than limiting poetry to the private, intrinsic operation of the work's meaning unto itself or on a single reader, Tolson expands literature and criticism to the work's extrinsic and public impact, which includes paratextual elements (a preface), critical reviews, events surrounding its release, and the continued resonance of these combined parts, or lack thereof. Tolson's rumor passed to Dudley Randall, the characterization of Hideho in *Harlem Gallery*, and his unpublished essay meant to publicize an excerpt of private correspondence with Tate are all examples of his mobilizing forces beyond the poem itself to reconfigure the poem's interpretation. Crucially, Tolson's insistence on the linkage of poetry to the world outside it also activated a broader decolonial philosophy that in his estimation could make possible a renewed and technologically ascendant African continent.[18] To reconfigure the circumstances surrounding Tolson's *Libretto for the Republic of Liberia* is to allow the poem's utopian political and historical vision to emerge. It is not that Tolson clears the way for poetry to enact such sweeping political-economic changes alone; he instead shows that poetry can be an integral part of a larger attempt to build anew material circumstances that support the potential realization of Black radical visions—what Robin D. G. Kelley has termed "freedom dreams."[19]

Tolson saw literature as essential to understandings of the political economy of capitalism. Upon seeing the table of contents for his friend Oliver Cromwell Cox's book *The Foundations of Capitalism*, he commented in a 1955 letter, "One thing is missing that would add much to the Table—a chapter on Capitalism as reflected in literature. This *must not* be ignored. It proves the whole theory of capitalistic specialization, as nothing else I know."[20] Tolson elaborated that poetry in its current form had been alienated and deskilled from its past formations, akin to that which had occurred in industry. Cox did not pursue Tolson's suggestion but, I suggest, Tolson pursued an argument about literature's entanglement with racial capitalism in his tête-à-tête with Tate. Tolson's argument produced a critique of the New Criticism and offered a sense of the world-changing order sought by decolonization movements.

To pursue Tolson's vision of literature's role in dismantling the color line central to capitalism's development, the chapter proceeds in two parts. The first part traces Tolson's efforts to undermine Allen Tate's defense of New Critical principles in the unpublished "Excerpts from a Letter to Allen Tate." Outlined in his preface to *Libretto*, Tate's defense disarmed Tolson's poem by emphasizing Tolson's—and by implication all Black writers'—belated arrival to a modernism that convened the poetic tradition rather than the sociological present. In response, Tolson suggests that Tate's own poetry failed to meet this standard, and that Tate could not maintain the disinterestedness required to discern it in his own work. In identifying Tate's "affectability" within his poetry and his criticism, Tolson implies that both critical and racializing principles are applied unevenly. By suggesting that Tolson deems Tate affectable, I signal that Tolson positions him within the subjective framework that has been forced upon Black people under the regime of racialization. As Denise Ferreira da Silva explains, under this regime there are two types of subjects: "the subject of transparency, for whom universal reason is an interior guide, and subjects of affectability, for whom universal reason remains an exterior ruler."[21] This subjective positioning assists in animating, justifying, and reproducing the color line that determines, among many other phenomena, understandings of Black poets and Black readers of poetry. In identifying a clear contradiction in Tate's reasoning, Tolson suggests that the principles of literary evaluation rely on assumptions about the social and political order, mainly regarding the level of education and taste of an imagined Black reader—or, put differently, rooted in assumptions about race and class. When Tolson reads Tate's work with his image of a Black reader instead of Tate's, he describes a vision for both poetry and the social and political order that racial capitalism renders as merely esoteric or impossible to understand.

To define more thoroughly that social and political order, and to suggest that Tolson's aesthetic "difficulty" is only difficult because it is read in a world actively shaped by racism and colonialism, I turn to the text of the *Libretto* in the second part of this chapter. There I highlight how the epic poem further elaborates on the imposition of a Western "question mark" on Liberia's—and more broadly Africa's—historical significance.[22] For Tolson, the reconfiguration of the rules of a falsely universal American whiteness supported by the New Criticism could suspend the self-splitting and geopolitical racial order sparked by the color line. This reconfiguration can only be achieved by destroying the two worlds brought into being by the color line, and opening out a world shaped by what has unfolded in the fleeting space, which previously existed only in between those worlds. The result is a radically new vision for Africa and the world, effectively abolishing Europe's colonial taxonomy and the dilemma of the Black artist.

TOLSON'S TAXONOMY OF CRITICISM

When Tolson received a copy of Tate's preface to his *Libretto for the Republic of Liberia* in 1950, he identified that Tate's observations relied on long-standing conventions regarding the relationship of poetry to the material world, the capacity for Black poets to disengage from the exigency of their immediate social and political circumstances, and how race and class manifest art's form and reception. In these areas, Tate largely offered a favorable judgment, concluding his brief preface by admitting, "I found that I was reading *Libretto for the Republic of Liberia* not because Mr. Tolson is a Negro, but because he is a poet, not because the poem has a 'Negro subject' but because it is about the world of all men. And this subject is not merely asserted; it is embodied in a rich and complex language, and realized in terms of the poetic imagination."[23] After earlier raising his hackles regarding the resistance of Black poets like Langston Hughes and Gwendolyn Brooks to assimilate "the Anglo-American poetic tradition," Tate's authentication of the *Libretto* as indeed a poem proves his highest compliment.[24] Tolson's poem supplies an occasion for a brief statement from a prominent New Critic on the relevance of race to the definition of poetry.

Tolson had seeded this assessment of *Libretto*, suggesting it to Tate himself in their correspondence. When Tolson solicited Tate in 1949,

he wrote, "It seems that belatedly I have initiated the modern movement among Negro poets."[25] Tolson's boast became the thesis of Tate's
preface: "For the first time, it seems to me, a Negro poet has assimilated
completely the full poetic language of his time."[26] Admittedly, Tolson's
approach seems far from challenging Tate's inherited view. Tolson traf-
fics in the same assumption about the belatedness of Black art that Tate
exercises in his preface and, for that matter, delivers that very argument
to Tate. Tolson appears to agree with Tate regarding the conditions
that have led to a stylistically delayed Black poetry, but Tolson gently
pushes back on the idea that this difference can be accounted for by the
reticence of Black writers to adjust to the preferred norms of the poetic
imagination. Tolson suggests that in Black writing "the contradictions
of the society are sharper . . . because of the pressures from above and
below. If the vanguard White poet is isolated, his Negro fellow is annihilated between the walls of bi-racialism."[27] In other words, the difficulty of white poets is animated by alienation brought about by an
increasingly fragmented modernity, while Black poets are trapped in
an existential and material struggle by anti-Black racism and capitalism.
Tolson attributes this distinction to "biracialism," the term coined by
the white supremacist Lothrop Stoddard to mark the physical separation of the races in his 1927 book *Re-Forging America*. The inability
to resolve the tensions wrought by the color line explain for Tolson
what Tate describes as the "provincial mediocrity" of Black poetry, a
term that Tolson says he "likes."[28]

There is a clear tension in Tolson's appreciation of Tate's comments.
On the one hand, by liking what Tate has to say about the so-called
provincial mediocrity of Black artists, Tolson confirms as fact the un-
varnished past of Black letters. The "provincial mediocrity" in this lens
can be seen as record of the historical weakness of Black art. On the
other hand, as W. E. B. Du Bois formulated in *The Souls of Black Folk*,
the striving state of Black culture and Black life is not "weakness,—it
is the contradiction of double aims."[29] By emphasizing that what has
up to the *Libretto* "annihilated" the Negro poet are the walls of "biracialism," Tolson invokes a favorite concept from Du Bois: double consciousness. When Du Bois defines double consciousness, he does so
not to evaluate the condition of Black history and Black life, but to describe and explain it, to give language to another way of knowing the
world.[30] Du Bois describes the manifestation of double consciousness

for a number of Black figures, including the artisan, the minister, the doctor, and the artist. In characterizing this for the would-be savant, for instance, Du Bois writes that he "was confronted by the paradox that the knowledge his people needed was a twice-told tale to his white neighbors, while the knowledge which would teach the white world was Greek to his own flesh and blood."[31] In drafting his admiring response to Tate, Tolson suggests that what Du Bois has described remains part of the paradox for a Black writer adopting the present poetic idiom of modernist difficulty: "Some of my friends put it like this: 'How do you expect the average Negro to understand your poems?' This means *you ought to write down*."[32] Tolson expresses frustration with this idea, both because it is what holds back the acceptance of his work by some Black critics and because it condescends to "the average Negro."

When Tolson suggests that Tate's preface arrives at some of the same conclusions as Du Bois in *The Souls of Black Folk*, it becomes clear that part of his pleasure with Tate's document requires reading against its grain and reading into it the forceful critique articulated against biracialism by thinkers like Du Bois.[33] Whether or not one sees it as successful, Tolson's adoption of an allusive, encyclopedic, and dense poetics in *Libretto* was an effort to reconcile such unreconcilable strivings, an effort to reach the people of a Black nation and to simultaneously be recognized as fully modern while challenging modes of Garveyist nationalism that, at least to Du Bois, seemingly endorsed aspects of a biracial world. To achieve both of these things would require a rewriting of the very concepts he engages—the nation and modernity—themselves.

Reading Tolson's embrace of Tate against the grain means attending to Tolson's recognition of what Nahum Chandler identifies as the "logic *of* the other" within the articulation of Du Bois's double consciousness concept. For Chandler, when Du Bois begins *The Souls of Black Folk* with "between," the word "would be the nonlocatable site of at least double meanings (and thereby never only double), taking sense from the play of forces (always) beyond or otherwise than strictly delimitable site."[34] To gloss Chandler's reading, Du Bois's "between"— the positionality of a Black person amid two worlds—signals not just opposition to either world, but the opening of space that is of neither world and the movement within and without that space. The neither-wordly space is difficult or impossible to define unless stated within the otherwise flickering "logic *of* the other." This applies to Tolson because of his frequent invocation of Du Bois's reference to this logic—double consciousness—and because Tolson pursues the destruction of the two worlds by means that confound key players in each respective world.

In his correspondence, Tolson makes an argument for how his play of forces in *Libretto* will yield something beyond the two worlds presently registered under the regime of the color line. In a letter to Tate, Tolson suggests that the preface had started a "revolution in Negro Letters," evidenced by Langston Hughes's epic poem "Prelude to Our Age: A Negro History Poem," which Tolson heard at the dedication of the Schomburg Collection in Harlem in 1950.[35] Tolson's invocation of Hughes's "Prelude" offers perspective on what Tolson may have meant by revolution. Tolson read in "Prelude" Hughes's embrace of a "modern" style similar to that of *Libretto*. That style was evidence that Tate's preface and a section of Tolson's poem, which were published in *Poetry* in 1950, opened the door to a wider adoption of this dense and distinctive aesthetic. What was truly revolutionary then was that Hughes's "modern" poem had a willing and committed Black audience. For its audience Tolson's *Libretto* had the people of Liberia. Hughes's "Prelude" had the dignitaries assembled at the Schomburg and the "our" whose age was imminent within Hughes's poem. No longer did Black poets have to, in Tolson's words, "write down." The imagined impact of the *Libretto* and Tate's preface create a Black radical world for modern poetry in which Tolson's poetic idiom is the heart.

Tolson also read his exchanges with Tate and Tate's preface as proof of how *Libretto* reconfigured understandings of white poetics. In the opening of his preface, Tate marvels at, but ultimately cannot grasp, how Tolson's poetics might support the political operation of a state.[36] He writes, "One can imagine, in Washington, during the New Deal, a patriotic poem being read by the late Stephen Vincent Benèt; but not, I assume, by the late Hart Crane. That may be one difference between the literary culture of official Washington and that of Liberia: Mr. Tolson is in the direct succession from Crane. Here is something marvellous indeed."[37] Tate's invocation of Crane indexes a sense of wonderment at Liberia's elevation of the type of romantic epic poetry that Tate hoped to keep out of the United States.[38] In this respect, Tate's endorsement of the *Libretto* marks a key success for the poem as it reconfigures the definition of modern poetry and Tate's sense of what the nation can or should be. In Tolson's estimation, his poem carves out a wide Black audience for a modern poetics, reshapes a sense of the historical order of Black modes of political and aesthetic organization, and redefines white perspectives on poetry and the nation.

As he continued his correspondence with Tate, Tolson soon got the sense that his reading of the preface was not the same as Tate's. Tolson would attempt to outline the wrongheadedness of Tate's reading and why he was correct in his Du Boisian interpretation in an essay. To do so Tolson began drafting an essay in November 1950. Not long after receiving feedback from Tate, he indicated that he planned to send the finished version to the major New Critical journal Tate had once edited. Had the essay been finished or published, it would have further heightened the stakes for the full release of Tolson's *Libretto*. (Despite its title, Tate's "Preface" first appeared as a postscript, with the publication of one of *Libretto*'s nine sections in the July 1950 issue of *Poetry* magazine. The full edition of the *Libretto* would not be published until 1953.)

Enclosed in Tolson's papers at the Library of Congress in Washington are more than seventy pages of draft material for the essay, in addition to his initial dissenting letter to Tate and another letter that expresses his intent to send the completed essay to *Sewanee*. The many drafts indicate that Tolson never completed the essay. The longest draft reaches the middle of a fourteenth page, but it ends abruptly and the bottom half of the page consists of typed single-spaced notes for additional material, distinct from the clean double-spaced prose above it.

Tolson sought to disassemble the arbitrary assumptions that delimit the historical and aesthetic holisms that structure literary critical and Western thought. This project required historical, sociological, and literary investigation. In this respect, Tolson's essay resembles a version of the chapter he would ask the sociologist Oliver Cox to write in *The Foundations of Capitalism* seven years later. Tolson identifies what literary critical and sociological thought on race leaves out in its efforts to make poetry and racism inwardly focused phenomena: a deliberate attention to the structuring forces of capital's political economy, and the ongoing Black left challenge to its reproduction. In this sense, Tolson takes up a compromise position between Du Bois's Marxian arguments in books like *Black Reconstruction* or *The World and Africa*, and Oliver Cox's materialist though less explicitly Marxist critique of

Gunnar Myrdal's foregrounding of the caste school of race relations in
Caste, Class, and Race. Tolson discerned that Tate reinforced the racialized and classed dimensions of modern poetry when he indicated skepticism of working-class Black readers and writers aspiring to its heights.
Further, Tolson rooted Tate's error in his understanding of the conflict
of the Civil War. Like Du Bois and Cox before him, Tolson insisted
that the Civil War was about slavery, a political-economic conflagra-
tion, rather than a moral one about disagreements in hearts and minds.

The germ of Tolson's critique of Tate, sociology, and the institutions
they stood in for was in an anecdote Tolson relayed to Tate about something he had witnessed several decades before.

> On a wintry afternoon in Detroit, I was browsing in the public library
> on Cadillac Square. I remember a strike was going on, and a number of
> dull-eyed workingmen were in the reading room. Among them was a
> venerable colored man absorbedly reading a book of modern poetry.[39]

The scene in the library casts a Black reader absorbed in modern poetry
while the working people surrounding him break from a prominent
action of resistance, likely the massive demonstration of nearly 150,000
people supporting the Flint Sit-Down Strikes in 1937. Tolson highlights
the tension between the people and the possibility for Black private
life, as well as the tension between Black readers and modern poetry.
He also alludes to the role of Southern Lost Cause-ism—the venerable
Black reader is absorbed in Tate's "Ode to the Confederate Dead"—in
upholding the exploitative order of racial capitalism, against which the
workers gather.

Tate's response to the anecdote signals a bracketing of the labor
struggle surrounding the Black reader, while questioning the scene's
viability:

> I have told several times to friends your story of the Uncle Remus in
> the library in Detroit reading my Ode to the Confederate Dead—
> always with great effect. One solemn sociologist, on one occasion,
> asked: "Shouldn't he have been informed that the heroes honored in
> that poem were anxious to keep his people in slavery?" I leave the an-
> swer to you. . . .[40]

In Tate's telling, Tolson's anecdote comes to be about the capacity for
Black readers, stereotyped as "Uncle Remus," to grasp the historical

complexities of poetry. By questioning the interpretive acumen of Black readers of modern poetry, Tate offers a more general comment on the relationship between Blackness, poetry, and modernity. Tate's suggestion of the incompatibility of Black readers and modern poetry invokes the wider strategy employed in Tate's preface and by academically trained readers to minimize the ambit of Tolson's revolutionary poetics.

That Tate displaces aspects of his own understanding on to a "solemn sociologist" highlights the purchase of midcentury sociologists to describe the "Negro problem." Gunnar Myrdal's *An American Dilemma* (1944) is perhaps the best known of these works; it argues that "at bottom our problem [the American Negro problem] is the moral dilemma of the American."[41] Tolson's colleague and friend from Wiley College, Oliver Cox, directly challenged Myrdal's understanding of American racism. In *Caste, Class, and Race*, Cox devotes an entire chapter to refuting Myrdal's central thesis, insisting that "racial antagonism is essentially political-class conflict" and arguing that racism is a practice tied to capitalist exploitation, rather than "an abstract, natural, immemorial feeling of mutual antipathy between groups."[42] Cox was only one skeptic of many challenging the central aspect of Myrdal's report. Even so, Tate's solemn sociologist directs to the venerable Black reader the same condescension and exclusion marked by the "our" in Myrdal's description of "the American Negro problem." That is, despite their emphasis on morality and ethics, white sociology and white readers reduce Black practices of knowledge making and understanding as ill-informed. This casting of a political economic structure as a moral one reproduces the exploitation and antagonism it otherwise seeks to redress.

This can be further glimpsed in the transposition of Tolson's "venerable colored man" reader to Tate's "Uncle Remus in the library." In turning a man into the fictional character created by Joel Chandler Harris, Tate and his sociologist friend mobilize anew the early-twentieth-century craze surrounding Uncle Remus. Bryan Wagner argues that the character offered a way to redefine "what counted as culture and what counted as politics," because the Uncle Remus character mediated theories about African cultural development, the African American retention of African culture, and Black criminality.[43] Tate uses Remus this way in his correspondence, as did midcentury sociologists of "the Negro problem" who used, for instance, the occasion of white-

led riots to diagnose the pathology of Black criminality.[44] Though Tate
and his sociologist never comment on the context of the strike in which
the venerable Black reader sits, their Uncle Remus reference implicitly
places blame on and enforces a need to police the Black reader, perhaps because this reader might, as Du Bois did, see the Civil War as a
"general strike" of Black workers, not entirely dissimilar from the action
happening outside the library.[45] Or, put differently, Tate and his sociologist fail to register the revolutionary character of Tolson's scene: that
the labor uprising and the Black reader investigating the Confederate
imaginary index a proletarian revolt against capitalism, a revolt which
in an earlier form had defeated the very Confederate soldiers in Tate's
poem. The convergence of sociology, literary interpretation, and their
material ramifications on Black life marked the stakes for Tolson's essay.
Tolson's Detroit reader shows what it might mean for class, aesthetic,
and racial assumptions to be attuned to the revolutionary implications
of what unfolds in the streets and in the library.

Tolson envisioned his essay as an extended excursus of a compact
four-page letter dissenting against Tate's understanding of Tolson's
Detroit anecdote, and would title it "Excerpts from a Letter to Allen
Tate." One reason why Tolson may not have finished the essay is its
expansive scope. Judging from his manuscript pages and notes, Tolson
hoped to link three threads in the essay, all of which stem from Tate's response to the Detroit anecdote. First, Tolson expounds upon a history
of the ode form, mainly focusing on the prepositions used in ode titles.
He invests significantly in the fact that Tate's poem, which the Black library reader scans, is an ode *to* the Confederate dead. This preposition
stands quietly in opposition to the fact that Tolson's *Libretto* is not *to*
the Republic of Liberia but *for* it. To some, this difference might prove
too small to note. Yet for Tolson this distinction prompts questions
of Tate's interpretive methods on multiple fronts. These questions
lead him to taxonomize the political and aesthetic logic buried within
something so minute as a titular preposition. Tolson argues that the
"for," which he employs in the *Libretto*, demands a connection between
the poem and the world beyond it, while the "to," deployed by Tate,
isolates the poem and limits poetry's political capacity.

Second, Tolson uses the occasion of Tate's anecdote to suggest that
the Black Detroit reader may offer a more sophisticated reading of
"Ode to the Confederate Dead" than Tate's "sociologist" friend. This

thread highlights materialist assumptions about the Black reader's capacity to be truly absorbed in a poem that is set in historical and political opposition to that reader and written in the style of modern poetry. Finally, the sociologist's reading gives Tolson occasion to counter Tate's reading of the "Ode," outlined in Tate's essay "Narcissus as Narcissus." That 1938 essay attempts the ultimate exercise of New Critical detachment: a critic reading his own poem not through his intentions, or through psychological history, but by the idea that "the poem is a real creation . . . a kind of knowledge that we did not possess before."[46] Tolson suggests that Tate fails at the task, a failure made even more damning by the fact that a Black reader (Tolson), like the "venerable colored man" in Detroit, can identify the full scope of Tate's errors.

Woven together, these threads would have enforced the fact that Tate's interpretive approach to the *Libretto* and more generally to literature was limited by its insistence upon a historical and aesthetic purity. Tolson's critical reading, which draws on expansive literary historical knowledge, social and political encounters, and close reading, emerges as a clear alternative that embraces holding multiple ideas and histories together simultaneously to yield a reading. Though Tate's preface is not mentioned explicitly in the draft text of the "Excerpts" essay, Tolson's focus on undoing New Critical principles, sociological race thinking, and troubling assumptions about race and class in reading poetry suggest that Tolson's essay was a direct response to Tate's take on the *Libretto*.

In the drafts of "Excerpts," Tolson sketches a taxonomy of the function of prepositions in the titles of odes. These little words are important, Tolson suggests, because "as an idea of relationship, it gives the tone of the poem, it augurs its loftiness and fixity of purpose; it indicates the poet's basic attitude toward his subject, his theme, his reader, his age."[47] In short, Tolson takes the preposition in the title as an index of authorial intention, as well as the connection of the poet to the world beyond the poem.

Tolson suggests that the preposition "to"—like that in the title of Tate's "Ode to the Confederate Dead"—serves as a device "to make the reader concentrate on the poem, as poem" because it points a "straight line" to the emotion and subject of the poem.[48] He makes clear that "to" is the preferred preposition of the New Critical establishment in large part because of its ability to isolate the poem as the matter at hand. But the "for," which Tolson prefers in his *Libretto*, is "riskier." He writes:

> Since *for* indicates the cause, motive, or occasion of the odic act, it runs the hazard of incorporating the didactic or propagandistic without converting the base metal into gold through the alchemy of the imagination. *For* fawns on pro and snubs con, and this is the way to the *adola mentis*.[49]

Tolson's definition of "for" lauds the preposition's capacity for positive definition and its potential for incorporating social and political material within an otherwise lofty style. Tolson indicates that these tendencies of the "for" are set in opposition to the New Criticism. A note written on an earlier draft shows that Tolson sees Tate and the New Criticism as only engaged in a mode of negative definition: "I discover (with a shock) that your Ode verifies my premise by being almost an attested copy of definition by negation."[50] At the same time, Tolson suggests that motive and occasion—another way of invoking the New Critical bugbear of authorial intention—cannot be avoided in a poem marked by "for." He concedes that this may lead to a "didactic or propagandistic" mode, like the kind that several Black writers have argued of Robert Penn Warren's efforts in his 1965 book, *Who Speaks for the Negro?*[51] In contrast to Warren, the potential that Tolson locates in "for" is not to speak on behalf of, but rather to speak in dedication with. The political connotation of speaking with, Tolson implies, allows for a simultaneity of a dense, allusive poetics with radical political potential.

Tolson positions his work at the intersection of political and poetic complication, mainly through his seemingly opaque reference to what he refers to as the "adola mentis." This reference directs a reader to Tolson's unique shorthand for Francis Bacon's "idols of the mind," which Tolson would deploy in his 1951 poem "E. & O. E.," the poem that would later become the private effort of Hideho Heights in 1965's *Harlem Gallery*. In a note to "E. & O. E." Tolson indicates that adola mentis can be tracked to sections 38–44 of Bacon's *Novum Organum*, a text which supplied a method for observing scientific truths in the natural world.[52] The relevant sections from Bacon's *Novum* describe idols that push back against truth when truth enters the mind.[53] For Bacon, these are idols that must be defended against. Tolson coins the phrase adola mentis seemingly to generalize the various idols that Bacon otherwise distinctly defines in these passages.

While Tolson's syntax is ambiguous, I read his line about the "for" offering the way to the adola mentis as suggesting that "for" allows a writer and a reader to approach a place where the idols of the mind can be dismantled. This interpretation is supported both in Tolson's elaboration on this issue in letters and in his references to the adola mentis in other poems. In his correspondence, Tolson intimates that his understanding of the idols is akin to that of ideology, that which gets in the way of the idea of a poem. He writes, "Most critics confuse and interchange *idea* and *ideology*."[54] In other words, ideology, or the adola mentis, reduces acts of Black poetic imagination to the didactic or propagandistic usages labeled by the New Critics. Indeed, Tolson suggests in "E. & O. E." that the idols figuratively dig the foundation for the defenses of a Roman city of "the Great White World." The poet's speaker, caught between Black and white definitions of identity, topples this foundation to save a woman who has been sentenced to the guillotine.[55] Like Bacon, who writes that identifying the idols is crucial to their defeat, Tolson suggests that "for" provides a path to glimpse the adola mentis and undo their figurative fortress.[56] Put differently, Tolson suggests that a Black poet toeing the color line can reach and dismantle the foundations of the white world because the ideology that must be defeated is yoked to empire. As usual, Tolson's allusive register is dense. When it is followed, what becomes clear is that Tolson aligns his poetics with a politicized "for," a preposition deliberately set against the "to" of Tate and the New Criticism. Tolson implicates the New Critical "to" as an ideology supplying prejudgment toward particular works and clouding any observations a critic might make in attempting to discern the poetic idea, thus silently reproducing the existing political economic order. Meanwhile, the New Criticism feeds the idols of the mind, who offer a defense of "the Great White World," and who mark and diffuse the imaginative force of a Black poetics with the claim of didacticism and propaganda.

By clarifying the functions of titular odic prepositions, Tolson lays the groundwork for his explanation of what distinguishes the interpretive practice of the Black reader in Detroit. Like the allusion to the adola mentis, this explanation also points beyond the edges of the "Excerpts" essay and into Tolson's poetry, particularly the *Libretto*. When Tolson suggests that the "for" "runs the hazard of [not] ... converting the base metal into gold," he invokes a crucial footnote and a direct reference to Cox from his *Libretto* ("the ferris wheel / of race, of caste, of class") that spells out Tolson's views on the philosophy of history. Tolson suggests that this philosophy is the key to the Detroit reader's interpretive practice while it also marks the limitations of the epistemologies of Tate and his sociologist. This historical understanding offers a way to both write *and* read poetry with the radical potential held in the "for."

Tolson expounds upon the historical and revolutionary resonance of his metal metaphor in a lengthy footnote to the concluding section of the *Libretto*:

> ... [History] remains a Heraclitean continuum of a world flaring up and dying down as "it always was, is, and shall be." Some moderns have turned this ancient seesaw figure of a crude dialectics into a locomotive of history.[57]

In this part of the note, Tolson argues that history for the moderns has moved a practice of past, present, and future understanding into simple determinism, which he refers to as the "locomotive of history."[58] Like Tate and the New Criticism's preferred preposition, this historical mode only moves in a straight line, a teleological track that reduces temporal and spatial complexity to a single dimension. Tolson continues, "By the Law of Relativity, history will always have its silver age as well as its golden, and each age will contain some of the other's metal."[59] In addition to affirming Tate's and the New Criticism's potential short-sightedness because of their intention toward historical purity, Tolson bolsters his idea that history is an alloy, the melding of multiple metals to which only those who employ the "for" can potentially identify. Tolson's footnote from *Libretto* states that his poem takes up this understanding of history, one that the rest of the poem suggests has particular rootedness in Black ways of knowing.

In "Excerpts," Tolson aligns the ability to read for the "for" and its radical historical potential with the venerable Black reader in the Detroit library. He illustrates that Tate relies on his sociologist friend to mediate the difference between culture and politics, as well as the philosophy of history that abstractly and institutionally authorizes

Tate's critical practice. Tate turns to the sociologist to make a historical point—"Should [the Detroit reader] have been informed that the heroes honored in that poem were anxious to keep his people in slavery?"—that would otherwise be beyond the pale of Tate's literary criticism. In Tate's reading of "Ode to the Confederate Dead," he argues that the poem is about the "solipsism" of its speaker, and even admits that this subject "and the Confederate dead cannot be connected logically, or even historically."[60] Tolson argues that the Detroit reader seizes on the gap between these two distinct interpretations, one historical and the other solipsistic. The Detroit reader asks what happens if the soldiers in Tate's poems are compared to the "Negro soldiers in George Washington's army, . . . the historic Senegalese in World War I, . . . in French West Africa, . . . [or] the Negro heroes of the Twenty-Fourth Infantry in Korea."[61] These are all groups that may have had complicated political affiliations with respect to the cause of the side for which they were fighting, and which therefore did not act out of narcissism. Their reason for enlistment is not immediately discernible.

In his essay, Tate admits that the otherwise disconnected themes of solipsism and the Confederacy are connected via "the experienced conflict which is the poem itself."[62] Neither the Detroit reader nor Tolson can locate such a conflict in the poem, as there is little particular evidence given as to individual soldiers' positions on slavery. Tolson argues that the only way the sociologist (and Tate) can arrive at the idea that the soldiers in the poem are fighting distinctly for slavery (and not because they are ordered to do so by their superiors) is that he "salts the mine, stacks the cards, loads the dice!"[63] In Tolson's reading of Tate's ode, "the man at the gate tells us that he saw *the inscrutable infantry*— that he bore witness to a martyrdom which defied his efforts to understand and only frustrated him."[64] That is, Tolson's interlocutors inject something into the poem that is neither there in its text, nor indicated by its prepositional intention. Further, Tolson introduces uncertainty into Tate's confident interpretation of the various motivations of what were predominantly white working-class Confederate soldiers, hinting at the fact that their interests were potentially distinct from the planter aristocracy.[65] By asking a cutting historical question, the venerable Detroit reader challenges the sociologist's reduction of Black capacity for complex historical understanding, as well as the sociologist's failure to read the dynamics of capital into the Civil War—all while questioning whether the political history the poem invokes can justify Tate's solipsistic interpretation.

His critique established, Tolson seeks to go one step further. He intimates that Tate might be relying on the tropes and traditions of what Du Bois called the "colored peoples of the world," a claim that torques Tate's work to align with Tolson's decolonial arguments. The sociologist is the main offender in reading "*into* the poem his reading of a non-poem," but Tolson also suggests that the origins of Tate's metaphorical imagery shows allegiance not to the Southern soldiers, but to Africa and Asia. In Tolson's reading, the ode's "sagging gate" draws on the same African proverb that Tolson engages in the "Sol" section of his *Libretto*—mainly, that a gate "sees both inside and out."[66] More significantly, Tolson sees in Tate's gate what he hopes to create in his poetics: "an authentic picture of the interrogating mind: it sees neither the black nor white of things; it sees the evidence for and against."[67] Tolson reads into Tate's gate the space between the biracialism he associates with Du Bois's double consciousness, as well as the historical simultaneity that can be two at once, for and against. While elliptical, Tolson's reading asserts that Tate's poem is informed by material extrinsic to its borders. This means that Tate falls to the same warnings of affectability that New Critics lob at Black writers. Tolson's suggestion that Tate is governed by irrationality echoes Cox's insistence in identifying the "mysticism" of Gunnar Myrdal's reliance on caste, "a misapprehension of the whole basis of race relations," because of its failure to recognize the political economic history of race's development.[68] It also means that the body of Tate's poem betrays its titular preposition's unidirectionality—or, as Tolson puts it, "The Ode is a flagrant deviation from the ante-bellum Party Line!"[69] He insists that Tate's poem reaches to the historical realm and betrays the Confederate desire for white purity by deploying African and Asian poetic tropes. Tolson concludes that "Ode to the Confederate Dead" operates in the political rather than literary realm.

Though it was never completed fully, what we have of Tolson's "Excerpts from a Letter to Allen Tate" outlines a significant critique of the New Criticism. More importantly, it offers an implicit critical alternative that centers Tolson's desire to destroy the two worlds demarcated by the color line by expanding what Nahum Chandler refers to as the "nonlocatable" space between them. Both Tolson's critique and his critical practice rely on disassembling the arbitrary assumptions that delimit the historical and aesthetical holisms that structure literary critical thought and, more broadly, Western thought.[70] He does so by refashioning an idea from natural science—Bacon's idols—to describe the unnatural world. In his drafts of the "Excerpt" essay, Tolson types the following as the final statement of a brainstorm: "A poem is a mental bomb. A poem is a synthesis of idea and image and rhythms. A naturalistic work is unnatural."[71] In these declarations, Tolson highlights both the goals for his poetics and his critical practice. The poem should explode the received dividing lines of thought; it should synthesize things as they are with aesthetic principles; and even as the poem is whole and made natural, it is also a product of adola mentis, the material world, or simply humans and the messy social and political world in which they live. In distinct contrast to Tate's New Criticism, all these principles in concert are important for interpretation and knowledge creation.

THE *LIBRETTO*'S "ABOLITION OF ITSELF"

In the *Libretto for the Republic of Liberia*, Melvin Tolson suggests that his poetic and interpretive principles derive from the multifaceted struggles of Black people and the exemplary story of the nation of Liberia. Before being named Liberia's poet laureate by President William Tubman in 1947, Tolson had never been to the western African nation or had much of a connection to it. In Liberia's national story, however, Tolson found a country caught between the poles of two worlds. Liberia's existence speaks to the questionable and violent interruption of African foundations—what Dionne Brand has discussed on a diasporic scale as "the Door of No Return"—for American Black people, as well as Black Africans stolen yet again from the then illegal transatlantic slave trade.[72] The anti-Black auspices of the American Colonization Society founded Liberia in 1822 as a solution to America's race problem; the ACS would send freed Black people to the country as a way to encourage their broader departure from the United States, a solution that was endorsed by key federal figures including Thomas Jefferson, Francis Scott Key, and later, even Abraham Lincoln. At the same time,

Liberia was founded despite the claims to the land by those who already lived there. Returning people seized from Africa to a place already inhabited by Africans highlights the complexity of African foundations and returns in imagining some forms of Black nationalism.

Tolson embraces this complexity because the geopolitical story of Liberia mirrors the idea that the color line has made a return to a world not divided by it impossible. The path forward is in the destruction of the two worlds and the embrace of the simultaneity found within Tolson's embrace of the odic "for." Put differently, Tolson's *Libretto* suggests what Tolson would later call "the dialectic of / to be or not to be / a Negro," the dilemma of the Black artist expanded far beyond the sphere of literary criticism governed by Allen Tate; this scenario had roots in a broader geopolitical domain, which his poem also targeted for reconfiguration. Tolson's intimation is that when linked to these worlds beyond the literary, poetry carried the capacity to initiate broader world-shattering measures. In the remaining pages of this chapter, I offer a brief reading of Tolson's *Libretto* to suggest that his interpretive practice and his poetics command a Black radical challenge to the institutions of literature and the racial and colonial order those institutions necessarily support.

The first section of the *Libretto* signals the poem's political investment in upending the color line's status quo, while also reckoning with the philosophical positioning of American Blackness vis-à-vis Africa. Each of the seven stanzas of the poem's first section begins with a line that reads simply *"Liberia?"* The only way the poet can answer this question is to invent a grammar that shuttles between negation and affirmation. On the basis of my earlier reading of Tolson's exchange with Tate, it is clear that this waffling highlights that the poem opens in the social and political world of the color line. The poet cannot choose the "to" or the "for," as one preposition leads to potential critical success with the white establishment by limiting poetry's political capacities, while the "for" marks a riskier path that may be subsumed by the logic of the "to" if the poem cannot achieve the generative destruction it seeks. For example, the poet expounds that Liberia is not "a micro-footnote in a bunioned-book," but is the "lightning rod of Europe."[73] That is, the history of Liberia is not something to be quickly passed over; it is instead a site that attracts the charge that animates Europe, and can thus provide a thoroughgoing narrative of Western imperialism and racial capitalism. Nowhere is this flickering between negation and affirmation more clearly apparent than in the final lines of this section. They read, "You [Liberia] are . . . Liberia and not Liberia."[74] Tolson's seemingly contradictory grammar here is the point; it is only in the contradictions and the impossibilities of that which for Du Bois is unreconcilable that the method and world Tolson hopes to achieve in and through his poem can be articulated.

The seven sections that follow *Libretto*'s first affirm this epistemological reality, and attempt to draw the reader closer to the affirmative definition that the poem's titular "for" demands. A consistent theme of Tolson's poem is the push and pull of a dialectic between Africa and the West, and it is encapsulated within the poem's structure. Tolson's 770-line poem is divided into eight sections, each marked with a corresponding scale degree of the major diatonic scale, noted by "sol-fa" syllables. Invoking the Western major scale, Tolson notes the universalism bestowed upon music by the West and seemingly that which may be attributed to his poem by the New Criticism. (Recall Tate's preface: the *Libretto* "is about the world of all men.") Yet the whole- and half-step intervals that mark the major scale are not the only distances between pitches. There are the quarter-tone bends of jazz and blues, as well as the microtonal melodies of South Asian and Middle Eastern musics that fall between the possible notes in the twelve-tone scales. At first glance, Tolson's embrace of sol-fa syllables appears as a contradiction to Tolson's aim of eluding forms of Western modernity and the universal, but it turns out to be just another instantiation of attempting to outline what has been made impossible in a world divided by racism.[75] Put differently, Tolson strives for universalism, but not Western universalism—or, more simply, the universal, but not as it is.

Tolson pushes against the idea that the universal he seeks is a synthesis of Western and African forms by critiquing a vulgar understanding of Hegelian dialectics. This misunderstanding implies that one mode of life must assimilate and assume the form of the other. Indeed, to recognize the Western universal as a compromise between or synthesis of the operative dialectic of the white and colored worlds as such is to fall trap to the "crude dialectics" that mark the locomotive of history, which Tolson cites in the aforementioned footnote in *Libretto*'s final section. Like the first section, the poem's final section is titled "Do"; but rather than return to the approach of the original

"Do," Tolson challenges the frame of the poem's potential universality and seeks a new definitional approach. In this respect, he works to situate Africa and Liberia as a site for a generative and affirmative utopian present, not solely as a site to mine for revisions to European formulations or for diasporic return. In effect, Tolson holds apart the two worlds divided by the color line, refusing, in Du Bois's language, "from being torn asunder" by fully resolving these "warring ideals." Like the genre-bending, discipline-confounding experimentation of Du Bois's work, Tolson seeks to create a new language and a new world in the standstill between these worlds; a language that would lead to the destruction of such a division; a language that to this point did not exist.

In one stanza, Tolson directly targets the colonizing effects of universal epistemologies in math, science, music, and language, some of which his own poem seems to employ elsewhere via its broad, encyclopedic scope:

> worldmusic's sol-fa syllables (*o do de do de do de*)
> worldmathematics' arabic and roman figures
> worldscience's greek and latin symbols
> > the letter killeth five hundred global tongues
>
> > before esperanto garrotes voläpuk *vanitas vanitatum*[76]

Tolson suggests that the same universalized science, math, and music he employs as important metaphorical repositories can have a morbid impact on the diversity of human cultures. This impact occurs only when operating in concert with the force of the "letter"—that is, the humanities disciplines. In this assertion, Tolson deviates from other midcentury poets who, according to Peter Middleton, made an uneasy alliance with scientific discourse in order to shore up "methodological credit" within the research university. These poets could use physics as a metaphor to make up for the fact that they tended to operate "outside the institutional networks" for the legitimation of knowledge.[77] Tolson's stanza suggests that this alliance would only further threaten "global tongues" by the valorization of the universal that would come through the use of scientific discourse. Even though the universals of letters and of science are at odds—Esperanto is strangling another international language, Voläpuk, as a result—the destruction wrought is undeniable and yet another vainglorious act of Western humanity.

The final "Do" commits to a multimodal movement through time and space as an attempt to enact the grammar established by the opening section's articulation of Liberia as "Liberia and not Liberia." Such movement is previewed in the "Sol" section, a preview that makes musical sense as the dominant scale degree demands resolution by returning to the tonic ("Do"). In "Sol," Tolson aligns the voyage of the *Elizabeth*, which brought the first African Americans to Liberia, with Gunnar Myrdal's *An American Dilemma*, and the Middle Passage. The poet chants, "This is the horned American/Dilemma" and "This is the Middle Passage."[78] The "American Dilemma" line carries a footnote that mentions Cox's *Caste, Class, and Race* as well as Herbert Aptheker's *The Negro People in America*, another work critical of Myrdal, which included an introduction by Doxey A. Wilkerson, the director of curriculum at the Jefferson School of Social Science. The reference intimates that Myrdal's work fails to register a fundamental understanding of what constitutes the Middle Passage; as Cox put it, "The slave trade was simply a way of recruiting labor for the purpose of exploiting the great natural resources of America."[79] Contrary to Myrdal's work and the era's dominant sociological approaches to the "Negro problem," these lines highlight the poem's movement between multiple events in the history of racial capitalism, a way of layering the poem's unfolding within three historical frames simultaneously.

Nowhere does this devotion to simultaneous and multimodal historical movement come clearer than in the poem's final lines. Tolson imagines a new continental African ethics and politics as a transportation system, and it is to this section that Tolson's footnote about the "crude dialectics" of the Western philosophy of history is appended. Flirting with ideas of modernity while casting them aside, Tolson shows Africa completely connected in all directions and in varying grains of the past, present, and future. There is the Futurafrique, an automobile from Liberia motors; the United Nations Limited, a bullet train; the Bula Matadi, a diesel-powered quadruple-decker ship; and *Le Premier des Noir*, the flagship of Pan-African Airways. These vehicles traverse African terrain in different shapes and at different paces, providing a multimodal glimpse of a Black utopia. Unlike the poem's opening, this future is defined affirmatively, each vehicle described with active, present-tense verbs. This tense suggests that by the end of *Libretto*, the reader has arrived at the previously unimaginable present, simultaneity left wanting by the poem's vexing opening grammar.

At the top of the poem's final stanza, Tolson's speaker offers up an explanation for what he has created. He states, "The Parliament of African Peoples signets forever / the *Recessional of Europe* and / trumpets the abolition of itself."[80] The lines express a complex operation. The first two suggest that by using sovereign authority, Tolson's invented African parliament enforces a now subdued role for Europe. The third line, however, makes clear that with the signet highlighted two lines earlier, the African parliament also abolishes itself. As in the atom bomb metaphor Tolson used to describe his poem with Tate, there is in the beginning of the poem's final statement a sense of mutually assured destruction: when Africa declares Europe's end, Africa too ends. These lines highlight, on the one hand, that Europe and Africa through Western eyes are mutually constituted; the color line, a symbol for the violent colonization and racialization brought forth by the hands of Europe, shapes these two worlds. To eradicate one is to eradicate the definition of the other as it has been established by European power.[81] In the wake of the destruction of these social constructs, however, a different possibility emerges: "and the / deserts that gave up the ghost / to green pastures chant in the / ears and teeth of the Dog, in the Rosh Hashana of the Afric / calends: *'Honi soit qui mal y / pense!'*"[82] The destruction wrought by Europe's recessional creates a new year, and in "calends," a new beginning: the first day of a new month.

There is then another recessional that occurs within Tolson's final lines. With each page turn of the *Libretto*, an official sovereign poem for the Parliament of African Peoples broadly construed, Allen Tate's preface, a voice from Europe, recedes to the background. The final stanza suggests that it is only by the end of the poem—the poem's abolition of itself—that Tate's relevance might cease. The poem doesn't fully achieve this escape velocity by its own measure; the "for" is fraught—or, as Tolson puts it, "Each age will contain some of the other's metal." Indeed, the green pastures of this new day are still haunted by the motto pasted on the garter that surrounds the shield of the royal coat of arms of the United Kingdom ("Honi soit qui mal y pense").

The poem's final stanza cements the fact that Tolson connects Tate and his preface not only to a literary critical apparatus that has the power to authorize or demote the work of Black writers, but also to the various machinations of Europe that continue to enforce and instantiate the global color line. Tolson's attempt to negate and reconfigure Europe by affirmatively, grammatically reinventing Black poetry, poetics, and philosophy of history highlights his connection to the Black radical tradition, especially through his efforts to exercise the praxis of W. E. B. Du Bois. Cedric Robinson argues that the Black historiographical and intellectual radicalism arises out of a recognition that Black people, not the urban proletariat, are the universal subject of Marxist history. Robinson suggests that Du Bois is crucial in this project because, he argues, "It was the slaves . . . and other agrarian workers who had mounted the attack on capitalism. It was, Du Bois observed, from the periphery and not the center that the most sustained threat to the American capitalist system had materialized."[83]

Tolson takes up Du Bois and the work of Oliver Cox to further challenge the false universalizations of Western historiography. For one, Tolson's ideal scene of reading in his letter to Tate is one that centers a Black reader in the midst of a major anticapitalist demonstration. That reader comes equipped with his own framework for reading poetry, a framework that elides the various divisions of discipline, taste, and culture set out by the Western world, and that insists upon literature's contact with the political action the reader undertakes. The *Libretto* expands on this intervention. It suggests that a political-economic revolution proceeds from Liberian shores, and that this seemingly incomprehensible poem becomes newly legible under that imagined but yet to be realized decolonial frame. Beyond providing occasion to register himself as engaging with the Black radical tradition, Tolson suggests that poetic innovations can occur while Black literature and criticism performs a mode of political theory and political organizing.

Tolson kept returning to the conditions which necessitated his critical, poetic, and political intervention throughout his career, including in the character of Hideho Heights and in his rumor to Dudley Randall. These returns suggest that his singular poetic and critical interventions in the *Libretto*, Tate's preface, and his unpublished "Excerpts" essay were not enough on their own. There is, as Tolson argued, a risk to the radical affirmation of the "for," and one of those risks admittedly is the ease with which some of its commitments can be misconstrued to serve the logic of the "to." Tolson's poetry has long been memorialized as "in between" literary periods of African American literature: too late and too modernist for the Harlem Renaissance, not seemingly nationalist enough for Black Arts.[84] Yet to see Tolson as only a Black modernist underestimates his Black radical challenge to the contours of the definitions of poetry and literature as they stood. At a Black writers' conference at Fisk University in 1966, Tolson and Robert Hayden sat with Arna Bontemps and Margaret Walker on a panel titled "Poetry from the Negro Renaissance Till Today." During the session, Hayden hesitated to identify as a Negro writer, but rather called himself a "poet who happens to be Negro."[85] Speaking after Hayden and responding directly to him, Tolson reaffirmed his critique of poetry's isolation and his emphasis on the directionality that poetry provides. As David Llorens recounted in his essay on the conference in *Negro Digest*, Tolson "roared: 'Nobody writes in a vacuum or out of a vacuum—when a man writes, he tells me which way he went in society.'"[86] Tolson continued, "I'm a black poet, an African-American poet, a Negro poet. I'm no accident—and I don't give a tinker's damn what you think."[87] Tolson backed up his affirmative response by endorsing the idea that LeRoi Jones was a "symbol of the times" not just on matters in Harlem, but for those of "an entire civilization."[88]

Tolson's comment reinforced the themes of his essay on Allen Tate drafted fifteen years earlier, by suggesting that poetry is necessarily connected to the exigencies of immediate social and political circumstances. It also addressed how race and class manifest in art's form and reception, something that Amiri Baraka would take up in his work. In this, Tolson would update his earlier master's thesis, which focused on the earlier spat about "Negro poets" between Hughes and Cullen, to suggest that Baraka took up the torch of Hughes, "the idealistic wanderer and defender of the proletariat."[89] (As we will learn in the next chapter, Hughes faced severe scrutiny for this position and had to craft new ways of articulating it in the same years that Tolson waged his war of correspondence with Tate.) Finally, Tolson's statement suggested that Hideho's embrace of the "private poem in the modern vein"—and Tolson's too—was a political project to break beyond the dialectic of "to be / or not to be / a Negro," a project to generate an affirmative, directional grammar through and against the social and political order that literature and criticism had both supported and established.

⊙ 3 ⊙

Tactical Criticism

In June 1950 Mozell E. Hill, the editor of the journal *Phylon*, wrote Langston Hughes to solicit an essay on "poetry of 'The Old Guard'" for a special issue titled "The Negro in Literature: The Current Scene." Hughes declined the request for an essay, but agreed to a phone interview that would be published if the questions were sent by airmail in advance.[1] Hill sought answers to questions such as "Are there any special problems which the Negro writer is likely to encounter which do not face the white writer?" in order to address a roiling debate as to whether Black writers were limited to, and perhaps even should avoid, treatment of "Negro themes."[2] The questions reflected wider concerns about the universalism of Black writing that have made this 1950 issue of *Phylon* a subject of much scholarly scrutiny in the early part of the twenty-first century. Kenneth Warren retrieves it from the archive to support his claim that African American literature has a terminus with the legal end of segregation, which would begin in earnest just a few years after the issue was published.[3] Lawrence Jackson argues that "The Negro in Literature: The Current Scene" stood as a chorus affirming "the ethos of universalism by way of idiomatic difficulty" in Black writing. To Jackson, in favor of an aesthetic more amenable to a New Critical literary establishment, nearly all of the issue's contributors cast aside protest literature, as well as the contemporaneous Black left political struggles involving W. E. B. Du Bois, Paul Robeson, and two groups of Black men accused of rape in Trenton and Martinsville.[4] Or most simply, as Mary Helen Washington puts it, the issue and its contributors were among many Black writers in the era "promoting conservative race politics," meaning those who focused on "racial progress" despite the state's maintenance of inequality.[5]

Neither Washington, Warren, nor Jackson gives much time to the Hughes interview, likely because despite Hughes's leftist past, they see it as reflecting the larger theme expressed in the issue: Black writing, in Jackson's phrasing, "painfully lacked a critical tradition."[6] When the editors of *Phylon* asked Hughes the areas where "the Negro writer" had yet to make a significant contribution, he responded:

> Well, let me put it this way: it seems to me that there is a crying need for good literary criticism. I can't give the reasons for it, but our great deficiency is this dearth of really good critics. We have almost no books of literary criticism—certainly not recent, competently-done books.[7]

While this statement appears to disparage the state of Black criticism, when situated in the context of Hughes's midcentury investigations of critical practice, a different understanding emerges.

In this chapter I suggest that Hughes identifies a link between conservative race politics and the New Criticism, and sets out to generate a mode of literary criticism suited to Black and left literature. Read in a wider frame, his insistence that there is a "dearth of really good critics" points to the fact that there are few Black *New Critics* of merit, not that there are few Black critics. In the years before and after the "Negro in Literature" *Phylon* issue, Hughes offered his tongue-in-cheek appraisal of "good" writing in reviews, speeches, and correspondence advising Black writers. He suggested that "good bad" writing was simply that which white critics and white people enjoyed, writing which often relied on the stereotypical portrayal of Black people. This evaluative measure of the racialized good operates in the so-called universal and objective realm. I show that Hughes troubled the definition of good offered by white critics and publishers via a sarcastic and therefore obscured challenge that could, when necessary, be denied. Hughes was a particularly visible target for anticommunist and anti-Black scrutiny, both of which animated fears about the transgression of norms governing race, class, and sexuality. To make a critique of these literary critical, political, and social forces, Hughes generated a contextually dependent definition of "good" criticism that could at one moment be plausibly deniable to liberal scrutiny and at another be politically useful to Black leftists. He pursued this different measure for criticism most explicitly in his closed-door testimony before the McCarthy commission three years after the *Phylon* publication and—less explicitly, because closer to public view—in correspondence, writings, and speaking engagements throughout the 1950s.

The *Phylon* issue only offers an obscure hint to the type of criticism Hughes admires. He cites "[E. Franklin] Frazier, John Hope Franklin, [Horace] Cayton and [St. Clair] Drake" as exemplars for what significant contributors to literary criticism might look like.[8] What unites the work of Frazier, Franklin, Cayton, and Drake is a deliberate attention to how the historical force of slavery and the ongoing development of racial capitalism continues to structure and divide the material circumstances of Black life along vectors of race and class. A criticism informed by their work would take seriously class and gender divisions among Black people, the practice of Black life in urban space, and the legacy of slavery. But even when this mode of scholarship was avowedly against communism, as it was in the case of John Hope Franklin, it still attracted political scrutiny. Throughout the 1950s and '60s the FBI would open intelligence files on Franklin, Frazier, and Drake. Hughes's reference to these writers suggests an admiration for their methods and aims, as well as an expression of what might be possible in the restrictive institutional framework of the university and the state in the era of racial liberalism. Elsewhere, Hughes suggested that there was a material dimension to performing literary criticism that necessarily drew upon the particularities of the institutions in which it was performed. On the one hand, this allowed him to identify that the white understanding of Black literary intention established by the New Criticism generated and supported the anti-Blackness and anti-communism of the US liberal state. On the other hand, this meant for Hughes that Black literary critical interpretive acts must be written for an institutional context to come, in which academia, the publishing world, and the state were materially reconfigured. Hughes imagined this material configuration, and proposed steps that would make it possible.

Hughes's approach to criticism and his resistance to Black universalism may make the most sense when understood as an expression of what in the twenty-first century Stefano Harney and Fred Moten call the undercommons. Harney and Moten offer the following as a description of the undercommons: "the downlow lowdown maroon community of the university . . . where the work gets done, where the work gets subverted, where the revolution is still black, still strong."[9]

The ties of the undercommons to the longer genealogy of the Black radical tradition suggests that Hughes's lament about Black criticism marks a similarly complex navigation of academic and state affiliation and form throughout the 1950s. Hughes's observation about the state of Black literary criticism is "in but not of" the networks of authorization and affiliation of a conservative, universalist approach to racism that came to be the official antiracism of the US order in this period. Harney and Moten make clear the subversive and dangerous dimension of undercommons planning. Hughes's path to describe a world that might sustain Black literary criticism highlights why the description itself may need to take on a multivalent and ephemeral form. Hughes insists upon outlining his Black critical practice behind closed doors, often with a sardonic tone that allows for an obfuscation of his aims. Bemoaning the "dearth of really good critics" fits comfortably within a universalist push in Black literature, at the same time as it identifies the failings of what dominant institutions mark as good criticism. This mode of critique becomes possible by reconfiguring the function of the McCarthy hearing and calling forth Black cultural workers and revolutionaries to assemble despite their forced absence from the institutional sites of criticism.

With this in mind, I see Hughes's "crying need for good literary criticism" as identifying the formal evaluative structures for literature, which have been established by the New Critics, as the only path for Black literary critical success in a white liberal-capitalist world. When Hughes singles out the lack of "literary essays and books of criticism," he highlights that these are the forms by which literary criticism is recognized as "good." These forms, however, are not the only ways in which literary criticism can be practiced, nor are they necessarily ready at hand for Black writers with restricted access to academic employment and matriculation, and to avenues for publication.[10] A reading of Hughes's testimony informed by the undercommons suggests that these imposed limitations mean that in 1950 Hughes intimated that literary essays and books of criticism were not the sites where Black literary criticism could be found. This idea can be confirmed elsewhere in the special issue of *Phylon*. Blyden Jackson, for instance, calls J. Saunders Redding's *To Make a Poet Black* and Hugh Gloster's *Negro Voices in American Fiction*—both prominent books by Black critics— "mere prolegomena for the hard, serious, tedious labor of giving our literature the sort of scholarly and critical framework which adds the needed marginal dimensions to the established European literatures."[11] Blyden Jackson takes issue with the quality of Black critical work based on New Critical standards. He points to the limits put on the time of Black critics by institutions that demand "teaching loads . . . too great and facilities for research too meager."[12] The uneven labor demands of the university system across racialized institutions connect to the New Criticism's tendency to devalue the imaginative work of Black writers. By midcentury it had become clear that literary success was possible for Black critics and Black literature if, and only if, those writers absconded to the dominant literary determinants of value institutionalized in the white American academy. Hughes deplored this reality and sought to change it in the face of being trapped by the discursive and enforcement arms of anti-Black and anticommunist racial liberalism.

In the first section of this chapter, I lay out how Hughes challenges the conservative universalist model of race and the New Critical interpretive imperative in his writing and correspondence in the early 1950s. That Hughes might elliptically articulate his point about where a distinctly Black literary criticism unfolds is supported by his response to the increased scrutiny of his leftist political positions. Hughes also had a longer history of encounter with the material restrictions of New Critical thought that led him to be especially suspicious of the movement's prominence and supposed objectivity. The second section of this chapter examines Hughes's closed-door testimony before the Senate Permanent Subcommittee on Investigations in 1953. Unlike in the public hearing, Hughes actively challenged the committee's method for reading his work as an index of his politics, and invoked an interpretive method distinct from the New Critical one loosely adopted by the state. Importantly, Hughes's method, which I call tactical criticism, does not appear as a "literary essay" or a "book of literary criticism," but as the spoken delivery of an autobiography. In this critical performance, Hughes drew on the repertoire of Black social life's challenge to and exposure of the limitations of the white, liberal citizen subject of the United States. In the final section, I show that this form of Black literary criticism draws on a repertoire of tactics that Black writers on the left employed to form a socially based political criticism of literature, a new definition of Black literature, and a sketch of a world that might accommodate such definitions and practices.

THE RACIST INTERPRETATION COMPLEX

Among the first encounters that Langston Hughes had with the inchoate New Criticism was in Nashville just two years after the publication of *I'll Take My Stand*. In 1932, James Weldon Johnson invited Hughes for a poetry reading at Fisk University. Across town, Vanderbilt English Department faculty member Tom Mabry decided to throw a party for the event, and invited Hughes and Johnson as guests of honor. Allen Tate would not have it. He wrote an open letter to Mabry, which he circulated to other members of the English faculty. "Johnson and Hughes are both very interesting writers," Tate wrote, "and as such I would like to meet them.... This would be possible in New York, London, or Paris, but here such a meeting would be ambiguous.... My theory of racial relations is this: there should be no social intercourse between the races unless we are willing for that to lead to a marriage."[13] Tate's "theory of racial relations" relied on intense fears of miscegenation, and on the spatial segregation of African Americans; it could easily stand as a textbook definition of racism, as well as an articulation of the unspoken reasoning for arguing a Southern return to an agrarian society.

Tate's theory is foundational to what I call the racist interpretation complex. Fears of sex between Black men and white women fueled anticommunist and prosegregationist sentiment, and became foundational largely because of the CPUSA's defense of nine Black boys accused of rape in Scottsboro, Alabama, in March 1931.[14] Tate would likely have associated Hughes with this event. Hughes wrote about Scottsboro first in his drama "Scottsboro Limited," which was published in *New Masses* in October 1931, and then in four poems that were published with the play and illustrations by Prentiss Taylor in an edition released by the Golden Stair Press in 1932. In an effort to govern social space on the terms of racism and sexual panic, Tate deployed his theory of racial relations that reenforced borders between Black academic institutions and white ones. As the scholar Michael Bibby notes, this episode is often told to highlight "the segregationism of southern academic institutions."[15] Bibby, however, goes on to suggest that the response to this theory, guided by both racism and sexism, continues to shape modernist studies and literary inquiry more broadly. The "personal prejudices" of New Critics like Tate are beyond personal; they structure the field of literary inquiry even as literary studies sought to "diversify the canon and the curriculum."[16] Tate's "personal prejudices" did, in fact, have broader material consequences. After the incident, the Vanderbilt English Department chose not to renew Mabry's junior faculty contract. Mabry subsequently took a job at Fisk, where he worked as an assistant to James Weldon Johnson, a move about which Robert Penn Warren commented, "Mabry has definitely decided to commercialize his talent for nigger-loving."[17] The overt racism of Warren, Tate, and the faculty of the Vanderbilt English Department made a lasting impact on Johnson, and presumably on Hughes as well. After the episode, Johnson wrote, "The South as an Institution can sink through the bottom of the pit of hell."[18] Though still nascent in 1932, the New Criticism would come to be a key arm in what Johnson referred to as the "Institution" of the South. The practice of enforcing the theory of racial relations that subtended it would not be limited to the South. As I argued in the first chapter of this book, New Critical interpretation would be adopted by the US state in a revanchist fight to maintain the racial capitalist order during the Cold War. Hughes would eventually encounter this mature formation of the racist interpretation complex when he met the Subcommittee on Investigations.

The New Criticism, its connection to the US state, and their joint impact on Black writing remained a topic of interest for Hughes long after his 1932 trip to Nashville. Two decades after the run-in with Tate, Hughes and his longtime Nashville ally Arna Bontemps expressed significant skepticism about any great change in the racial theory of the New Criticism, while also acknowledging the movement's significant power. Less than a week before his 1953 Senate hearing in Washington, Hughes reached out to Bontemps to express his hesitation about the publication of James Baldwin's essay "Everybody's Protest Novel" alongside another essay by the young Black critic Richard Gibson in the Lionel Trilling–edited and Ford Foundation–funded *Perspectives USA*. The essays by Gibson and Baldwin were printed under the same heading: "Two Protests against Protest." (This was the third time Baldwin's essay had been published. It was first printed in the small Paris-based English-language journal *Zero* in spring 1949, and reprinted in the June 1949 issue of *Partisan Review*, which also contained an essay by Allen Tate that addressed the Bollingen controversy.) Hughes states, "I think it is encouraging to see them trying to leap fences and get out of pens—even if they do fall into lily ponds. Baldwin's critical pieces are much better than his fiction, and I think he writes beautifully."[19]

According to Hughes's biographer, Arnold Rampersad, "'lily ponds' was his term for New Criticism, art that evaded its social context, and Black snobbishness of the more flaccid white artistic values."[20] From a New Critical perspective, the beauty of the lilies, or poems, stands apart from the mud, stink, and morass that ultimately generates and creates them, the process and the material that goes into the making of beauty. A number of scholars have followed Hughes in suggesting that Baldwin's "Everybody's Protest Novel" supported a New Critical approach. Lawrence Jackson, for instance, argues that the pivotal essay worked "as a primer for new criticism," employing "the same catalog for writing used by Lionel Trilling in *The Liberal Imagination* and also by Cleanth Brooks in *The Well Wrought Urn*."[21] Jackson's and Hughes's readings highlight how the New Critical context of the publication of Baldwin's essay in *Perspectives USA* reconfigure the essay's argument. That is, the enduring force of the New Criticism and its institutions subsumes and adopts Baldwin's essay to endorse its methods.

In his reading, Hughes sympathizes with Baldwin's analysis of the conundrum of Black writers living in an anti-Black United States, but less so with where that analysis takes Baldwin. Baldwin's essay unfurls a searing critique against the most prominent writer on the Black left, Richard Wright, and against Harriet Beecher Stowe's *Uncle Tom's Cabin*, a book for which Hughes had just written a favorable introduction. Baldwin suggests that Wright has written Uncle Tom's exact "opposite" because Wright has seemingly been trapped in the "deadly, timeless battle" of Black's evil and white's superiority.[22] This likely was not what was controversial to Hughes. He had expressed his own impatience with Bigger Thomas's stereotypical portrayal. Thirty years prior to Baldwin, Hughes had laid out his own account of this "deadly, timeless battle," but had offered a different cultural prescription. In "The Negro Artist and the Racial Mountain" (1926), Hughes identifies the "desire to pour racial individuality into the mold of American standardization . . . to be as little Negro and as much American as possible."[23] Hughes's ideas about American standardization resonate with what Hughes would later identify as the fence Baldwin and Gibson leap. Hughes's own flight from this fence in "The Negro Artist" consisted of an embrace of the eternal "tom-tom of the Negro soul" that both cries and laughs. Hughes rooted the Black struggle against American racism in the race and class consciousness found in popular forms like jazz and the blues. Baldwin's theorization of the path forward in "Everybody's Protest Novel" was cast in admittedly more abstract terms. Baldwin locates the "power that will free us from ourselves" in a "web of ambiguity, paradox."[24] On their surface, the terms "ambiguity" and "paradox" show Baldwin adopting the language of the New Criticism, and support latter-day readings that position his essay as an endorsement of New Critical practice.

But Baldwin's paradox is not that of Cleanth Brooks. Baldwin seeks to lace his with "hunger, danger, darkness." In Hughes's reading, the context of the essay's publication in *Perspectives USA* overwhelms Baldwin's recasting of these terms. The result is that Hughes perceives Baldwin to endorse a more socially, politically, and racially autonomous literature than Baldwin himself practiced. Several months after reading "Everybody's Protest Novel," Hughes wrote to Baldwin about his recently published novel *Go Tell It on the Mountain*, saying "Man after reading your piece in 'Perspectives' I didn't expect you to write such a colored book."[25] Hughes recognized that *Go Tell It on the Mountain* was not fully aligned with the New Critical principles that "Everybody's Protest Novel" seemed to endorse. This recognition suggests that the apparatus surrounding the essay—the journal in which it was republished, that journal's editor, et cetera—recast its terms to support the dominant US critical movement, a context that influenced Hughes's skeptical reading.

Hughes's sense that Baldwin was writing in line with the New Critics would have only been intensified by reading "Everybody's Protest Novel" after Richard Gibson's "A No to Nothing." Gibson had attended Kenyon College while John Crowe Ransom headed the *Kenyon Review* there; "A No to Nothing" was the first essay by a Black writer to be published in the prestigious New Critical publication. At the end of the 1950s, Gibson became embroiled in a scandal when he wrote a letter with William Gardner Smith that supported Algerian revolutionaries using the name of the cartoonist Ollie Harrington without permission; it put Harrington at risk of deportation from France. Richard Wright, E. Franklin Frazier, and Julian Mayfield accused Gibson of being a CIA operative, a claim which Gibson has publicly denied.[26] Though *Perspectives USA* is not known to have received direct funding from the CIA, Greg Barnhisel has argued that its efforts to "depoliticize and aestheticize" literary modernism were of a piece with US government-backed efforts in the Cultural Cold War.[27]

Printed by Trilling as a prelude to Baldwin's "Everybody's Protest

Novel," Gibson's essay analyzes an imagined dialogue between a Black
writer and a white liberal editor in which the Black writer is convinced
to write a book that deals with "the Problem." The Black writer is not
able to "write about what you know," what would become a creative
writing maxim, because the only thing he is assumed to know is "Jim
Crow, sharecropping, slum-ghettoes, Georgia crackers, and the sting
of his humiliation, his unending ordeal, his blackness."[28] Gibson's suggestion of where the young Black writer should turn is distinct from
Baldwin's: "The young writer might do well to impress upon himself
the fact that he is a contemporary of Eliot, Valéry, Pound, Rilke, Auden,
and not merely of Langston Hughes."[29] Gibson's aesthetic preferences
fill in the gaps left by the abstraction of terms like "ambiguity" and
"paradox" in Baldwin's essay. He embraces the New Criticism's tendency toward a certain mode of literary modernism, while shunning
Hughes's work directly.

As their correspondence continued on the *Perspectives USA* matter,
Hughes and Bontemps suggest that neither Baldwin nor Gibson were
aware of how New Critical categories attached to powerful institutions
were among the material forces that perpetuated the "deadly tireless
battle" Baldwin identified. Responding to Hughes's "lily ponds" comment, Bontemps wrote:

> You are very generous to the boys in PERSPECTIVES USA. They do
> have some talent, especially Baldwin, but in my opinion it remains to
> be seen whether or not the New Critics, under whose influence they
> have fallen, mean them any good. That group traces its genealogy to
> the Fugitives of Nashville, the group which produced I'LL TAKE MY
> STAND, a very anti-Negro book. Not all have been reconstructed. Nat-
> urally they have their own reasons for opposing protest in fiction writ-
> ing. They are ready enough to protest the things they don't like. They
> simply object to protesting the disabilities of the Negro in America.[30]

Bontemps spelled out explicitly what Hughes had intimated in the
letter before. Baldwin and Gibson had been caught, wittingly or not,
within the ambit of the New Criticism. Bontemps's contextualization
suggests that he believed Baldwin and Gibson were perhaps not fully
aware of the racist background of the Agrarian New Critics. Bontemps
made clear that the "anti-Negro" position of *I'll Take My Stand* had suf-

fused the group's literary preferences, and suggested that without explicit interpretive care, the work of Black writers and critics could be
torqued to endorse the depoliticized aesthetic ideals of the New Criticism as well as their social, political, and even sexual vision. In Bontemps' estimation, the New Criticism and the racial liberal state had
the capacity to redirect Black writing to support its aesthetic, institutional, and political economic aspirations.

Bontemps would elaborate these concerns in a 1954 lecture delivered
at Peabody College, just across the street from Vanderbilt in Nashville.
In the lecture, titled "Some Recent Writings by Negroes," Bontemps
examined work by Hughes, Wright, and Ellison to "draw a bead on the
New Criticism which holds that neither folk materials nor sociological
questions are proper for serious art."[31] Bontemps's culminating claim
in "Some Recent Writing" was that the common denominator of Black
writers publishing recently was "the way the authors have addressed
themselves severally to that tenant of the New Criticism."[32] Bontemps
went on to suggest that the New Criticism was "the special problem
of the Negro writer in the United States today" because New Critical
principles were a "device for excluding [the Negro writer's] works from
the *best* literary company. The anthologies and the textbooks, for example."[33] Like Hughes, Bontemps saw the New Criticism as a device to
be engaged or challenged by Black writers *and* a material obstacle for
Black writers hoping to make it into print and to the increasingly lucra-
tive university market. Segregation impacted the resources available to
Black critics and scholars, as Blyden Jackson argued in *Phylon*. It also
kept Black writers from the anthologies that supported college teaching, as Hughes had addressed in a 1952 *Chicago Defender* column and
in his work with Bontemps in editing an anthology, *The Poetry of the
Negro, 1746–1949*.[34] What Hughes identified as "good literary criticism"
held back Black writers in terms of aesthetics and the institutions that
supported the valuation and circulation of those aesthetic principles.
Because literary criticism was paired with segregated institutions, an
institutional and material response was necessary to address and challenge its racist practice.

Hughes was imminently aware of the challenges of navigating the increasingly dominant racial liberalism that was held up in part by New

Critical aesthetics and institutions. While he had long been under investigation by the FBI, the demands of the postwar racial liberal order
led to increased suspicions about Hughes's leftist poetry of the 1930s.
The aftermath of World War II had thrust the United States forward
as the unifying global power of capitalist democracy and, as such, as
Nikhil Pal Singh argues, "black inclusion in the nation-state was an
index of U.S. world ordering power."[35] Rather than prompting a rectification of long-standing material inequalities between Black and
white people, this prioritization of nominal freedom and equality led
to growing demand for Black leaders to marshal Black people to adopt
white "American" social and cultural norms. There was the prevailing
sense that the ideal form of the Black subject was of "white men with
black skins," a sense that defined the era.[36] The push for universalism
found in the *Phylon* issue is a clear outgrowth of this official mode of
antiracism. The force of racial liberalism was expressed by members of
the Black bourgeoisie in white-led sociological studies on "the American Negro problem," and in literary critical essays.

   Black leaders and institutions who sought to work within the racial liberal order came to question Hughes's overt expressions of Black
self-determination and Black culture in his explicitly Leninist poems
of the 1930s. These poems included "Goodbye Christ," "Good Morning Revolution," and "One More 'S' in the U.S.A." among others.
Hughes's Leninist vision was informed by Harry Haywood's "Black
Belt thesis," adopted by the Communist International in 1928, which
suggested that Black people in the United States constituted their own
nation and thus had their own right to self-determination.[37] Despite
the geographical articulation of Haywood's position—it pointed to a
particular area of the US South that constituted the Black Belt—the
biggest impact of Haywood's thesis was, in Robin D. G. Kelley's view,
an opening of "space for creative expressions of black nationalism and
race pride."[38] Hughes's ready valorization in his poetry of the "BLACK
WORLD" and of international, interracial coalitions of workers constituted what might as well have been the exact opposite of midcentury
liberal universalism.[39] The "BLACK WORLD" that Hughes called for in
1930s poems like "Air Raid over Harlem" suggested that a path to peace
relied on organizing "BLACK AND WHITE WORKERS" on the chance
that "Harlem see red," rather than a continued expansion of colonialism. Hughes's poetry called for a political order defined by the Black

working class and international communism, mediated by the production of culture, poetry, blues, and film.

In the 1940s and 1950s the US state was far less tolerant of these political positions. To critique the white critical establishment, their institutions, and the state, Hughes had to craft a different register to make these critiques, even if this discursive register had to endure the linked aesthetic and political scrutiny of the period. As early as 1944, US citizens, Black and white, began writing to the FBI to ask about Hughes's politics. Many of these queries centered on Hughes's 1932 poem, "Goodbye Christ," which declared Christianity "dead" and replaced it with "A real guy named / Marx Communist Lenin Peasant Stalin Worker ME."[40] The poem proved so inflammatory that J. Edgar Hoover interpreted it in a lecture he delivered to Methodist ministers. When citizens would write to Hoover inquiring about Hughes's political affiliation, the FBI director would personally respond and enclose a pamphlet with his own interpretation of "Goodbye Christ."[41] The scrutiny clearly weighed on Hughes. He tried to stay out of the press, to speak at Black institutions because the appearances would draw less attention, and to avoid endorsing explicitly leftist causes, including the support of W. E. B. Du Bois after Du Bois was indicted in 1951 on claims that he was a Soviet agent. Even as Hughes pulled back from Marxism-Leninism, he revealed an ongoing sympathy with Black leftists. His poem "Lenin" was published in *New Masses* in 1946 (despite having been written several years before), he eventually wrote in support of Du Bois, and he allowed the Communist Party of New York to reprint his *Chicago Defender* column that defended the twelve CPUSA leaders being tried for violation of the Smith Act in 1949. Further, while he was writing frequently for the increasingly liberal *Phylon*, Hughes advised and contributed to the new *Harlem Quarterly*, a journal whose masthead carried the names of leftists Black and white, including Shirley Graham, Herbert Aptheker, Harold Cruse, and Ernest Kaiser.

Hughes delivered his thinly veiled and even caustic critique of the limitations that the New Criticism placed on Black writers in his address to the 1959 Negro Writers Conference of the American Society of African Culture (AMSAC). Though AMSAC was a CIA front, the writers conference was organized by John O. Killens, a Black leftist and nominal head of the Harlem Writers Guild.[42] Much to the dismay of AMSAC's conservative leadership, Killens arranged for a number of prominent Black leftists to speak, including Alice Childress, Frank London Brown, and Lorraine Hansberry, whose *A Raisin in the Sun* was set to premiere on Broadway two weeks after her AMSAC closing address. After the conference, with the encouragement of Harold Cruse, who by then had become an aggressive anticommunist, the AMSAC board excluded the most radical addresses from the published proceedings of the meeting. Mary Helen Washington argues that the conference stands as "a crossroads moment for black leftist writers," because the censorship of these Black, leftist positions marks a significant excision of these views from the record of midcentury Black literature.[43]

Hughes's paper did make it into the volume, likely because his speech trafficked in an irony that seems to have been lost on the universalist AMSAC leadership. Hughes's remarks, titled "Writers: Black and White," can be read as a statement advocating that Black writers pursue white themes in their literature. For instance, he argues that Black writers can only be successful if they depict Black people in their fiction "with white eyes," and if they seek out universal (i.e., non-Negro) subjects. However, he maintains throughout the essay that writing of this kind might yield commercial success but will ultimately be "bad writing." He advises, "Try becoming a good *bad* writer or a black *white* writer, in which case you might, with luck, do as well as white *black* writers do."[44] Hughes bemoans the fact that midcentury publishing success requires Black writers to adapt to the demand for "bad" writing by white writers that often circulates and relies upon negative stereotypes of Black people. As Hughes suggests, "Blackness seen through black eyes may be too black for wide white consumption," because there are "no black literary magazines, no black publishers, no black producers, no black investors."[45] The New Criticism and racial liberalism had made universalism the rubric for literary valuation and success, therefore further directing the publishing industry away from Black writers. As Hughes suggests in his AMSAC remarks, this universalism relied on projecting white perspectives as universal, as well as enforcing and reproducing the negative stereotypes of Black people that white perspectives tended to require. Hughes's riffing on the good and the good bad throughout his remarks—he even begins by saying, "To sell bad writing you have to be good"—can explain his suggestion in *Phylon* about the lack of good literary criticism. When Hughes referred to the "good" in *Phylon,* he likely meant what he called in 1959 the good *bad* of the white universalist principles of the New Criticism. The New Criticism's institutional prominence led the bad to be dropped from the "good *bad*" just as it prompted the elimination of the modifier "white" ahead of universalism. Moreover, both the good and the universal relied on the logic of Tate's "theory of race relations" or, more simply, the logic of racist stereotype. In this analysis, the "dearth of really good critics" became a political and economic problem in addition to a methodological one.

Compounding the idea that Hughes's AMSAC remarks are skeptical of the New Critical literary establishment rather than complementary, the speech holds within it a number of references to Hughes's radical past, and to his more explicit critiques of US racial liberalism and the white universalist literary world. The talk's primary advice is recycled from a sardonic listicle Hughes wrote for *Harlem Quarterly* in 1950. Item two of "How to Be a Bad Writer (in Ten Easy Lessons)" reads, "If you are a Negro, try very hard to write with an eye dead on the white market."[46] Additionally, the title of his AMSAC presentation recalls the name of the movie for which Hughes traveled to the Soviet Union to work as script supervisor in 1932.[47] That Hughes enfolds these obscure references to his leftist past in his AMSAC address highlights how here, too, he harkens for a different set of criteria for literary valuation and affiliation.

Hughes's sardonic challenge to New Critical and racial liberal norms is nowhere clearer than in the closing image of his AMSAC talk. The image directly connects to Hughes's 1953 encounter with the Senate Permanent Subcommittee on Investigations. It is the same as the one Hughes employed in a poem written in the '50s that described the McCarthy panel and would be published in his final poetry collection, *The Panther and the Lash* (1967). The speaker of "Un-American Investigators" insists that the assembled committee "shivers / with delight / in its manure," suggesting the scatological ecstasy experienced in authorizing authoritarianism as democracy. At AMSAC, likely unbeknownst to the audience assembled, that manure makes another appearance. This time, instead of surrounding the committee, the manure inundates the Black writer working under the universalist premises of the New Critical literary scene. He writes, "You say you are mired in manure? Manure fertilizes. As the old saying goes, 'Where the finest roses bloom, there is always a lot of manure around.'"[48] In both cases, the shit is the sticky and noxious decomposition of the false premises of egalitarian American democracy. The forms ready at hand for Black writers are determined by the means of survival (the growth of the rose), as they are by the world in which those forms emerge (the manure). Hughes's manure metaphor sutures the state's scrutiny of subversive thinkers red and Black to the means that Black writers, who are always understood to be against the order of the midcentury racial liberal state, can survive and succeed.

The manure, of course, also recalls the New Critical lily ponds that Hughes referenced in his correspondence with Bontemps. At AMSAC and in "Un-American Investigators," his focus on the manure highlights that Hughes's criticism must necessarily foreground the processes that cultivate the flower's bloom and its continued existence. In addition to centering the social, political, and institutional processes that go into the making of a work of art, Hughes connects through a complex network of metaphor the New Criticism, the Senate Permanent Subcommittee on Investigations, the state adoption of racial liberalism, and the market for Black writing. These connected entities can be seen as institutions reproducing the midcentury racist interpretation complex.

From these connections, I see Hughes's appearance in the *Phylon* issue devoted to racial universalism in Black literature as an experiment in finding a means to articulate Black radicalism within the universalist language of racial liberalism. The racist interpretation complex explains Hughes's dread of being called before McCarthy, or of having to negotiate the inevitable marginalization of a Black, leftist, queer writer writing protest poems. To speak before the Senate Permanent Subcommittee was to perform at a state site where the rules for making meaning for literature were meant to strip Black writers of value and subjectivity, and to subdue communist horizons of political possibility.[49] Against this state-sponsored racism, Hughes spoke plainly that which he otherwise addressed elliptically before and after: his means for literary and political interpretation.

A LESSON IN LITERARY CRITICISM

Three years after the publication of the *Phylon* interview, Langston Hughes was served a subpoena that required his appearance before

Senator Joseph McCarthy's committee on March 23, 1953. The blank on the subpoena to indicate the reason for Hughes's appearance was left unfilled. Hughes immediately wrote to the infamous senator, asking that his appearance be postponed because he had not "been informed why or what you wish to question me about," nor had he been given sufficient "time to be present."[50] The committee reluctantly delayed the testimony one day to Tuesday, March 24. In the interim, Hughes found a lawyer, Frank D. Reeves, one of the architects of the *Brown v. Board of Education* case, which had been argued before the Supreme Court four months earlier. Hughes had to scramble for funds to fly to Washington. The steady defaming of Hughes by J. Edgar Hoover and by the press had led to the cancellation of many of his speaking appearances and left the poet financially strapped.

Over the course of three days of private and public sessions with the Executive Committee of the Senate Permanent Subcommittee on Investigations, Hughes learned that he had been accused of writing pro-communist poetry in books that had been purchased by the federal government. The purchased books were held in foreign libraries managed by the International Information Administration (IIA), which would later become part of the United States Information Agency. According to Senator Everett Dirksen, the IIA had purchased Hughes's books, "which allegedly delineate American objectives and American culture," in order to "propagandiz[e] our way of life and our system."[51] The point of calling Hughes to Washington, it seemed, was to have him speak to the meaning of the works that were purchased by the federal government. As expressed by the committee, the goal of their questioning of Hughes was to find an authoritative statement on the "general objective of some of [Hughes's] poems, whether they strike a Communist, rather than an anti-Communist note."[52]

To get an answer about the communist dimensions of Hughes's work, the committee set out to consult the author directly. Vera Kutzinski has argued that the general situation of the hearing was oriented around the question of "intent."[53] Intent was pivotal for the rationale of government readers in their approach to African American literature. In their view, literature was an index of the potentially subversive political views of its writers. As William Maxwell has shown, this meant that J. Edgar Hoover and the Senate Permanent Subcommittee performed a type of "inverted Marxism" in reading, "identify[ing] the poem's radical speaker with Hughes, and Hughes with the poem alone,

pigeonholing him as the lyric confessor of communism at its most sac-
rilegious."[54] The federal government did not abide by the rules of intention laid out by the New Criticism, but neither did the New Critics,
especially when it came to works written by Black writers or works that
rankled their politics. The government's approach to Hughes's work
reveals what might otherwise appear as a contradiction to the New
Criticism as well as a contradiction within it: regardless of the author's
intent, Black literature always was political, and therefore subversive.
This contradiction signals that artistic intention is inconsistent by
definition. That same inconsistency became a central component of
the racial liberalism against which Hughes had to fight. Yet both New
Critical and government readers rendered intent as a consistent, objective fact that could be confirmed or denied. Hughes's critical strategy
targeted inconsistency and contradiction as the fulcrum that united
and balanced New Critical and federal scrutiny of Black writing, and
offered as an alternative a critical mode directly rooted in traditions of
Black social struggle against liberal bounds on personhood.

Hughes laid out his argument for a different definition of literary interpretation in the closed-door hearing on March 22, 1953, the transcript
of which remained under seal for fifty years. Unlike in his public testimony, where he made certain concessions about his past political positions—a testimony that Arnold Rampersad characterizes as "largely
passive, perhaps supine"—Hughes actively contested the reading and
interpretation of his poetry and of his past in the restricted session.[55]
In the closed hearing, Hughes was questioned by McCarthy's chief
counsel, Roy Cohn; the chief consultant to the subcommittee, David
Schine; and the junior senator from Illinois, Everett Dirksen. The committee's initial means to determine the "general objective" of Hughes's
poetry was to identify the political objective of Hughes the man. The
first question lobbed at Hughes was the most predictable: "Have you
ever been a Communist?" Yet Hughes' response was anything but.
Instead of providing a simple yes-or-no answer, Hughes troubled the
question's false simplicity and, in the process, began his course in the
perils of interpretation. He asked to know the committee's definition
of communism and, while they were at it, the definition of "all isms."
With this, Hughes implored the committee to agree upon a critical lan-

guage to which he, too, hoped to contribute meaning. Cohn called on Hughes to "interpret it [the definition of communism] as broadly as you want."[56] The imperative failed, because for Hughes, interpretation could not be a broad act defined by an abstracted institution. Instead, interpretation was a contingent and social act defined among the parties on the scene.

Hughes's emphasis on the situational definition of concepts—and the subsequent contextual definition of all concepts, invoked by his reference to all "isms"—gestures toward the fact that not only would Hughes resist the committee's definitions, he would also posit an alternative epistemology. If Black literature and Blackness under federal and New Critical eyes always carried the potential of subversion, then Hughes made the case that intent must play a different kind of function in interpretation. By denying the committee's predetermined definition of terms—of communism, of criticism—Hughes argued that such terms must be defined in relation to the situation of the hearing as well as the bodies assembled under its heading, thus implying that the meaning of these terms—and poems, by extension—shift. This process allowed Hughes to generate a critical work of his own in his testimony, while also showing that his poetry broke the mold of New Critical definitions of autonomy. Hughes's poetry can neither be read as a clear, objective statement on its author's politics, nor be thoroughly separated from the author who creates it. Hughes, in other words, works to demystify the literary object by highlighting that authorial intention neither entirely defines nor can be fully excised from a work. This leaves a poem as neither an object unto itself nor one synonymous with its author, thus troubling its ontological status and requiring a process-based, materially attentive practice instead.

I term Hughes's process and attunement toward reading literature "tactical criticism." Michel de Certeau defines a tactic as that which "play[s] on and with a terrain imposed on it and organized by the law of a foreign power."[57] Contrary to strategy—the dominant means to make history and space legible—tactics act from "the absence of a proper locus," which is to say that tactics must function through a space unmade by power, or a nonspace. Put differently, "The space of a tactic is the space of the other."[58] Robin D. G. Kelley has suggested that de Certeau's vocabulary of tactics gives shape to how workers, especially Black workers, constitute an analysis of capital and the state in their means of everyday resistance.[59] Hughes's approach was tactical for three reasons. First, it was defined through and against the terrain of authorial intention and the ontological stability of the literary object and the human. Second, Hughes generated his critical practice beyond the limits of the imagined possibility of what poetry could be, those limits being that poetry is a pure expression of its author's personhood or an object unto itself. Finally, out of this "absence of a proper locus," he would develop, through his attempt in the hearing at what he terms "full interpretation," a contingent and shifting form of critical practice. This practice reveals a wider critique of the links between capital and the state through a revelation about the limits placed on Black expression and interpretation premised on a temporary claim to the time and space of the hearing.

More recently, Stefano Harney and Fred Moten have described the undercommons as a "nonplace" where the "maroons" of the university steal its resources to make another world for those parties exploited by the university, the state, and the contemporaneous forms of capital. The ephemerality of the undercommons is itself a tactic; to be temporary and difficult to pin down is to elude the valuation frameworks of institutions devoted to preserving their permanence. It is also a means to avoid being detected as a threat, "buying time" for planning, which Harney and Moten define as "the ceaseless experiment with the futurial presence of the forms of life that make such activities possible."[60] Harney and Moten's account of the futurial dimension to presently practiced tactics suggests that Hughes lay a foundation for Black criticism in the hearing that was meant for an audience beyond its walls in another time.

Despite the private nature of Hughes's closed-door session, word of Hughes's approach to the committee managed to circulate. His private testimony became a rumor, something that Hughes himself may have leaked to the *Amsterdam News* to make it clear that he did not endorse red-baiting.[61] With this framework, we can understand how Hughes's testimony and his midcentury career—even if not fully realized—sought to articulate his definition of Black criticism and Black literature against that of the New Criticism and the US state. Hughes's closed-door testimony drew on the Black radical tradition, stole the tools of the university and knowledge making, and fugitively created a space of his own oriented to a world-to-come. Tactical criticism is the development of an interpretive practice and a political economic organization of a future world free of conquest in an anti-Black present that is not yet ready for either.

Quickly getting the sense that Hughes's tendency toward definition and negation would thwart his explicitly political queries, Roy Cohn moved in the closed-door hearing to a line of questioning regarding the objectives of individual poems. Hughes immediately signaled that here, too, the committee would be stymied. Hughes challenged the possibility of objective, true answers about literature. "I don't think you can get a yes or no answer entirely to any literary question," Hughes stated; a poem could "mean many things to different people."[62] The unstable definition of literature that Hughes suggested was different from the one held by the committee, and from the one held by the prevailing definition of literary studies as formulated by the New Critics. In arguing that the poem is an object unto its own, the New Critics figured the task of the critic as one of reconstruction and observation, which could create some variation; but in the end, because of the object-nature of the poem, that variation could only be measured against the object's reality. Hughes saw instead that a poem could have multiple meanings, and that those meanings were made by different readers. Questioning the ontological stability of the poem made possible through its excision of intent meant that those borders that separate a poem from the world—and make it an object unto itself—were a mere critical construction. That is, New Critical ambiguity relied on the ontological closure of the poem, whereas Hughes's multiple meanings generated via reading implied that a poem and its meanings were made a process and a practice that could be, as it was in the hearing, a social project.

When the committee asked Hughes for an interpretation of his poem "Ballad of Lenin," the poet agreed to provide one only if he was allowed to reread the poem. He made this request because to interpret the poem was to read it anew in this particular situation. A different reader in a different context might unfurl a different, valid meaning. Hughes defined this as context: the conditions surrounding the reading and the writing of the work. He further outlined this definition when Roy Cohn asked him to respond to a particular sentence of a *Chicago Defender* column in which he lay out a defense for the twelve Communists charged under the Smith Act in 1949. Hughes responded that "one can not take anything out of context."[63] At first, Hughes' statement indicated that Cohn had the context of the work's publication wrong; Cohn cited the column as having come from the *Daily Worker* rather than the *Chicago Defender*. After being reminded that he was under oath, however, Hughes elaborated on why reading one sentence from an essay did not meet his contextual standard: "If that statement is from a column of mine, as I presume it probably is, I would say that I believed the entire context of the article in which it is included."[64] In this statement, Hughes upheld two contradictory realities to New Critical and federal readers. On the one hand, he suggested that a single sentence of an entire article could not be understood unless it was interpreted as part of the whole article, seemingly affirming that the article was a whole of sorts, determining its parts. On the other hand, the article was part of an "entire context" that expanded beyond that whole, including such relevant material as the publication in which it was printed, the social and political realities that surrounded its composition, and the writer's understanding of that varied material. In other words, Hughes's responses to the Permanent Subcommittee point to the fact that an article had meaning via a number of factors that New Critical and federal readers could not hold together all at once. What must be taken into account included the work itself, the situation of its reading, and the "entire context" of the work, which included authorial intent and social and political background. This definition of context, shuttling between writer and reader, highlights that interpretation is as much an interactive and social process, as it is a solitary and objective one.

Hughes further outlined the significance of context when he endeavored to give what he called "a full interpretation" of his poem "One More 'S' in the U.S.A." He requested that he not be interrupted, a request that the committee grudgingly accepted. By attempting to suspend interruptions, Hughes made time and space of his own design within the confines of the hearing. And since this space and time belonged to Hughes—not to the committee members—it also operated beyond the confines of the hearing. It was precisely in this claiming and morphing of space and time that Hughes summoned a repertoire of interpretive efforts from the Black radical tradition to engage in the practice of tactical criticism.

He began:

All right, sir. To give a full interpretation of any piece of literary work one has to consider not only when and how it was written, but what brought it into being. I, sir, was born in Joplin, Missouri. I was born a Negro. From my very earliest childhood memories, I have encountered very serious and very hurtful problems. One of my earliest childhood memories was going to the movies in Lawrence, Kansas, where we lived and there was one motion picture theater, and I went every afternoon. It was a nickelodeon, and I had a nickel to go. One afternoon I put my nickel down and the woman pushed it back and she pointed to a sign. I was about seven years old.[65]

At this point, Cohn interrupted:

I do not want to interrupt you. I do want to say this. I want to save time here. I want to concede very fully that you encounter oppression and denial of civil rights. Let us assume that, because I assume that will be the substance of what you are about to say. To save us time, what we are interested in determining for our purpose is this: Was the solution to which you turned that of the Soviet form of government?[66]

After this question, Hughes sparred with Cohn about the committee's broken promise to allow him unlimited time to give a full interpretation. Eventually, he continued his autobiographical narrative for two and a half transcript pages before being interrupted again. At this point in his full interpretation, Hughes had only reached the 1920s, fifteen years before he had published the poem in question. Cohn and the committee reclaimed the hearing and left Hughes's "full interpretation" seemingly unfinished, permanently fugitive.

A reading of Hughes's interpretive attempt offers a glimpse of his critical practice, its invocation of the Black radical tradition's challenge to ontological stability, and its attempt to bring forward a future world subtended by institutional and interpretive forces of a different kind. Hughes begins his full interpretation by attending to the limits on his personhood, because his racialization as "the Negro" impacts and violates Hughes the man. I suggest that in this, Hughes draws on a Black autobiographical tradition that similarly highlights the incongruity between Black life and Western ideas of humanity and citizenship. Frederick Douglass, for instance, situates his *Narrative of the Life* as animated by this tension. Douglass writes that at the "turning-point in my career as a slave," he recognizes that "however long I might remain a slave in form, the day had passed forever when I could be a slave in fact."[67] Douglass crafts this with writerly attention, but it is occasioned through an action that generates a different shape of the world: a strike against Covey, a white renter of and known breaker of men. This moment of Douglass's narrative, of course, rests seemingly in opposition to its otherwise firm argument for the power of literacy—a metonym for what Western liberalism terms reason—as a force for Black uplift. Rather than a contradiction of two poles, Douglass's narrative can be read as troubling the binary rubric by which humanity is defined; his autobiographical contradiction reveals that there might instead be a way of imagining humanity beyond the static bounds of those terms. This has led Fred Moten, for instance, to term works that, like Douglass's, place in close contact the contradictions that undergird "the unities of lawful, gentlemanly, regulative understanding" as *an*autobiographical. The prefix "an-" orients these works as without, or in a nonspace with regard to the autobiographical genre that otherwise narrates the forming of a liberal subject.[68]

Hughes seized on this Black tactic to surface the "manure" that the committee members otherwise sought to suppress. His testimony shows how he was called back into the form of "the Negro" again and again, including in the moment when the movie-ticket seller pointed to the sign that presumably read, "Colored not admitted."[69] By offering his narrative of these repeated violences, Hughes earns a concession from the committee: the state openly recognizes its role in ignoring and supporting the "oppression and denial of [his] civil rights."[70] But an admission of this fact is not enough. Unlike Cohn, who deploys this concession as a way of silencing Hughes rather than granting him rights, Hughes expands the moment so as to allow for a different mode of criticism and a different understanding of blackness. Indeed, the continuation of his testimony beyond the committee's time-saving measures suggests that the meaning of his poem may exceed the administrative demands of the state. "A deep background," as Hughes put it, "does not come in a moment."[71] His escape to the depths of the lily-pond swamp starts to build an interpretive practice supported by a vision of the world that has yet to arrive. Hughes's latter-day reflections that invoke the imagery of the swamp at AMSAC and in *The Panther and the Lash* suggest how he positions his testimony as entering in a small way into the historical projects of marronage and slave revolt.

In his interpretation of "One More 'S'," Hughes demands more than an empty complicity with oppression. His poem can only be interpreted when the central assumptions and the very structure of the hearing are redefined. Hughes's testimony, like his poem, chronicles the violent encounters that thwart Black solidarity and, importantly, interracial solidarity among Black and white people. He highlights times in his life when a Black and red vision of the world seemed possible, times that even recall severe oppression:

> Some of my schoolmates stoned me on the way home from school. One of my schoolmates (and there were no other Negro children in the school), a little white boy, protected me, and I have never in all my writing career or speech career as far as I know said anything to create a division among humans, or between whites or Negroes, because I have never forgotten this kid standing up for me against these other first graders who were throwing stones at me.[72]

In "One More 'S'," Hughes offers a broader example of interracial solidarity as a prospect for a different, more democratic future:

> But we can't join hands together
> So long as white are lynching black
> So black and white in one union fight
> And get on the right track.
> By Texas, or Georgia, or Alabama led,
> Come together, fellow workers!
> Black and white can all be red

Before the Senate Permanent Subcommittee, Hughes at once unfurled a new autobiography with material that he had not discussed in *The Big Sea*, and a full-interpretation of "One More 'S' in the U.S.A." His poem and his testimony recalled moments of interracial solidarity that might have led to the creation of what Kate Baldwin describes as a "new people under a rubric of 'red.'"[73] The interpretive making enacted in this moment relied on targeting existing means of state-supported and socially practiced oppression. It also necessitated that Hughes, however briefly, make the chamber into his space, not the committee's, to attempt his "full interpretation."

Because Roy Cohn, David Schine, and Everett Dirksen denied Hughes the opportunity to finish his full interpretation, it is not clear whether Hughes would have returned to these lines from his poem.

Nor is it clear whether Hughes would have described his encounter in Nashville with Allen Tate and the New Critics, an encounter where he was offered a small gesture of solidarity by Tom Mabry. That encounter echoes in the stanza of "One More 'S'" quoted above. When the speaker expresses that Southern states can lead the red interracial coalition, Hughes dismisses Tate's idea that an integrated gathering in Nashville is cause for the expression of anxieties about miscegenation. The South can be, and is, something other than what the Agrarians imposed upon it—Black communist organizers in Alabama in the 1930s, for instance, offered evidence of a different a vision of the South. Readers of the closed-door testimony are left to wonder the full extent to which Hughes would call for a revolutionary reconfiguration of the racist interpretation complex, including the liberalism that supported it. At the very least it is clear that in this private hearing, his approach invoked and built upon the Black radical tradition and its simultaneously literary, critical, and political acts that evaded the encompassing strategic inquiries of the dominant order, and which made space beyond that order to build and imagine a Black radical world.

"TOWARD A NEW ROMANTICISM"

Hughes was not alone in his struggle with the midcentury racist interpretation complex, or in forging a tactical criticism against it. The racist interpretation complex describes the entanglement of the institutionalized New Criticism and the racialized anticommunism of the US liberal state. This entanglement animates assumptions about literary from and intent as material barriers for entry to the "good" literary world, and sets criteria for nonsubversive citizenship. While some Black writers would take on this complex more directly with the formation of counter-institutions like the Jefferson School of Social Science—something I discuss in the next chapter—others, like Hughes, addressed the problem in a variety of venues in different levels of disguise. In this final section, I argue that tactical criticism against the interpretive method of the federal government expanded beyond Hughes's closed-door hearing. The demands of the racial liberal state and the interpretive demands of the New Criticism became a live object in Black writing, even among Black writers hesitant to state explicitly their affiliation with communism and the interracial solidarity aggressively promoted by the CPUSA after Earl Browder's departure in 1944. For instance, the conflicts between liberalism and communism, between authority and chaos, and between white and Black that animate Ralph Ellison's *Invisible Man* are navigated throughout the novel by what its narrator deems a "new analytical way of listening to music."[74] As Kenneth Warren argues, "The novel's advocacy of a pattern of order that anticipates, makes room for, or otherwise acknowledges chaos, seeks to find its authorization not in logical argument, but rather in aesthetic practice."[75] The point of this brief reference is not that Ellison arrives at the same conclusion as Hughes, or even that he formulates the connection between political economy and aesthetics in precisely the same way. Instead, my point is to show that the connection of these otherwise separated realms had an animating function in Black imaginative writing, even in the work of those who explicitly turned away from communism. With this in mind, when we read Hughes's 1950 *Phylon* statement as a call to locate where a Black literary criticism was developing in midcentury, one place to find it is within Black literature.

Published in the same year as Hughes's hearing before the Senate, *The Narrows*, Ann Petry's final novel, elaborates on Hughes's tactical approach within and beyond the category of literature. In *The Narrows*, Petry registers the danger of challenging the racist interpretation complex and recognizes that such challenges often occur piecemeal and behind closed doors. Petry herself did not face the same level of federal scrutiny regarding her politics as Hughes did regarding his; the FBI never opened a file on her, for instance. Yet she maintained a number of left political commitments. In addition to modeling the protagonist of *The Narrows*, Link Williams, on prominent Black radicals, Petry drew on her friendship with Dollie Robinson, an active Harlem leftist, as inspiration for other characters in the novel.[76] By the time Petry was writing *The Narrows*, she had left Harlem for Connecticut and had stopped regularly spending time with the left-leaning literary circles she had previously frequented, including the Negro Women Incorporated and the offices of the *People's Voice*. Nevertheless, these obscured affiliations and Petry's writing on the social function of the novel provide traction for a reading of *The Narrows* in terms of the entanglement of the dominant institutions of literary criticism and publishing, and the anti-Black and anticommunist US state.

Petry's expansive novel narrates collisions of and romance across class, race, and gender taboos at the same time as it depicts a spatially segregated Connecticut commuter town called Monmouth. The climax of the novel pits Link Williams, a Black Dartmouth grad working to complete a book on the history of slavery, against the mother and husband of his white lover, Camilo Treadway Sheffield. Camilo is the heiress to a munitions factory fortune, and to uphold her reputation, her mother and husband baselessly accuse Link of raping her, in an echo of the 1932 Massie Affair.[77] Farah Jasmine Griffin argues that Link "links" Blackness and communism; she suggests that his character invokes W. E. B. Du Bois and Paul Robeson, embodiments of the Black left and the state's willingness to repress it.[78] At the same time, several of the novel's characters frequently express anxiety about miscegenation as tied to anti-Black and anticommunist forces, expanding Kate Baldwin's argument about how "the political pressures of anticommunism must be seen in tandem with the social pressures of sexual conformity."[79] Link's eventual murder by the Treadway clan and their henchmen results from the well-funded circulation of interpretive practices that intensify and suture anticommunism, anti-Black racism, and racialized sexual panic, like that exhibited by Allen Tate in Nashville in 1932 and challenged by Hughes in his tactical criticism.

In the novel Bullock, the white editor of the *Monmouth Chronicle*, states the connection between these phenomena plainly while circulating and reinforcing their criminalizing function. He says, "What difference does it make . . . whether we here in Monmouth hunt down Negroes or whether we hunt down Communists? . . . There is a difference, though at the moment it escapes me."[80] What prompts Bullock's confusion about the difference between Black and red is his decision to print an aggressively stereotypical image of Black criminality in his newspaper, after earlier refusing to print a damning photo taken by Jubine, a communist photographer and friend of Link's. Jubine's photo has provided proof that Camilo Treadway struck a Black child with her car. Bullock hasn't printed the photo, but a New York newspaper has. Ever since, Bullock has been under pressure from the Treadway family to heighten his paper's depiction of the danger of the Narrows, the Black neighborhood in Monmouth, as a way to divert attention from

Camilo's growing legal trouble. Specifically, Camilo's mother threatens to withdraw her company's advertising from the *Chronicle* unless Bullock begins "emphasizing, spotlighting, underlining these stories about crimes committed by Negroes."[81] The image Bullock prints in response literally embraces Mrs. Treadway's request. If the image itself is not enough, the headline that accompanies it provides a generic description of its contents: "NEGRO CONVICT SHOT." The categorical aspect of the headline suggests that this image might as well be a stock photo of Black masculine criminality that could be reinserted on repeat use.[82] It undercuts leftists who seek to highlight white people absolved of their violence by wealth and skin privilege, while simultaneously justifying the state's violence against Black people. In fact, the man depicted in the generic photo was shot and killed by police after he escaped the nearby prison.

While Bullock publishes the photo of what he knows will be seen as "the crazed black animal," he expresses some reticence over whether it is acceptable to print news for the purpose of circulating racist stereotypes. After all, his paper "started as an abolitionist newspaper."[83] This history, paired with his refusal of Jubine's photograph, highlights how capitalism mobilizes and indirectly profits from portraying Black criminality as objective fact, while suppressing stories of white violence endorsed by the state. Bullock's situation anticipates Hughes's 1959 advice for being a white *black* writer and a good *bad* writer; he chooses to see Black people through "white eyes," and prompts others to do the same.

To view Black people through white eyes in literature was to recognize the monopoly of New Critical thought on how literature was to be read and appreciated, as well as to acknowledge how the Nashville group had come to organize the literary world. For Hughes, the circulation of this perspective was driven by the sense that the publishing industry pursued "wide white consumption" and might only be interrupted by the founding of Black institutions. Bullock dramatizes this observation. He is a white publisher printing white *black* writing and white *black* images, and must do so more intently only after the image of a world through the eyes of a communist photographer has undercut the apparent objectivity and universality of those images. He and his paper produce an interpretive source that, like the New Critics, circulates a form of Black criminality to reinforce the borders around whiteness in order to imbue it with additional value.

Hughes's idea of the "good *bad*" writer points to an intersection between the positive valuation of white universalism under midcentury liberalism (the good) and the simultaneously political and aesthetic challenge to that valuation (the bad). This tension manifests in the situation of another of the novel's characters, Malcolm Powther, the Black butler of the Treadway family. Powther is fascinated by white upper-class life and, as such, is torn between the trappings of whiteness and his erotic attachment to his wife. In a scene seemingly straight from a McCarthy hearing, Powther is expected to point out Link Williams to Camilo's mother, husband, and two henchmen so that they can kidnap him. (I think here of questions like this one that David Schine asked Hughes: "Will you give the committee at this time the names of some Communist party member whom you know?") Powther feels trapped in this situation. To comply is to betray Link Williams, who he realizes was not guilty of anything other than sleeping with a white woman. Powther's affiliation with Link operates primarily through race because, in a parallel to the Captain, Camilo's white husband, he also believes—incorrectly, in Powther's case—that Link is sleeping with his wife, Mamie. But for Powther not to comply would be to position himself within the "NEGRO CONVICT SHOT" photo circulating in the *Chronicle*. Watching for Link, Powther thinks, "I have to prove [Link] wasn't my brother. Prove to these people in this car, that all Negroes are not criminal, some of them are good, some of them are selfrespecting, some of them are first class butlers named Powther."[84] Powther's appeal to the "good" morality of white liberalism rewards him in the end. Upon fingering Link, he thinks that he has "achieved a kind of togetherness" because he and the Captain are now "equals."[85] Powther wagers that redirecting ideas about Black (and red) criminality is a pathway to the equal playing field of "American standardization," as Hughes refers to it in "The Negro Artist and the Racial Mountain." In other words, Powther aligns himself with whiteness for personal gain, and it contextualizes his proprietary relationship over his wife as well as his hypersexualization of her in terms of white supremacy; it is, in effect, the force of the liberal-individual over collective political interest. Petry draws Powther's gesture as fundamentally empty, though seemingly determined by his class aspirations—he is a "first class" butler after all—and by the inescapable threat of lethal violence should he not comply. The primary way for Powther to be "good" and to protect himself from white supremacist violence is to circulate, act on, and, ultimately capitalize on ideas of Black criminality and leftist subversion that are rendered essential for bourgeois aspirations.

The collapse of interpretive norms, anti-Blackness, and anticommunism is intensified in the novel's climax. Link Williams is interrogated before a committee of Captain Sheffield (Camilo's husband) and Mrs. Treadway (her mother). The Captain and Mrs. Treadway hope to cajole Link into a confession that he raped Camilo. Their hope is that the story of interracial rape will both supplant and explain Camilo's vehicular assault. Link, however, is reticent to provide this confession. He didn't do what they claimed. When they ask him to interpret his acts, unlike Powther, he supplies an autobiography that details the fact of being thrust into the form of Black criminality, an autobiography similar in form to Hughes's "full interpretation":

> "I stole a lollipop when I was five, stole it in a candy store named Mintz. I ran away from home when I was eight. I went a long ways, too, just across the street." He stopped again, thinking, well I might as well at some point name the complication, the inflammatory complication that the choreographer rang in on the old rigadoon of adultery and cuckoldry, because The Race with his deathshead face unmasked walked right in here with us, with me. "But the distance that I went was farther away from where I had been living than if it had been the coast of Africa where your rapacious Christian ancestors went to kidnap the Guinea niggers who were my ancestors."[86]

Link's autobiography at first hesitates to articulate the origin of his supposed Black criminality—an everyday redistributive pursuit against the order wrought through racial capitalism—but then explicitly names it. Link figures that this situation stems from the intersection of the Middle Passage, a pivotal chapter in the development of racial capitalism, and the panic based on the imagined hypersexuality of Black men. To invoke "the inflammatory complication" of the formation of Blackness in this moment is to alter the false premise of moral authority thought to be inhabited by the Captain and his mother-in-law. Link's spoken confession prompts his interrogators to glimpse their reality in an entirely different vein. His voice, which does not "sound like AmosAndySambo," makes Mrs. Treadway realize that Link and Camilo were in love, that a consensual sexual relationship between the two was possible. As Lindon Barrett reads this moment, "The sound of Link's voice disturbs the scopic evidence of his racial blackness. It asserts what Mrs. Treadway understands as fully rational and perceptive personhood, which she, as does U.S. culture, most routinely equates with racial whiteness."[87] Link's autobiography of supposed Black criminality reveals what Allen Tate called his "theory of racial relations" to be vapid, an expression of power hinged on accruing value to whiteness. The Captain and Mrs. Treadway cannot register the truth of this in their usual interpretive framework. Upon speaking the unspeakable truth of the matter—that he and Camilo "were in love"—the Captain returns the situation to order by shooting and killing Link.

Like Langston Hughes in his testimony, Link uses a version of autobiography, a history of Black life, and a brief claiming of time and space in an effort to reorient and redefine the terms upon which he is being interrogated. What made Hughes's criticism tactical was his challenge to ontologically stable definitions of poetry and the human, his assertion beyond the limits of the imagined possibility of what poetry could be, and, finally, out of this nonspace, his development of a shifting form of critical practice. Link's moment of confession translates those interpretive acts to be an even more direct interpretation of how literary and state forces reduce Black life to Black criminality—a reduction that relies upon the intersection of racist, anticommunist, and miscegenationist fears, themselves an echo of Tate's "theory of racial relations." Even though the particulars of Link's murder aren't exposed to the wider public, his tactical interpretation of his situation extends beyond the confines of the committee room. When Link's mother thinks, "To them, all of them, he's the Negro," she accepts an invitation to interpret the conditions that culminated in Link's execution, a cloud of anticommunism, liberal white universalism, and an unwavering belief in the reality fashioned through the circulation of racist assumption.

For Farah Jasmine Griffin, *The Narrows* is "Petry's novelistic example of the ideas she espouses" in an essay called "The Novel as Social Criticism." There, like Arna Bontemps in his Peabody College lecture, Petry explicitly targets the New Critical understanding of literature as the object of her displeasure. She writes, "Being a product of the twentieth century (Hitler, atomic energy, Hiroshima, Buchenwald, Mussolini, USSR) I find it difficult to subscribe to the idea that art exists for art's sake. . . . It seems to me that all truly great art is propaganda. . . . The novel, like all other forms of art, will always reflect the political, economic, and social structure of the period in which it was created."[88] Recalling W. E. B. Du Bois's "Criteria for Negro Art," Petry identifies fiction as inevitably tied to the world in which the work is a part. In this, she expresses a clear articulation of a literary politics that other Black left writers were actively pursuing. This builds on her depiction of the acts of writing, confession, and image making as trapped between the forces of anticommunism and anti-Blackness, as well as in a struggle with intent, universality, and racial stereotype. The struggle between these forces casts in a new light Alan Wald's account of Petry as moving between the modernist literature to which she was exposed to as a student in the writing courses of Mabel Louise Robinson and Helen Hull at Columbia, and her "extraordinary grounding in African American history and culture," including background in the blues and in the career of Camilla Williams, an African American opera singer.[89] A work like *The Narrows* shifts the political valence of modernist aesthetics to afford attention to race and class, thus challenging the New Critical and state interpretive practices that worked to outfit this aesthetic as universal through favoring the white American middle class.

Petry's clear statement on the expectations of Black criticism, as well as the elaboration of the situation, possibility, and consequence of its unfurling in *The Narrows*, would be echoed at the AMSAC conference where Hughes gave his "Black and White" talk. At AMSAC, Lorraine Hansberry would register the tactical dimensions not only of Petry's articulation of criticism and the necessity for situating it within the theatre of the nuclear age, but also of Hughes's subversive testimony. Hansberry closed her remarks there by offering another autobiography in miniature that challenged the racist interpretation complex subtended by the institutionalized New Criticism:

> I was born on the South Side of Chicago. I was born black and a female. I was born in a depression after one world war, and came into my adolescence during another. While I was still in my teens the first atom bombs were dropped on human beings at Nagasaki and Hiroshima, and by the time I was twenty-three years old my government

and that of the Soviet Union had entered actively into the worst conflict of nerves in human history—the Cold War.

I have lost friends and relatives through cancer, lynching and war.
I have been personally the victim of physical attack which was the offspring of racial and political hysteria. I have worked with the handi-
capped and seen the ravages of congenital diseases that we have not
yet conquered because we spend our time and ingenuity in far less
purposeful wars. I have known persons afflicted with drug addiction
and alcoholism and mental illness. I see daily on the streets of New
York, street gangs and prostitutes and beggars. I have, like all of you,
on a thousand occasions seen indescribable displays of man's very real
inhumanity to man; and I have come to maturity, as we all must, knowing that greed and malice and indifference to human misery, bigotry,
and corruption, brutality and, perhaps above all else, ignorance—the
prime ancient and persistent enemy of man—abound in this world....

I have given you this account so that you know that what I write is
not based on the assumption of idyllic possibilities or innocent assessments of the true nature of life—but, rather, my own personal view
that, posing one against the other, I think the human race does command its own destiny and that that destiny can eventually embrace
the stars.[90]

In Hansberry's statement—not published in scholarly journals or
"competently-done books" until 1981—one finds the circulation of a
tactical critical tradition, a Black radical tradition that is both grounded
in the politics of the present and utopian by design. Hansberry called
this position a "new romanticism," and her name for her critical perspective targets the antagonism the New Critics harbored for romanticism. Beyond that, Hansberry makes a clear suggestion that a different
aesthetic engagement with her writing requires the making of a different world.

Typically for a tactical critical act, Hansberry's remarks only created a temporary space for her "new romanticism." When the AMSAC
conference proceedings were published, her speech was not included
because it was too radical for AMSAC's universalist board. In her public
and explicit articulation of a different path for Black literature and Black
criticism, Hansberry differs from writers like Hughes, Petry, and Bontemps, who attempt to formulate race radical interpretive methods in

the language of racial liberalism. Those writers pursued that path for a variety of reasons, many of which intersected with the fact that when New Criticism's definition of literature combined with the state's red-baiting and anti-Blackness, a contextually rooted Black criticism and literature could carry no permanent institutional space. For Hughes, Petry, and Bontemps this lack of a permanent institutional space for truly good Black criticism resulted from segregation and the related lack of Black wealth to fund such institutions. It was about material restrictions and the government's scrutiny of subversive institutions as much as it is about a critical dearth. Yet Hansberry makes more explicit the fact that, until there is broad-based social and political change to upend the yoked oppressions of race, class, gender, and ability, such tactical interventions will inevitably be temporary. To be something other than "in but not of" requires the making of something entirely different in which to be.

Hansberry's direct articulation of the intersections of anti-Black racism, capitalism, environmental degradation, and uneven exposure to disease suggests that radical statements folded into the rhetoric of racial liberalism may not be the only way to pursue an eventual "embrace of the stars." As I will show in the next chapter, Hansberry associated with Black writers, Black leftists, and communist affiliates who sought to build institutions around the critical study of Black literature. This was an effort designed to counter the New Critical grip on American interpretive institutions, and to foster an interracial coalition to challenge the ills of racial liberalism and American capitalism. It was undeniably a radical vision of what was possible—the best way for Hansberry to state its potential was to "embrace the stars"—but the lens of history carved by the racist interpretation complex has made the imagining of such efforts, and the efforts themselves, appear improbable.

◦ 4 ◦

Culture as a Powerful Weapon

On April 13, 1956, at the Hotel Whitcomb in San Francisco, W. E. B. Du Bois addressed a crowd offering its support to defend the California Labor School. Citing the McCarran Act, the federal government demanded that the school register as a subversive or un-American entity, a legal requirement that in the heightened anticommunist climate would effectively shutter the institution. Du Bois's talk was suited for the occasion. He planned to discuss "the deterioration of education in the United States," a topic that the event organizers provocatively titled "The Know-Nothings Ride Again."[1] According to the FBI informant in attendance, Du Bois argued that the California Labor School and New York City's Jefferson School of Social Science "were the only two schools who tried to teach the people about the Negro position in their relation to the nation and the world."[2] This was not the first indication that Du Bois held the California Labor School, the Jefferson School of Social Science, and institutions like it in such high esteem. In a 1954 letter, Du Bois wrote that the Jefferson School, where he was offering a class on "Reconstruction," could be considered on par with "Princeton, Chicago University," and the many other institutions in "the east, middle west, and west" where Du Bois had lectured previously.[3]

The California Labor School and the Jefferson School of Social Science were two of nearly a dozen labor schools that appeared in US cities in the mid-1940s. Unlike most universities at the time, these schools had open admissions policies and were highly affordable; the cost of an eight-week course ranged from two to eight dollars. These policies meant that labor school student bodies included a significant number of women as well as Black and working-class people. While these schools didn't offer degrees, they anticipated the significant need for continuing education. The US Department of Education approved the California Labor School as an institution where veterans could use their GI Bill benefits. In a number of ways, labor schools anticipated the expanded function of two-year institutions proposed in the 1947 Truman Commission report, *Higher Education in American Democracy*. The report offered that a two-year institution should be referred to as a "community college" rather than a "junior college," in part because the commission envisioned these types of institutions as "people's colleges."[4] Founded before the end of the war, labor schools were often described as "progressive people's schools," a euphemistic way of indicating their Marxist educational platform, and a code for the fact that they were often staffed and financed by members of the Communist Party.[5]

Over its thirteen-year existence, the Jefferson School—the largest in the system—had approximately 120,000 enrollments at its main building in Manhattan, and thousands more in extension courses in ten neighborhood branches throughout New York City.[6] The vast majority of those enrollments occurred prior to the 1950 passage of the McCarran Act and before the most intense red-baiting of the mid- to late 1950s. People's schools were initially founded during a period known as the Popular Front, when under the leadership of Earl Browder, the Communist Party USA (CPUSA) allied with liberals to support the defeat of fascism. The alignment of a left political program with liberal American nationalism is reflected in the names of these schools. Many were named for well-respected American figures including Thomas Jefferson (New York), Samuel Adams (Boston), Walt Whitman (Philadelphia), and Abraham Lincoln (Chicago). These gestures of patriotism—and the CPUSA's alignment with liberalism—would prove facile in the face of a growing state regime for isolating and ostracizing Marxist thought in the United States.[7] Yet even as the federal government worked to close these institutions, Du Bois and a number of other Black radicals saw potential for how the Marxist education they offered presented a model for a politically and historically situated understanding of Black culture. That model insisted that literature and the arts were not separate from intensifying social and political struggles, but a necessary and potent rallying cry.

As Du Bois argued at the Hotel Whitcomb, labor schools were important because they were the only institutions where students could learn about Marxism and could expand Marx's considerations about the entanglement of capitalism and colonialism. In a different lecture at the California Labor School, this one in March 1948, he stated succinctly the role of the American university system and, ultimately, what it failed to teach: "In the world at large the white worker was long convinced that civilization and high wage depended in the suppression and control of the colored world where most human being live."[8] The university system did the "convincing" that ensured the continued uneven development of its labor forces and global geography. More bluntly, there was an economic and political gain to a university system that perpetuated racism via anti-Blackness and white chauvinism, as well as reinforcing misogyny and class hierarchy.

In these people's schools lectures, Du Bois examined how the world historical arguments he outlined in *Black Reconstruction* manifested in the higher education system of the United States. As summarized by Lisa Lowe, *Black Reconstruction* "told a history of the consolidation of northern industrial finance capitalism and southern planters, and of ruling-class whites aggressively recruiting poor southern whites as their allies, dividing the black and white workers to prevent their joining in common struggle."[9] By the mid-1940s, the Agrarian New Critics, the US state, and American universities had forged a similar north-south alliance to incorporate the massive influx of American GIs into the university system via its "democratizing" pedagogy and its centrifugal push for the formation of a unified national culture. As Du Bois suggests of Reconstruction and the mid-twentieth century—what Manning Marable has periodized as "the Second Reconstruction—these reconfigurations merely established a "new capitalism and a new enslavement of labor."[10]

To challenge the liberal capitalist education system of the United States, labor schools pursued a program of material antiracism and a call for interracial unity. People's school leaders thought interracial unity was essential because capitalism had made racism a necessity for the continued availability of cheap labor, imperial expansion, and state-protected free enterprise. When Du Bois argues that what labor schools seek to teach is "the relation of the workers of the world to modern society," he refers not just to white workers, but to a coalition of those forced into a "new industrial slavery of black and brown and yellow workers in Africa and Asia," in addition to workers of color in

the United States.[11] This "new industrial slavery," its history, and its operation, Du Bois argued in his 1948 lecture, was precisely "the truth
which the universities of America ~~admire but~~ hesitate to teach."[12] Du
Bois's argument registers that the system of American education had
long been entangled in the recasting and reproduction of American
racial capitalism, and his strikethrough indexes the danger of saying
the quiet part aloud.[13]

For Du Bois, labor schools could shape a future world attendant to
Black life, and could challenge the world that had long sought to ex-
tinguish it. The scientific study of capitalism, imperialism, and racism
would defend against turning a Black student into a "capitalistic ex-
ploiter among Negroes." Further, this study could yield a future buoyed
by "planned economy, the development of art and literature and an understanding of socialism."[14] Across his labor school lectures in California and New York, Du Bois insisted that these institutions were centers
for ensuring "the Future of the American Negro" by offering a Marxist
education in arts and culture, economics, and sociology to a racially,
ethnically, and economically diverse student population. These efforts
were part of an elaborate material challenge to New Critical principles
of literature's ontological isolation and the broader social and political
system that those principles supported and upheld. This occurred even
as documents like the Truman Commission report attempted to redirect—or, to use Roderick Ferguson's term, strategically incorporate—
the progressive language of the people and of democracy embraced
by the CPUSA, not to mention the language of minority difference, to
stand for the state-supported university system and racial capitalism.[15]

In this chapter I examine how US labor schools emphasized Black
culture and its creation as a means of challenging the anti-Black, anticommunist status quo, or racial liberalism, supported and reproduced
by the American New Criticism. In doing so, I build on Du Bois's claim
that the Jefferson School and the system of progressive people's schools
were the only higher education institutions devoted to grasping the
contours of anti-Black racism in the United States and abroad. Beyond
the fact that the existence of these schools—let alone the particulars of
their operations—are not widely known, the Black radical ideas that
were fostered in them relied on the ways that the Black women and
men who developed them reshaped these institutions from within.[16]
The histories of these institutions show a struggle between the largely

white Communist Party, which provided funding, advertising, and administrative support for the schools, and the instructors and some administrators, many of whom were people of color. Departing from the relatively small body of scholarship on these institutions, I suggest that out of this tension materialized a groundbreaking pedagogy for the study of Black culture.

This approach to the study of Black life and culture is groundbreaking because these institutions proposed an institutional and ideological basis for Black studies distinct from that which had preceded them and would proceed from them. Nick Mitchell has argued that turn-of-the-twentieth-century calls for Negro history by the American Negro Academy and the Association for the Study of Negro Life and History developed a "race-first" conception of the field that suppressed intraracial difference, especially in terms of gender and class. Based on the purchase of scientific and anthropological claims, these early-twentieth-century organizations positioned the Black intellectual in a privileged and separate position to speak initially on behalf of those studied in the "field," a formation that later became "the Black community." Further, Mitchell highlights that this basis for Black studies positions the field as an "object for philanthropy" that disciplines and incorporates alternative conceptions of Black studies on behalf of the university. This occurred even when conceptions of Black studies were asserted in protest.[17] The study of Black culture at schools like the Jefferson School, the Carver School, and the Frederick Douglass Education Center evade some but not all, of the masculinist and middle-class formations of the Black studies field formation Mitchell identifies. These institutions foregrounded thinkers who saw gender and class as central to understanding Black life, including Claudia Jones, Louise Thompson Patterson, Gwendolyn Bennett, and Paul Robeson. Because of the communist foundations of these institutions, and the fact that many faculty and students were blacklisted from the mainstream higher education system, they rejected the forms encouraged by liberal-capitalist philanthropy—including, for instance, the New Criticism. In this respect, these institutions formulated an institutional and ideological field construction distinct from that of the Black studies which would emerge in the late 1960s. This midcentury construction was attuned to differences in class and gender, as well as to the influence of the racist interpretation complex—the confluence of the state, higher education, and private philanthropy—on acceptable knowledge production in the mid-twentieth century.

How Gwendolyn Bennett, Doxey A. Wilkerson, and others enacted these shifts requires an understanding of the contemporaneous operations of the Communist Party, the federal government's efforts to mark progressive people's schools as subversive, and how these institutions formed as a result of political purges within the American university system. In the first section of this chapter, I outline a brief history of the Jefferson School and its related institutions in Harlem with an eye toward its development of a mode of Black study. The Jefferson School was the flagship of the labor school system in these years, enrolling the most students and attracting the most attention from federal agencies and the press. Internal documents in the Jefferson School's remaining archives, held in the Tamiment Library at New York University and in the Wisconsin Historical Society, show that the school worked tirelessly to distinguish its pedagogy and curricula from those of the bourgeois American university system. While nearly every people's school regularly offered a class on "the Negro Question," the Jefferson School offered more courses on "Negro culture" than did any other labor school in the United States. And this is why it is my primary focus here.

In the second section of this chapter, I address how Black writers, thinkers, artists, faculty, and students pushed the Jefferson School in New York to make the study of Black life and culture one of its signature functions. The Jefferson School offered many courses on "Negro culture" because its size and resources allowed it to carry forward the aims of a people's school in Harlem, the George Washington Carver School. Led by Gwendolyn Bennett, the Carver School had emerged from the organizing efforts of the National Negro Congress (NNC) and the Southern Negro Youth Conference (SNYC). While these efforts certainly tapped well-known Black communists like Paul Robeson and Max Yergan (before he disavowed the left), they also drew on the support of everyday Black people from Harlem who offered money and time to start the school. When the Carver School was forced to close due to financial issues brought on by the US attorney general listing the institution as a subversive organization, the Jefferson School provided assistance, and soon hired Doxey A. Wilkerson as director of its faculty and curriculum in January 1948. The move garnered attention from the Black press as far away as Baltimore and Philadelphia, because Wilkerson was widely known for his 1939 study *Special Problems of Negro Education*, which he had conducted while teaching at Howard University.[18] Wilkerson left the faculty of Howard to join the Communist Party in 1943. This was when Howard faculty, including Rayford Logan, Ralph Bunche, E. Franklin Frazier, Alain Locke, and Merze Tate, were offering, according to Robert Vitalis, "early and relentless critiques of the supposed truths of racial science and the role racism played in sustaining imperialism."[19] This "Howard School" grew from the trajectory of the American Negro Academy's engagement with theory of race development, spearheaded by Du Bois's early essay "Conservation of the Races." To leave Howard at this time meant that Wilkerson sought a different approach to education and to defining an alternative genealogy of Black culture, even one that was actively critical of Black academic thinking on race. At the Jefferson School, Wilkerson left his mark by facilitating sessions where students and faculty could push the institution on certain shortcomings in its offerings on people of color and women. More importantly, Wilkerson took the recommendations that emerged from these conferences to reimagine the school's cultural curriculum and its recruitment practices for students and faculty. These changes only increased the demand for another independent labor school in Harlem. Black organizers opened the Frederick Douglass Educational Center in 1952.

The efforts of Wilkerson, Bennett, and others to develop socially and politically attuned means of studying Black culture and Black life was explicitly set against the interpretive practices of the New Criticism, as well as those of the American university system, including institutions like Howard. Indeed, spearheaded by Wilkerson, faculty in the cultural departments at the Jefferson School saw that the methods promoted by the New Critics harbored "racialism" in the interpretation of culture, and denied the fact that cultural works could have social and political efficacy. Such arguments were promoted by teachers who took Black literature as a specific topic for extended study in labor school courses, including Lorraine Hansberry, Augusta Strong, and Yvonne Gregory.

These ideas circulated beyond the classroom walls of the progressive people's schools. In the final section of this chapter, I argue that the novel *Youngblood* by John O. Killens adopts many of the pedagogical and theoretical approaches to Black culture as a wider tactic for the Black freedom movement. *Youngblood* shows how Black self-determination generates a form of Black literature intimately connected to the social and political struggles of Black people on the left. That literature, like the labor schools themselves, envisioned a coalition of Black and white people, north and south, to challenge the "new industrial slavery" established by ruling-class whites after Reconstruction. Literature was crucial for developing in the progressive people's schools what Du Bois insisted could not be generated in the mainstream American university system: a "philosophy of life" to displace the "intense and subtle propaganda, backed by religious teaching and intense belief that only white folk were really human, . . . [propaganda maintained] to crush the workers of Africa and Asia for the honor and glory of white imperialism."[20]

THE HISTORY OF
THE JEFFERSON SCHOOL

The mid-twentieth-century American university subjected its faculty, students, and personnel to a set of implicit political tests brought on by a growing anticommunist fervor. Despite nominal opposition to political persecution, many universities actively cooperated with government investigators and fired faculty members who refused to testify before newly assembled state and federal investigatory committees meant to root out "subversives." New York, for instance, passed legislation in 1940 to establish what came to be known as the Rapp-Coudert committee, charged with investigating the state's education system. Nearly forty faculty members of Brooklyn College, City College, Hunter College, and Queens College either resigned or were fired due to their refusal to testify before the panel. Several of those ousted during the Rapp-Coudert purge formed the School for Democracy, including Howard Selsam, who had previously taught philosophy at Brooklyn College, and Philip and Jack Foner, who had worked on labor and Black history at City College. The School for Democracy and the Worker's School, which were located in New York City, became landing pads for those newly blacklisted from academia or those who had been previously receiving state or private funding. After being told by Columbia University that his communist politics would keep him from ever being hired in academia, Herbert Aptheker found a role at the School for Democracy. Gwendolyn Bennett also began teaching at the School for Democracy after she had been forced out of the directorship position of the WPA-funded Harlem Community Art Center because of her affiliations with the left.

Clearly sympathetic to and supported by the CPUSA, these schools quickly became hubs for radical thought that universities ultimately refused to accommodate. In her history of academic freedom, Ellen Schrecker suggests that in the early 1940s, liberal academics "said that they were opposing Senator McCarthy and the more rabid red-baiters of the period. Yet, when given an opportunity to transform that opposition into something more concrete than words, almost all of these essentially liberal academics faltered."[21] Schrecker sees the emerging use of the term "academic freedom" in this moment as dictating "the permissible limits of political dissent."[22] To reframe this point, the failure to defend radical left ideas in the academy suggests that the study of left ideas about literature, history, and the like must necessarily be found in other institutional formations. Because of academe's alignment with liberal state interests in preserving and promoting capitalism while squashing communism, leftist writers and thinkers grew frustrated with this arrangement. During the anticommunist fervor, Mary Helen Washington reminds us, Blackness was perceived as contiguous with communism, a disorderly threat to the reactionary capitalist state.[23] The alignment of racism and anticommunism provided the university system of the liberal state with an operative mode for excluding Black writers and thinkers as well as critical investigations of Black culture and history. Segregation kept Black scholars from teaching at many universities, and the anticommunist atmosphere made it nearly impossible, even for white intellectuals, to pursue scholarship about racism and Black revolutionary activity that did not offer a palatable solution to the "race problem" without risk of losing their jobs. The university was inhospitable to Blackness and Black people epistemologically, politically, and administratively. Those who had been forced out of the system, or who wanted to study racism, imperialism, sexism, and class struggle, had to create their own institutions.

The Jefferson School of Social Science opened its doors at 575 Sixth Avenue on February 14, 1944. Howard Selsam served as the school's

director, just as he had at the Jefferson School's predecessor, the School
for Democracy. Encouraged by the School for Democracy's growth to
1,100 students from just 400 at its opening, the Jefferson School formed
out of a merger between the School for Democracy and the Workers
School. The first advertisement for the Jefferson School published in
the *Daily Worker* announces the institution as "A New People's University for Economic, Social, and Political Democracy."[24] "Principles of
Scientific Socialism" was listed as one of the available evening courses
for the first term, and a variety of other courses were on offer, including "Creative Writing," "How to Listen to Music," "Negro in American
Life," and "Music and Drawing for Children."[25]

The *Daily Worker*, the New York organ of the CPUSA, situated the
school's opening as nationally significant. The article detailed that the
school had received "many letters from soldiers." A soldier from Arkansas thought the school's opening to be especially important because of "what he had seen in Arkansas in the way of Jim Crow and
poverty."[26] One GI even donated his extensive butterfly and insect
collection for use at the school. As the *Daily Worker* reporter put it,
if Harvard's founding was a significant event for American culture,
the Jefferson School's opening "is another milestone in the advance
of democracy."[27] The grandeur of the reporter's rhetoric indicates the
Communist Party's clear support for the school, but also the hope that
the Jefferson School was well positioned to intervene in America's system of higher education, its ongoing war stance, and its undemocratic
perpetuation of racism and poverty.

The Jefferson School's opening years were wildly successful. In its
first full year of operation, the school had more than ten thousand enrollments, and that annual number held steady until 1951. Selsam wrote
in the school's first annual report that "students come to us primarily because they believe we have an answer to the problems they find
no answer to elsewhere"—problems about maintaining peace after
the war, about "how the Negro people and all national groups carry
on . . . the fight for complete social, economic, and political equality,"
and about how to "work out a more adequate theory and to achieve
clearer criteria of evaluation in all fields of culture."[28] The institution's
rapid growth was supported not by the era's significant private foundation funding, but by a significant capital outlay by Frederick Vanderbilt
Field, who had been disowned by his family (he was the great-great-

grandson of Cornelius Vanderbilt) due to his active support for leftist causes. Field's funds were used to purchase the school's main building in Manhattan, previously a furniture warehouse, and to renovate it so as to support the growing number of students and faculty.

In addition to classroom space, the nine-story main building had a number of facilities for students to study and socialize. There was the Jefferson Bookshop, a café and lounge called Club Jefferson, and the school's library. The library carried more than forty thousand volumes; subscribed to a wide variety of leftist magazines from the United States, Asia, and Europe; and opened its doors to nearly thirty thousand visitors a year. Those visitors included Jefferson School students, scholars, writers, graduate students at New York colleges and universities, and labor union members.[29] The large number of annual visitors to the library was bolstered by its unique holdings related to left and labor issues. According to Henry Black, the school's librarian, the Jefferson School library was "the only Marxist institution or enterprise in the United States whose relations with corresponding public, academic, or governmental institutions is completely normal."[30] The school's facilities were frequently used to hold public events including lectures, weekly folk dances, film screenings, and evening banquets. Even for people not enrolled as students, the Jefferson School became a hub for those explicitly affiliated with or merely interested in leftist causes. For seventy-five cents, a person could join the Saturday Night Square Dance Series, or hear Jay Williams read Langston Hughes's long poem *Freedom's Plow*. These various activities quickly drew the attention of the FBI. In 1953 the poet Ted Joans decided against enrolling in the first seminar Du Bois offered, titled "Background of African Liberation Struggles," for fear of being photographed from the FBI surveillance post set up across Sixth Avenue.[31]

Many other Black writers and intellectuals made a commitment to the school as faculty, as students, or by participating in one of the many events sponsored by the school. Doxey A. Wilkerson, the school's director of curriculum and faculty, played a large part in encouraging prominent Black people to take part in the school's activities. The faculty at the Jefferson School included Black writers and intellectuals (Du Bois, Wilkerson, Bennett, Lloyd Brown, Alice Childress, Lorraine Hansberry, Augusta Strong, and Yvonne Gregory), Black visual artists (Elizabeth Catlett, Charles White, and Norman Lewis), and Black

political leaders (Ben Davis, Pettis Perry, Louis Burnham, William Alphaeus Hunton, and Louise Thompson Patterson). In addition, the
Jefferson School hosted public events and lectures with Claudia Jones,
Shirley Graham, Lawrence Reddick, Oliver Cox, Langston Hughes,
and Paul Robeson, among many others. This roster of faculty and affiliates connected the Jefferson School to important Black radical political
groups of the era, including the Sojourners for Truth and Justice (Gregory, Patterson), the Council on African Affairs (Du Bois, Robeson,
Hunton), the Southern Negro Youth Congress (Strong), the American
Negro Theater (Childress), and the Committee for the Negro and the
Arts (Du Bois, Graham, Hunton, Reddick, Robeson, White). A number of left, antiracist white writers, artists, and musicians also taught
or appeared at people's schools; among them were Herbert Aptheker,
Philip Foner, Myra Page, Dashiell Hammett, Howard Fast, Martha Mil-
let, Dorothy Parker, Annette Rubinstein, Pete Seeger, Bob Russell, and
Woody Guthrie. The Jefferson School and its affiliate institutions in
New York served as a cultural and intellectual hub for Black writers,
artists, and activists on the left, and for the left more broadly.

Because the school was meant to be an adult-education center,
nearly all of its courses were held at night to accommodate students
who worked. Many students only took one class a term, and there
were no degrees to work toward. A large proportion of students were
women—at times as many as 70 percent of those enrolled—and there
was a significant contingent of labor union members in attendance.
In addition to offering courses at the main building in Manhattan,
the school brought courses on basic political economy and the "Negro Question" directly to union halls throughout New York. From
its opening in 1944, the Jefferson School sought to recruit Black and
Puerto Rican students to its rolls. It offered scholarships to students
with those backgrounds, and to any who could not afford the course
fees. Faculty were instructed to "be on the alert for new students at
the School, especially industrial workers, Negroes, and Puerto Ricans,"
and to make a special effort to talk to these students after class or take
them for a drink at Club Jefferson.[32] Meanwhile, students and faculty
participating in a panel at the school's semiannual "self-criticism conference" in 1953 identified that the school needed to strengthen its curriculum in "the field of national groups." Using a distinctly Marxist lex-
icon, the panel suggested expanded offerings on "the Negro question,

the Puerto Rican question, and the Jewish question," and new courses on the "Mexican-American, . . . American Indian, . . . Irish-American and Italian-American questions."[33] The school could address these curricular gaps by "intensify[ing] efforts to bring more theoretically developed, experienced leaders of the working class, and of the Negro and Puerto Rican peoples, into the faculty of the School."[34] This expansion did not pursue diversity for diversity's sake. That is, the particular courses sought were not those that would make monadic claims about particular ethnic and racial groups, nor were the leaders sought those who set themselves apart from the people they sought to engage. Instead, the new curriculum was to account for the racial and ethnic makeup of the working class, and attention to the full field of national groups could "correct the abstract, academic nature of instruction that prevails in most classrooms."[35] These "self-criticisms" show that faculty were consistently challenged to adapt to a unique institutional function: to make ever apparent the concrete and material relationship of theory to practice, and to view education as a crucial element of social and political struggle.

For its recruitment efforts, the school actively tried to reach people who might be interested in the "world's problems" by advertising in explicitly communist venues, especially the *Daily Worker*; in Black newspapers including the *New York Amsterdam News*; and in more mainstream newspapers, namely the *New York Times*. The result was that only about half of the students were directly affiliated with the CP. Most party affiliates enrolled in a special intensive program at the school, called the Institute for Marxist Studies. A particularly breathless *Saturday Evening Post* reporter expressed special concern over the fact that "a majority of the students, far from being union toughs, imported bomb tossers or hardened social wreckers are, instead, run-of-the-mine young Americans between seventeen and twenty-five years old."[36] This synchs up with Shirley Graham's anecdotal observation that "many Africans who were studying in colleges around the city" ended up in classes taught by her husband, W. E. B. Du Bois, and by others at the Jefferson School.[37] *The Chicago Defender* reported that a white student from Columbia enrolled in the Negro history course at the Carver School because she wanted "background for racial equality to give her friends."[38] Indeed, a 1950 Jefferson School report states that 18 percent of its enrollments were from those who were currently students at other colleges and universities around New York.[39]

The Jefferson School soon encountered problems because of its open commitment to Marxist education. An intensifying anticommunist climate in the years after World War II meant that the school was under constant government investigation. In 1947 the attorney general of the United States, Tom H. Clark, included the Jefferson School on a list of subversive organizations maintained by the federal government. The list helped the FBI and the Loyalty Review Board established by President Truman ensure that those with communist affiliations were not working within the federal government. The institutions on the list faced a public stigma that made it difficult to operate normally. The *New York Times* refused ads from the Jefferson School after it was listed as subversive. The Carver School had to close after making the attorney general's list. These problems would only grow more complicated after the passage of the Internal Security Act of 1950; it mandated communist-affiliated organizations to register with the Subversive Activities Control Board (SACB), and to state clearly on any printed materials or mailers that the organization was in fact subversive. Soon after the passage of this act—sometimes referred to as the McCarran Act, after the Nevada Senator who had introduced the legislation—the Jefferson School ceased keeping records of the names and addresses of registered students.[40] After the attorney general filed a petition to register the Jefferson School with the SACB in 1953, the school undertook a legal battle to challenge the idea that it was a subversive institution. The challenge was largely in vain. After the McCarran Act's passage in 1950, the school's registrations declined by about two thousand enrollments per year until 1956, when, after the Jefferson School had lost its appeal to the SACB, the board of trustees decided to close the school permanently. The red-baiting activities supported by the McCarran Act, the Senate Permanent Subcommittee on Investigations, and the general social ostracization of communists eventually made it nearly impossible to operate a "people's university" on a large scale.

The Jefferson School argued to the SACB that it was a "legitimate" educational center, rather than a training ground for current and potential communists. As school officials suggested in a popular pamphlet titled "How to Study," the Jefferson School had an expansive but simple mission: "to encourage students to think for themselves and to reach their own reasoned conclusions."[41] This independent thinking was tied to a Marxist-Leninist education. The government's investigation of the school hinged on whether or not the curriculum and the pedagogy of the school held the orthodoxy of the CPUSA's party line. There are accounts that cut both ways. Some faculty members would later claim before the House Un-American Activities Committee that the school was "controlled lock, stock, and barrel by the Communist conspiracy."[42] Some students, however, offered a different view. In private correspondence, one wrote that "the conclusions I have reached are the result of using my own common sense and intelligence after weighing the merits of both points of view in terms of what is best for me and my children and for the great mass of the American people."[43]

Accounts from journalists framed these institutions as sites for indoctrination. In a memorable column in the *Pittsburgh Courier* about the opening of the Douglass Educational Center, George Schuyler jabbed that "it must be admitted that no more distinguished faculty was ever tracked by the FBI or had its passports snatched."[44] Often times these accounts framed everyday classroom activities as explicit threats to the national order. In one article, a student revealed that there is no such thing as a politically neutral classroom when she suggested that in her experience, "lying propaganda" came from her Hunter College professors, not from her teachers at the Jefferson School.[45] The *Saturday Evening Post* writer viewed this comment not as an indictment of the political climate of the mainstream university system, but as evidence of the kind of subversive education one might receive at the Jefferson School.

The Jefferson School's active questioning of the basic assumptions of American liberalism gave ample reason for the government to see the school as subversive. At the same time, as Julian Nemeth has pointed out in a thorough examination of the school's claims to academic freedom, the Communist Party's sway over the institution "helped lead to the production of innovative work that was out of step with scholarship at the time, but . . . also led to a seriously blinkered perspective on a whole range of issues" including Stalin's regime in the Soviet Union, Trotskyism, and schools of thought understood to be antithetical to Marxist-Leninist analysis, like Freudian psychoanalysis.[46] What was most threatening to the federal government was also what served as the school's intellectual ideal, according to its best scholarly chronicler, Marvin Gettleman: "that education should not be a vehicle for individual advancement or an ivory tower pursuit of knowledge for its own sake, but a social process in which teaching-and-learning were intended to be transformed into action—action that would hasten the advent of American socialism."[47]

The Jefferson School's commitment to an analysis of capitalism in terms of race, gender, and imperialism was shaped by larger changes within the Communist Party, particularly the appointment of Black women and men to roles that could shape its positions. Earl Browder, who guided the CPUSA through the Popular Front years, was ousted and replaced by William Z. Foster in 1944. Browder sought to continue the liberalization of the party by maintaining policies like the "no strike pledge," while Foster and others had a more radical vision for the party's future. Foster's tenure was defined by a large loss in membership, because of the increased federal scrutiny of communists, but also because a number of the party's official positions on women and African Americans were not endorsed by many of its white members.[48] After Foster's ascendance to the chairmanship, the CPUSA readopted the Black Belt thesis and Claudia Jones was promoted to a party policy-making role. Jones, a Black Trinidadian woman who frequently appeared at events at the Jefferson School and led the Institute for Marxism there in 1949, became one of the party's leading lieutenants on "the women's question." Building on the thought of Louise Thompson Patterson, Jones insisted that race could not be isolated from the question of gender, going so far as to argue that race preceded gender in understanding oppression. In Rebecca Hill's assessment of Jones's oeuvre, the foregrounding of racial oppression before gender oppression meant that "it was necessary for white women to fight their own racism before they could unite with other women."[49] In her essential examination of Jones's thought, Carol Boyce Davies suggests that Jones's signature analysis of the triple exploitation of Black women (as Negroes, as women, as workers) ultimately shaped Foster's thinking on issues of gender and race.[50] The party refused to see capitalism solely as an economic problem, and it opened its theory and practice to the ways race and gender were leveraged for the extraction of surplus value. According to Erik McDuffie, Black left feminists did not "allow the move toward the ultra-left of the CPUSA's leadership prevent them from building black Popular Front movements for human rights and the defense of black womanhood."[51]

The Jefferson School developed and embraced an interlocking analysis of race, gender, and class. This position informed the institution's curriculum and its approach to the public. Courses on "the Negro Question" were offered every term. After a 1949 conference on "the Woman Question," which had six hundred attendees to hear talks by Claudia Jones, Betty Millard, Eve Merriam, and Elizabeth Gurley Flynn, a class on the topic was offered regularly.[52] Further illustrative of Jones's influence on thinking about race, gender, and class together was the fact that courses on the Negro Question had at least one session on "the role of Negro women," as did the seminar on "the Women Question."[53] Even in courses where national questions were not the immediate focus, issues of class, race, and gender were foregrounded. The school's main introductory class, titled the "Science of Society: Introduction to Marxism," often devoted at least a week to women and African Americans. Some faculty at the Jefferson School employed Jones's analytic to transform courses that twenty-first century educators still struggle to consider within the framework of racism, sexism, and colonialism. Annette T. Rubinstein taught a class on Shakespeare that foregrounded "the democratic attitude toward the problems of poverty, woman's rights and racial equality" as a means to examine the Bard's plays.[54]

Skeptics saw the radical position of the Communist Party as dictating thought at the Jefferson School rather than facilitating study. They claimed that the anti-white and anti–male chauvinist positions were taken for the benefit of the party, not for those who were oppressed. Harold Cruse was one of these skeptics. Before he argued that "Communist influence became a retarding, divisive, and destructive political force" disconnected from the "Negro ghetto masses" in his 1967 book *The Crisis of the Negro Intellectual,* Cruse was a student at both Carver and Jefferson.[55] In his papers at the Tamiment Library are two separate copies of a syllabus for a Jefferson School course titled "Marxism and the Negro Question," taught in 1950. In his roman à clef titled *Education of a Rebel,* Cruse wrote about how Gwendolyn Bennett's "completely deceptive" personality lured him into the Communist Party at the Carver School. Part of Bennett's deception—and the substance of Cruse's later attack on Black leftists—was that "this Negro woman, albeit sincere, scholarly and full of zeal for Negro progress, was so thoroughly middleclass in social motivations that she succumbed and was swamped in the morass of Negro opportunism in post–World War II Communism."[56]

While Cruse may have been one of the biggest critics of the inter-racial unity platform of postwar communism, one of its largest boost-ers, Doxey A. Wilkerson, also disputed Communist Party positions. Wilkerson disagreed with the Black Belt thesis, writing in *Political Af-fairs* that the idea was "theoretically incorrect and, therefore, tactically disastrous."[57] As the director of curriculum at the Jefferson School, however, Wilkerson swallowed his critique and facilitated courses that examined and promoted the merits of the policy. Wilkerson's criti-cism of the Black Belt thesis cannot necessarily be reduced to white party leaders forcing the position onto a Black subordinate; a number of Black members of the party supported and called for the position's readoption, perhaps most prominently Harry Haywood in his 1948 book *Negro Liberation*. But Wilkerson's Black Belt concession stoked fears that intellectual heavyweights—not to mention the malleable-minded students, some of whom were engaged in higher education for the first time—would succumb to the party's bullying.

Read slightly against the grain, the same chapter of Cruse's *Educa-tion of a Rebel* offers a more favorable portrait of labor schools. The nov-el's protagonist, Clyde, suggests what the space made possible for its students and faculty:

> The atmosphere of the Harlem School dispelled all of his doubts about the Communist movement and he thought of the school as a most pleasant and edifying entrée to a constructive post-war life. Many Marxist and non-Marxist intellectuals lectured and taught here. The interracial relations had a certain camaraderie which pleased him. The librarian of the school was a white woman, whom he learned was married to a West Indian Negro and who had come from an affluent New England family (as Clyde recalls) which she had broken with for the cause of "Communism." The "interracialism" here in the school was also deceptive for the beginner in Communist racial etiquette, for the school was not openly dominated by whites as in the case of most Communist interracial organizations.[58]

Though seeded with suspicions—the deception of the school's inter-racialism, the librarian's affluent New England pedigree—that would mature into his critique in the pages that followed, Cruse's description of what happened in the Carver school was largely positive. It was not dogmatic, and it served a mostly Black student population. Cruse is first to signal that this atmosphere was not necessarily typical of larger labor schools like the Jefferson School. Yet through his account and those of others who had more favorable experiences at these institutions, it becomes clear that people's schools generated the social and intellectual space for interpreting and generating Black culture both outside the immediate dictates of the Communist Party and, perhaps more importantly, outside the consensus liberalism of the anti-Black, anticommunist American academy promoted by the New Criticism. Robin D. G. Kelley recalls that Cedric Robinson's work on the Black Radical Tradition in *Black Marxism* compelled him to consider "what black people . . . brought to the Left to make it their own."[59] Embedded within Cruse's otherwise critical account of the Carver school is evidence of Black people using the emerging CP labor school model as their own. This supports Du Bois's notion that the labor school was a site to pursue the "planned economy, the development or art and literature and an understanding of socialism" opposed to, of course, the "new capitalism and new enslavement of labor" which had grown out of the US racial liberal order. In the next section of this chapter, I show how these goals were set in part by the Black radicals, educators, and culture workers teaching, thinking, and studying at the Jefferson School. Moreover, the curriculum of the Jefferson School, the Carver School, and the Douglass Center embedded these priorities into a larger project of interpreting and making Black culture, which challenged the legitimacy of New Critical—and mainstream academic—claims about interpretation and the role of literature and culture.

BUILDING INSTITUTIONS
OF BLACK LEFT CRITICISM

When Doxey Wilkerson was appointed to be the director of curriculum and faculty, the Jefferson School's approach to studying, discussing, and teaching Black life and Black culture changed dramatically. Much of this change stemmed from Wilkerson's expertise in Black education; in addition to writing his 1939 book *Special Problems of Negro Education*, Wilkerson had studied the role of Black people in US higher education as part of Gunnar Myrdal's *American Dilemma* project. (Wilkerson had quickly grown frustrated with and isolated from

Myrdal when it became clear he held a vastly different understanding of racism than did the Carnegie-funded Swede.) Moreover, Wilkerson showed a willingness to adopt pedagogical and curricular approaches developed by his comrades working in Harlem, particularly Gwendolyn Bennett, the cultural polymath who directed the George Washington Carver School. This adoption was designed not to usurp the function of a Harlem-based progressive people's school, but rather to continue its approach to teaching Black culture after that school closed. Wilkerson's 1948 appointment to the Jefferson School occurred just a few months after the Jefferson School's board established a plan to pay off the Carver School's debt and undertake the operation of the same or a similar institution in Harlem. After being appointed, Wilkerson took rapid action to create space at the Jefferson School for the development of Black cultural work and critical interpretation, especially after course offerings in Black culture were curtailed in Harlem.

Wilkerson's developments sought to address institutional problems within the Jefferson School and settle debates within the communist left, yet they also explicitly challenged the prevailing norms that guided the study of Black life within the mainstream university system and by liberal Black intellectuals in the United States. In addition to developing courses for the study of Black culture, including Black literature specifically, the Jefferson School adopted pedagogies developed by Black people that were designed to foster contact between students, faculty, and prominent members of the Black and left communities across class and race boundaries. These encounters had several effects: they legitimized the particular knowledges of Black working people; they foregrounded the fact that revolutionary power did not stem as much from Black leaders as it did from everyday people enduring and fighting working conditions and the social restrictions of Jim Crow; and they defetishized the isolation of the literary from the social and political world in which they emerged—a defetishization that extended beyond literature to cultural work more broadly. Put simply, with the direction of figures like Wilkerson and Bennett, New York progressive people's schools developed a socially and politically rooted definition of culture, driven by the ideas and institutional arrangements determined by Black people. These formations sought to collapse the separation between the intellectual and the field that contemporaneous forms of Negro history implicitly endorsed. A 1955 photo shows the Jefferson School's leaders—Wilkerson, Selsam, and David Goldway, the executive secretary—conducting an administrative meeting beneath a prominent portrait of Frederick Douglass, suggesting that at the very least, Black leaders and thinkers were always watching over decisions about the school's operations during Wilkerson's tenure.

When the faculty of the Jefferson School's cultural departments met in 1950, they adopted in writing a number of principles that stemmed from practices established at the George Washington Carver School and from Wilkerson's reflection on those practices. Those principles could be summed up by the idea that "black culture [is] a social force," which Wilkerson had developed in an essay published a year earlier in the journal *Masses and Mainstream*. The cultural faculty wrote in their report, "Our instruction in this field must proceed from the premise that culture is a powerful weapon in the class struggle in general, and in today's struggles for democracy and peace in particular."[60] This is a generalized version of Wilkerson's particular argument about Black culture, and it has deep Marxist roots, both in the writings of Lenin and Stalin and in Marx's "Critique of Hegel's Philosophy of the Right." In that text, Marx makes a case for the material contribution of criticism to the class struggle. He writes, "The weapon of criticism cannot, of course, replace criticism of the weapons, material force must be overthrown by material force; but theory also becomes a material force as soon as it has gripped the masses."[61] The problem was that the techniques of cultural criticism taught at the Jefferson School, more often than not were reinforcing "an all-pervading 'classless,' idealist, and clearly non-Marxist, approach," inevitably preventing criticism and culture from becoming a material force.[62] This problem manifested in course descriptions that emphasized "appreciation" over political understanding, or that put technical skills before the work's social purpose. The faculty cited a description for a class on Shakespeare that taught *Hamlet* "as a work of dramatic poetry" as an offending example.[63] The term "dramatic poetry" invokes Cleanth Brooks's argument in *The Well Wrought Urn* that "the most helpful analogy by which to suggest the structure of poetry is that of the drama," bolstered paradoxically by Brooks's reading of *Macbeth* not as drama but as poetry.[64] The cultural faculty's frustration with New Critical reading indicates how they saw its principles as upholding the hierarchical logics of capital-ism and, in turn, the consistent means by which Black people or other marginalized groups were artificially barred entry into the arts. All the while, New Critical methods denied the possibility of criticism garner-ing any material force, because its conceptual framework was deliber-ately isolated from the social and political sphere.

In another collectively written document, the cultural departments' faculty directly invoked the New Criticism as the entity against which the Jefferson School defined its theoretical ideas and pedagogical prac-tices. In the faculty's eyes, the New Critics had trained scholars of liter-ature to defend "the fascist propagandist and anti-Semite Ezra Pound and the Tory, medievalist myth-purveyor and anti-Semite T. S. Elliot [*sic*]."[65] Just as concerning was the fact that the writing of those lead-ing this reactionary plea, including "men like Tate, Faulkner, Ransom, Warren," was "saturated with racialism, apologetics for slavery, delib-erate distortions of American history, explanation of the most bestial violence as being 'human nature.'"[66] The Jefferson School viewed the New Criticism as representative of academia's reproduction of a de-politicized understanding of art and naturalizing hierarchies of racial difference. In this, the school participated in a wider project by Black writers and some writers on the left who registered that the adoption of the language of liberalism by many Agrarian New Critics further en-trenched the racialization of literature and its study through its appar-ent universalization.

As a collective, the cultural departments' faculty generated peda-gogical principles to establish a clearer analytical understanding of rac-ism, sexism, and imperialism. They proposed an interpretive program that would be equipped for a world of "peace and democracy":

> In criticism we place works of art directly in the context of political, social, and philosophical struggles which they reflect in clear or dis-torted fashion. All world views, concepts of human being, society, human history and the human mind are class views, either those of a dying class or those of a class welcoming reality and building the future. We expose and attack all forms of anti-human thinking, chau-vinism and racialism, irrationality, degraded theories of society and

"human nature" disguise, disguised as "universal truths." They are the class thinking of the exploiters of labor, war mongers, and imperialists of today.[67]

Critical interpretation was an essential component of a struggle for anticolonial, antiracist, and feminist visions of the world, and not for a bourgeois exercise of appreciation. Effective critique in this vein would define how literature reflected and generated prevalent understandings of people, systems, and institutions that justified ongoing state and capitalist policies. The faculty's proposal for improvement centered around three decisive ideas: (1) to include "Marxist theoretical content" in all cultural classes, (2) to teach students to recognize "culture as a weapon in all political and related courses," and (3) to hire new personnel in an effort to increase enrollment in these programs.

In line with the tenets for the school's improvement, W. E. B. Du Bois would design his Jefferson School courses to give agency to his students, to encourage their learning, and to make clear that their study had an important role to play in wider social and political struggles. In his 1953 class, he gave lectures in the first two sessions of the course and then left the remaining five sessions to be driven by student reports on African liberation struggles. Those who were not as prepared for the effort required in this type of class grew frustrated with Du Bois's pedagogy. One teaching evaluation from his 1954 course on Reconstruction tersely reads that the class suffered from "a difference of opinion as to whether the object of the course is the development of the individual student or the presentation of a definitive body of information on the part of the teacher." The student who wrote the evaluation hoped for the latter, but Du Bois responded that he wanted his working students to encounter the challenge of "develop[ing] an intelligent point of view on a current subject, by thinking, reading and research."[68] This ambition presented a challenge for the school's students, many of whom had little time to study. Yet the faculty, Du Bois and Wilkerson included, saw that to demand any less would be to desert the institution's ambition to heed, as well as develop, the cultural, social, and political understandings of its students.

The Jefferson School's approach to pedagogical, institutional, and curricular practices had roots in Doxey Wilkerson's 1949 essay "Negro Culture: Heritage and Weapon." In the essay, Wilkerson outlines socially rooted commandments for the interpretation and making of Black culture that grew out of Black-led left educational institutions in midcentury, particularly the Carver School. Wilkerson's definition of Negro culture mandates the establishment of a criticism that is socially attentive to present struggles as well as to a longer-term cultural tradition. For Wilkerson, "Negro culture emerges from and develops as an expression of the struggles of the Negro people for freedom from oppression. It reflects, therefore, the problems and achievements of the developing national liberation movement from whose womb it springs."[69] This meant that the task for Wilkerson—both in the essay and at the Jefferson School—was "to interpret Negro culture as a social phenomenon, which emerges from, and reacts upon, the freedom struggles of the Negro people."[70]

Wilkerson's understanding of the production and interpretation of culture was guided by Marxist thought. He defined culture broadly as "the entirety of the superstructure which a society has developed on the basis of its prevailing mode of production."[71] This materialist understanding led Wilkerson to argue that the particular conditions of slavery and Jim Crow had generated two defining struggles for the production of Black culture: a struggle for literacy and a struggle for content.[72] By literacy, Wilkerson meant that Black people had been barred from "technical discipline in the arts." That restriction had produced expressive developments beyond the bounds of so-called technical disciplines, particularly the sorrow songs, blues, and dance forms. Even when Black people achieved success in the technical disciplines, Wilkerson argued, the subject of these works was necessarily shaped by the struggle to gain education in reading, writing, and the arts. The "struggle for literacy" registered both the so-called nontraditional forms of Black culture as imaginative expressions of organizing and struggle, but also that the growth of the technical skills of the Black artist in any medium was tied to the social and political fate of Black people more broadly. In Wilkerson's description, "To bar the path of technical growth for the Negro artist is to help keep the Negro people 'in their place.'"[73]

Meanwhile, the Black artists' struggle for content contends with the fact that "the highest goal of art is to express . . . the values cherished by the immense majority of working people everywhere."[74] In other words, how can Black writers speak beyond Black people to the greater universal proletarian mass? Invoking a common communist answer, Wilkerson suggests that Black artists turn to "realism" to solve this conundrum. Wilkerson identifies two areas where Black writers tend to reinforce certain modes of anti-Black oppression: the deployment of stereotypical characterizations of Black people, and the commercialization of Black culture for the benefit of white people rather than the mass of Black people. Avoiding these pitfalls requires a "theoretical understanding of Negro life and history," shaped from the ongoing effort to fight against modes of exploitation fostered by racial capitalism. That is, "Negro culture is much more than a mere reflection of the liberation struggles of an oppressed people; it is a social force which can do much to advance the freedom struggles of which it is an integral part."[75] In other words, Wilkerson seemingly anticipates the fact that later forms of Black studies will be rendered solely as protest, in part due to their institutional and ideological formation. His emphasis on "Negro culture" as a social force attempts to consider multifaceted formations of race and class to inform the development of interpretive inquiry.

In clear opposition to ideas that art was autonomous from its creator or from the society in which it was formed, Wilkerson defined Negro culture in its form and content as shaped by oppression. More precisely, the imaginative brilliance of Black culture emerged out of working within and against that oppression. The ongoing nature of that struggle necessarily meant that Black culture could not be disentangled from the project of persuasion and education, an idea likely formed by Wilkerson's expertise as an educational researcher and his longtime admiration for Du Bois. The educational capacity of Black culture—and, in Wilkerson's essay, it is admittedly ambiguous whether or not that capacity is directed at a proletarian audience, a Black audience, a white audience, or all three—moved the relevance of a particular work beyond the page, the canvas, or the concert hall to the streets, the picket line, and the barricade.

Other Black artists and writers working in progressive people's schools took a more explicit line on whether their work should be for a specifically defined Black audience. Both during and after her time teaching at the George Washington Carver School, Elizabeth Catlett, a visual artist then married to the muralist Charles White, spoke extensively about the possibilities afforded by the unique classroom environment created in Harlem. Those classrooms brought together

Black people from a number of different class backgrounds. Catlett fundraised for the school and taught sculpture, one of her signature media; but some of her most valuable experiences came from a popular class she led called "How to Make a Dress." What happened in Catlett's classroom went beyond a sharing of vocational skills, as Catlett remembered in an interview:

> When I worked at the Carver School, theoretically a Marxist institution, people said, "How do you teach Marxism making a dress?" And I said, "Well, while we're sewing, we talk. And when a lady says, 'I have to leave early to get my news,' I say, 'Do you know what the news thinks of you and black people?' And we'd get into a discussion of why newspapers are printed, and who reads them, what they support, what they don't support. . . .'" It was that way that we worked.[76]

These informal moments were part of what made the Carver School special for making new ideas about Black culture and Black life. For Catlett, these experiences led her to develop a new aesthetic that sought as its audience the Black working-class people with whom she worked at the school. "Everybody I met there was so hungry for culture—for art, for music, for dance, for theater," Catlett reflected, "and I felt that these were the people whom I wanted to address in my work."[77]

Catlett left New York for Mexico not long after the Carver School closed in 1946. When she arrived in Mexico she produced a series of etchings called *The Negro Woman*. The twelve linocuts combined aesthetic and political lessons learned at the Carver School with related trends in collectively driven Mexican Art. Catlett's etchings intercut images of Black women's lives with defiant titles about the exploitation that Black women faced. In her series, Black women are constantly working, not just in the fields or in the homes of white women, but also in study and in organizing against racism. The first work in the series, titled "I Am the Negro Woman," shows a Black woman with a furrowed brow looking forcefully to the right. As Melanie Anne Herzog, Catlett's biographer, states, for Catlett to declare in 1946 proudly and politically that "'I am the Negro Woman' . . . was a radical proclamation."[78] Making this bold and broad statement particular, other etchings elaborate on the political work Black women conduct. For example, the title of one etching reads, "My role has been important in the struggle to organize the unorganized"; and another, "I have studied in ever increasing numbers." Catlett sought to display the work in spaces accessible to the working African American women the series depicted: schools and community centers, rather than museums. That a work as politically and aesthetically significant as *The Negro Woman* grew out of Catlett's experiences at the Carver School encapsulates the force generated by the institution's unique approach to interpreting and making Black culture. Anticipating Wilkerson's argument, Catlett identified her cross-class experience of Blackness at the Carver School as a catalyst in orienting her art toward the Black radical tradition. Her series *The Negro Woman*, which crafted an aesthetic and a setting meant for Black working-class viewing, exactly provides an example of the propagandistic impulse within Black left definitions of Black culture while further developing a social and political understanding of Blackness.

The Carver School was able to foster an orientation toward the people of Harlem in part because it developed out of the efforts of people adjacent to the Communist Party, rather than the party itself. Founded in 1943, a year before the Jefferson School, the Carver School anticipated many of the challenges that the Jefferson School would face institutionally and with regard to its study of Black life and Black culture. Gwendolyn Bennett, the artist and writer whose work was included in important Harlem Renaissance publications like *FIRE!!* and *The New Negro*, and who had traveled with Langston Hughes to the Soviet Union in 1932, organized the founding of the school with support from the National Negro Congress. The NNC was a coalition-building organization, not necessarily communist, devoted to uniting Black labor movements and civil rights organizations. It often made these connections via its emphasis on the production of and education about Black culture.[79] Located at 57 West 125th Street, the Carver School fashioned itself as "A People's School," meant to serve the people of Harlem in a variety of ways. The school's course offerings reflect the variegated purposes of the institution: along with courses on art, Negro history, and Marxism-Leninism were courses called "Law for Your Use," "How to Write Good English," and "Your Problems with People: A Course in Psychology."

From the beginning, the school was largely Black-run, and most of its administrators were Black women. While the school was immediately popular with people in Harlem, it struggled financially. To gather additional funding, the board—made up of Black community leaders including Paul Robeson and Adam Clayton Powell—invited mostly white education experts from New York University to join the panel. Conflict followed almost immediately. The Black radical aims of the school were seen as naive by the education experts. In a last-ditch effort to wrest control of the board, the white educators, led by E. George Payne, the dean of NYU's School of Education, announced a mass resignation of six board members due to the fact that other members of the board and the school's administrators included "an element accused of being Communistic."[80] Payne's hope was that the controversy would shake up the organization to give white liberals and liberal Black leaders, among them Walter White of the NAACP, more sway. In Payne's eyes, an anticommunist Carver School would be more representative of Harlem. The move drew much press attention. There were multiple stories in the *New York Times*. and competing op-eds in Black and communist papers. This coverage made it incredibly difficult to obtain funding for the school, especially from members of the Black middle class who were hesitant to be affiliated with the communism. The white educator-administrative class was able to disrupt the Carver School's popularity by drawing on the "red menace," a rhetorical bogeyman that allowed them to mask their concerns about the racial implications of the school's philosophy of Black self-determination.

Though the Carver School was under siege almost before it opened its doors, it provided an important political and cultural experience for many. Among Gwendolyn Bennett's papers is a pamphlet called *Journey's Start*, which consists of poems and short compositions written in a poetry class likely taught by her husband, Richard Crosscup, who was white, at the Carver School in fall 1945. Fourteen of the fifteen writers included in the slim volume were women, and many of their works highlighted the role of poetry and writing in a struggle against what Louise Thompson Patterson called "the triple exploitation" of Black women as workers, as Black, and as women.[81] The creative compositions took on segregation and Black migration, among other topics. One composition recounts the first time the speaker caught a fish in Trinidad; another chuckles at the thought that a bus could go from Jamaica, Queens, to the island nation of the same name;

and yet another considers the tribulations of a young Black man who learns through trial and error that his mobility is restricted because he is Black. In aggregate, *Journey's Start* suggests that writing was taught as a vehicle for connecting one's personal observations to a broader social and political framework for the purpose of generating shared solidarity across the diaspora and, at times, across race.

The charge to "write what you know" in early university creative writing programs was about the expression of authenticity. The Carver School took this further: the creative writer was to draw from the well of experience to build social and political solidarity based on an understanding of known or unknown experiences of oppression.[82] This distinction between labor-school writing instruction and the emergent modes of academic creative writing is apparent in the penultimate composition in *Journey's Start*. The student-writer reflects on the strange and unique experience of taking this class, for only a small fee, in which somehow "everyone seemed intensely interested in everything." In this writer's view, this special feat could be achieved at the Carver School because there, "black and white persons were serving side by side to aid those of us who sought a better understanding of life and problems."[83] Writing—the production of and understanding of culture—was the means to achieve this "better understanding."

Courses about producing literature and art foregrounded the experience of Black people, working people, and women in an effort to generate a different understanding of art's purpose. Bennett advocated for a pedagogy that refused to set prominent artists apart from the larger communities from which they emerged. She developed these approaches first at the School of Democracy and then at the Carver School. Bennett taught a class called "Literature, Music, and Art of the Negro People" at the School for Democracy several times in the early 1940s. Her course situated the development of Black art and literature as part of a social and political struggle. To emphasize this, she designed the course around putting its students in direct conversation with some of the most accomplished Black artists of the era. Among the guests were Countee Cullen, Aaron Douglas, W. C. Handy, Langston Hughes, Alain Locke, Carlton Moss, and Max Yergan. These visits typically consisted of a lecture on the visitor's medium of expertise—Hughes on poetry, Handy on music, et cetera—followed by an open discussion. Sometimes Bennett prompted the guest luminary to reflect on how their work engaged with the longer history of Black life and art. For example, the artist Aaron Douglas came to the first session of the term to consider the questions "Where did the Negro come from and what cultural heritage did he bring with him?" and "What happened to the cultural gift of the Negro during slavery in America?"[84] Bennett's organization of the course emphasized the entanglement of political, economic, and historical understandings of Black life with the production of culture. It also acknowledged that social exchange among Black artists and Black working people would benefit both parties. This was not a matter of consulting the artist for authoritative answers about meaning or the direction that Black people should take. Instead, Bennett's pedagogy suggests that Black cultural workers were engaged in a struggle for democracy and peace *with* Black and white working people.

In early organizational meetings for the Carver School, Bennett, the head of the Curriculum and Faculty committee, suggested that a course called "Negro Life and Culture" be one of the five regular offerings at the school. Continuing her commitment to contact between students and significant Black cultural figures, she suggested a number of prominent Black writers, artists, and critics as instructors for the course, among them her close friend Langston Hughes, as well as Alain Locke, Lawrence Reddick (then curator of the Schomburg Collection in Harlem), and Canada Lee (a Black actor who played Bigger Thomas in the 1941 Broadway adaptation of *Native Son*, which was produced by Orson Welles).[85] The proposed course did not make it to the catalog, though the practice of bringing prominent Black politicians, writers, and artists came to be standard in classes offered at the Carver School. W. E. B. Du Bois was invited to speak in two different courses in 1945 and 1946. One invitation was for a class called "Meet the Author," facilitated by Elizabeth Adams, that focused on "What part does literature play in our thinking and living? What role does literature play as organizer for a democratic world? What function has literature in the betterment of race relations?"[86] The other invitation was for a course called "The Colonial Peoples," which engaged broadly the question of imperialism and had previously featured visits from Eslanda Goode Robeson, Alphaeus Hunton, and leading academics on colonial matters.

A note scribbled by Lorraine Hansberry while she was a student in Du Bois's first class at the Jefferson School provides a sense of what it

meant for some people's school students to be in class with an important Black intellectual and cultural worker:

> —Imagine then what [it] is for me a young Negro sprung from all the
> unrest and fervent searching & anxiety to sit before him
>
> His back against the light of May afternoons. Blue suit, line/d/ shirt,
> bow tie, pince nez, goatee & mustache—Relaxing back leisurely, full
> and confident in his vast knowledge and his splendid sense of interpre-
> tation of history–
>
> His voice coming always perfectly measured. His upper lip curling now
> and again in appreciation of his wit–
>
> Freedom's passion, refined and organized, sits there.[87]

Hansberry's admiration for Du Bois as a confident intellectual who,
like her, had "sprung from all the unrest" is immediately apparent.
Hansberry, who wrote a paper on the Belgian Congo for the class, soon
formed a close friendship with Du Bois and Shirley Graham, the Black
left writer and activist who married Du Bois in 1951. Alice Childress
was in the same class, and she too grew close to Graham and Du Bois.

Bennett's vision for people's school courses centered on the idea that
students could make cultural works that contributed to the liberation
movement. After the Carver School closed, Doxey Wilkerson installed
these principles as central to the Jefferson School's operations. Wilkerson pushed the institution to address racism in its course offerings
and in its treatment of Black, Puerto Rican, and working-class students
and faculty. For instance, none of the seven literature courses taught
during Wilkerson's first term, including a course called "The Contemporary Novel," mentioned any Black writing. Soon, however, the study
of racism, Black life, and Black culture was a central part of the Jefferson
School's curriculum, especially in its cultural offerings.[88] During the
first three years of Wilkerson's curricular leadership the school created
a two-term seminar on the Negro Question, honored W. E. B. Du Bois
during Negro History Week, held a course taught by Lloyd Brown, and
hosted, among other events, a multicultural town hall event attended
by 1,400 people where the Jewish People's Philharmonic Chorus performed pieces with text by Langston Hughes. These were the years
when the Jefferson School faculty declared that its cultural programs

were necessary to contest the New Critical interpretive program and the broader social and political order that program supported.

It would take the opening of another "new people's school in Harlem" to fully establish an array of specialized courses in Black culture, literature, and the arts. The Black faculty associated with the Frederick Douglass Educational Center, founded during Negro History Week of 1952, were able to illustrate the demand for and importance of the regular offering of courses on Black literature to students in progressive people's schools, a decade before similar arguments were made in the mainstream university system. These classes later became a staple at the Jefferson School in its final years of operation.

In January 1952, W. Alphaeus Hunton and Rosalie Berry organized a conference of twenty-five dignitaries to discuss a "new people's school in Harlem," which would eventually be named the Frederick Douglass Educational Center, located at 124 West 124th Street. At the time, Hunton was director of the Council on African Affairs and Rosalie Berry had done organizing in the South, worked with labor movements in Detroit and New York, and served as registrar of the Jefferson School. The delegates, Black, white, and Puerto Rican, assembled at the Skyline Room of the Hotel Theresa and included Herbert Aptheker, Lloyd Brown, Jesus Colon, Howard Fast, Philip Foner, Shirley Graham, Louise Patterson, Paul Robeson, and Doxey Wilkerson. They decided that the main aim of the school should be "the education of the workers on the why-is-it and the what-to-do about jimcrow living. A School that will be not only an educational center, but a cultural center for the people of Harlem."[89] While the school was Harlem-focused, the delegates were careful to recognize the neighborhood as a key node in the Black Atlantic, and the education offered there would be a means to "call forth the untapped strength of the Negro, West Indian, and Puerto Rican people."[90]

The opening of the Douglass Educational Center revived the work of the Carver School and tapped into the energy of a number of Black radical groups that had since been established. Most of these groups intersected in one way or another with the newspaper *Freedom*, a publication started by the Committee for the Negro in the Arts (CNA) to defend Paul Robeson and other prominent Black cultural figures against an intensifying anticommunist push from the federal government, as well as from liberal and conservative media.[91] Because it grew out of a cultural organization, *Freedom* quickly became a vehicle for emerging Black writers and crucial political reporting. Some of this reporting drew national attention to various cases of "legal lynching." Activist groups used the term to indicate the ways the courts and police were used to sentence innocent Black people to death. As part of the legal lynching coverage for *Masses and Mainstream*, Yvonne Gregory traveled to Georgia in 1951 to report on the case of Rosa Lee Ingram, whose two sons were sentenced to death after a one-day trial for killing a white man after he had begun an altercation with her. Coverage of state violence against Black people had long been a mobilizing force for the Communist Party in the United States. When CPUSA offered legal support during the 1931 Scottsboro trial, it legitimated the party's antiracist credentials. More importantly, perhaps, the wide publicity generated by this attention to anti-Black violence created an impetus for the growth and establishment of Black activist groups and outlets, some specifically for Black women. These groups, especially the Sojourners for Truth and Justice, generated national platforms for Black-led protest against anti-Black and anticommunist crusades.[92]

The faculty and course offerings at the Douglass Educational Center emphasized the commingling of Black political activism and Black cultural work. The school offered the first course devoted entirely to Negro Culture at one of New York's labor schools since the closure of the Carver School in the spring of 1952. It was taught by Lloyd Brown. Concurrently, the Douglass Educational Center facilitated intensive inquiries into Black liberation efforts both in the United States and abroad. Alphaeus Hunton taught a course on African liberation movements, Jose Santiago taught courses on "the Puerto Rican Question," and there were classes on West Indian liberation movements. The center also offered courses in Spanish to reach more students in Harlem, including "La Ciencia Social," "El Problema Del Pueblo Negro," and "Problemas Fundamentales en Estados Unidos: Sus Causas y Soluciones." There were also opportunities to learn about political organizing, including a course taught by Lorraine Hansberry called "Public Speaking for Progressives," which provided instruction in how to "speak from the floor, deliver a talk or report, and act as a chairman."[93] The school's "dedicat[ion] to Negro Liberation" meant that school administrators foregrounded the study of Black culture in multifaceted ways. Wilkerson described the school in an article in the *Daily Worker*: "Let substantial numbers of the people of Harlem come to understand the class character of their main oppressors. Let them grasp the super-profit motive which maintains the ghetto. Let them acquire strength from the historic struggles and rich culture which are their heritage."[94]

Starting with a course at the Douglass Education Center, the study of Black literature became a regular topic of study in the New York labor schools. This is especially significant because John Lash, citing a survey of university literature faculty in 1945, implies that only a handful of colleges and universities offered courses in Negro literature, all of them historically Black.[95] In the fall term of 1952, back from her reporting on the Rosa Lee Ingram affair in Georgia, Yvonne Gregory planned a class titled "The Poetry of the Negro People." Her description read: "The culture of the Negro people expressed through poetry: Folk songs, work songs, ballads, blues. How Negro poetry was and is used in the fight for freedom. From Phyllis Wheatley to Langston Hughes. Who are the makers of Negro poetry?"[96] Gregory's course description emphasizes that Black literature should not be disentangled from the "fight for freedom," and establishes a canon for Black writers engaged in this tradition.

Gregory's approach to writing poetry—both in its expressly social and political subject matter and in its aesthetic pattern—provides some insight into how she taught Black poetry. Gregory herself had turned to poetry to process the government's role in the Ingram case, with a poem called "Long Distance to Life," which *Freedom* published in its February 1951 issue.[97] The poem's most impactful stanza reads:

> *Our* government lynched the seven
> That GOVERNMENT want to LYNCH us all
> And send US ALL to 'heaven'—[98]

This stanza ironizes, through the use of italics, the political agency of Black people in terms of shaping the US government's action, while also creating a collective Black nation—"US"—out of the state's turn to violence. Skewering the tropes of racial liberalism, Gregory registers the fact that even the state's death sentence is couched within the false rhetoric of Christian grace. Indeed, Gregory expresses exasperation with the idea that liberation might only be achieved through Black death. She writes, "I want my people here on earth / My people want to live." Gregory's poetry grew out of Black, communist organizing, and her work demands the earthly realization of Black liberation. Her course's focus on the history of Black poetry's role in liberation struggles highlights that the definition of Black literature she crafted relied on the social and political valence of Black culture, in addition to its aesthetic qualities.

In the next academic term, Gregory taught a related course at the Jefferson School on Black literature of the first half of the twentieth century. At the time, the Jefferson School was responding to one of its many self-criticism sessions by opening a campaign to recruit more Black and Puerto Rican students for the school. The goal, as advertised frequently in *The Daily Worker*, was to make the Jefferson School "a fortress of Negro-White unity" by achieving five hundred Negro and fifty-five Puerto Rican enrollments for the winter term, which would respectively be 12.5 percent and 1.3 percent of the school's total projected enrollments. Such goals were particularly lofty because they outpaced the proportional representation of Black and Puerto Rican people in New York City and the nation.[99] In addition to offering Gregory's course and several other classes on Black and Puerto Rican liberation, the school achieved this goal by increasing its programming directed to Black students. During the same term as the recruitment campaign, Lorraine Hansberry and Gwendolyn Bennett spoke at an event offering a reading and analysis of "Working Class Poets of the Negro People." Claudia Jones gave a lecture titled "Negro Women in the Struggle for Peace and Democracy," and sat as the head of a conference titled "Women: A Mighty Force for Peace and Freedom." In this environment, Gregory's course on Black literature continued its emphasis on the role of Black literature in "the liberation struggle," and listed "Booker T. Washington, W. E. B. Du Bois, Paul Laurence Dunbar, James Weldon Johnson, Sterling Brown, Langston Hughes, Roy Ottley, Richard Wright, Countee Cullen, Theodore Ward, Arna Bontemps, Alice Childress, [and] Lloyd Brown" as the writers to be discussed.[100] The course also foregrounded how literature developed in Black social movements, a clear gesture toward articulating a creative and critical practice in understanding the social force of Black literature.

Versions of Gregory's course were soon taught on an annual basis at the Jefferson School. Lorraine Hansberry took over the class in fall 1953.

She kept the title and focus largely the same, but pared down the number of writers to be discussed. Augusta Strong, an important figure in the Southern Negro Youth Congress, and later editor of *Freedomways*, taught a class on the Harlem Renaissance in winter 1955, and Dolly Walker taught a class on poetry from Wheatley to Hughes at the Jefferson School in fall 1955. During the Jefferson School's final term, the artist Mel Williamson taught a class called "Negro Culture in the Struggle for Democracy" with a number of guest lectures, recalling Gwendolyn Bennett's work a decade earlier at the School for Democracy.

Black leftists within people's schools developed a sense that forging Black institutions for study could create favorable conditions for socially engaged Black culture and criticism while participating in a communist vision for revolutionary change. Wilkerson and others envisioned the production and interpretation of culture against and beyond New Critical institutional models as elemental to dislodging entrenched forms of racism not only within literary and cultural study, but in the broader and social political programs that New Critical logics subtended. In addition to expanding an academic imagination of what kind of study of Black literature and culture was possible in the midcentury, the history of Black women and men within labor schools shows how modes of Black self-determination could exist in and through communism in an era of intensive scrutiny for the Black and the red.

PEOPLE'S SCHOOL PEDAGOGY
AND BLACK LITERATURE

Just as this uptick in offerings in Black literature occurred, John O. Killens was finishing a novel, *Youngblood*, on which his experiences at the Jefferson School made a clear impact. In his biography of Killens, Keith Gilyard deems the institution one of Killens's "haunts" because of Killens's frequent attendance at Harry Haywood's lectures there, and his ardent admiration of Doxey Wilkerson's and Lloyd Brown's ideas about Black culture.[101] Killens also participated in a contentious conference on Black writing and culture at the Jefferson School in 1950. Harold Cruse called for the conference after the publication of Wilkerson's essay "Negro Culture," and this, in Cruse's words, led to "the first cultural conference on Negro problems that the Communist Party ever held."[102] The conflict at the conference largely stemmed from disagreements among Black writers about the role that Marxism should play in Black writing. Ernest Kaiser, for instance, gave a speech that expanded on his critique of Black writers on the left for their failure "to deal with Negro psychology," an argument that Douglas Field suggests anticipates Baldwin's in "Everybody's Protest Novel."[103] Lloyd Brown accused Kaiser of Trotskyism and offered a rebuttal so searing that he crushed Cruse and Kaiser's attempt to form a group of writers devoted to "anti-social" realism.[104] Killens, sympathetic to Wilkerson and Brown, saw the conference accordingly as an effort to "hammer out a liberation ideology for Black writers," an implicit endorsement of the Marxist side of the argument rather than the psychological side.[105] Killens took this goal as a catalyst to form an organization devoted to this project, called the Harlem Writer's Guild. He formed the guild with Philip Bonofsky, a white novelist and Jefferson School instructor, and there he would work through early drafts of *Youngblood*.

In *Youngblood*, Killens projects his midcentury admiration and hopes for East Coast Marxist education back into the first several decades of the twentieth century in Crossroads, Georgia, a fictional town modeled after his birthplace. This projection honors the historical trajectory from communist organizing in the South to the reconfiguration of labor schools in the North during the Popular Front era via organizations like the NNC, the SNYC, and the CNA, while muddying the contemporary interpretation of communism's exploitative interest in Black people offered by Ralph Ellison and Richard Wright. Killens would employ a similar anachronistic projection in his 1963 novel *And Then We Heard the Thunder*. As Alan Wald has shown, that book, despite being set during World War II, reflects "the race as well as labor and gender relationships of the civil rights movement of the late 1950s and the rise of Third World radicalism in the 1960s."[106]

With *Youngblood*, Killens suggests that the radical education possible in places like New York and Washington, DC, could reach the grassroots labor, educational, and social struggles in the deep South, leading to a circuit of Black radical ideas from north to south and back again. Killens's novel shows how radical Black education could create a North-South coalition of Black and white workers to challenge the rul-

ing class coalition that established what Du Bois called the "new industrial slavery" after Reconstruction. Killens does this by dramatizing the
approach to Black culture taught at the people's schools in two ways.
First, he builds on the idea that Black self-determination results from
teaching Black culture as a "force." Second, he suggests that interracial
unity in unionization efforts and in friendship was crucial for fighting
white supremacy and capitalism more broadly. *Youngblood*, therefore,
spotlights one of the Jefferson School's curricular goals: instruction
in literature and the arts "must proceed from the premise that culture
is a powerful weapon in the class struggle in general, and in today's
struggles for democracy and peace in particular."[107]

Killens first makes this point in *Youngblood* with the character of
Richard Myles, a Black teacher educated in Washington, DC, and New
York who travels to Crossroads to take a teaching job. Once he arrives,
Richard upends the established curriculum by providing instruction
on Black history and Black culture to his classroom of Black students.
His approach makes his immediate superiors uneasy. Richard later tin-
kers with the annual school-sponsored Jubilee Pageant, a move that
prompts significant social upheaval. For years, the Jubilee Pageant has
been an opportunity for Black students to perform what amounted to
a minstrel show for the white residents of Crossroads. Richard instead
undertakes a project of meeting with Black families to highlight the
fact that tactics to address contemporary social and political struggles
can be found in the spirituals performed. These interpretive moments
are then woven into the performance to create a defiant community-
building event that solidifies bonds among Black people, rather than
those among whites.

Richard's politics and educational tactics stem from the influence of
his college roommate at Howard, Randy the Radical. Randy prompts
Richard to participate in Black protests around DC, all while Randy
gives Richard "dangerous books" to read, including "Booker T. Washington's *Up from Slavery, The Life and Times of Frederick Douglass, Black
Reconstruction* by W. E. B. Du Bois and Karl Marx's *Das Kapital* and
Carter Woodson and many many more."[108] While Richard and Randy's
relationship may have roots in the radicalism of Howard faculty and
students in the 1930s, many of these texts and ideas about the necessity
for political action were being taught in a different context at the Jefferson School when Killens was working on the novel. A student in the

Jefferson School's "20-Week Seminar on the Negro Question" would have encountered nearly all of the texts mentioned by Randy in the course's third session, "The Negro People in the Era of Imperialism." One objective of that particular class was to examine "northern migrations and the persistence of the Black Belt."[109] The Jefferson School's inquiry into the "Negro Question" quietly informs Richard Myles's coming into revolutionary consciousness in *Youngblood*, and provides a Marxist-Leninist basis for grasping how education may cut against capitalist geography and white chauvinism.

When Richard moves to Crossroads, Georgia to teach, he carries with him the radical pedagogies that later would be fostered in progressive people's schools. His pupils in Georgia register this pedagogical method—which foregrounds culture not as something that can be neutrally appreciated, but as an element in the formation of a political consciousness—by reflecting on the many ways in which it is unusual to them. Sitting in Richard's classroom, Rob Youngblood, the youngest son in the novel's central family, thinks:

> Mr. Myles really had a new way of teaching. Nobody ever taught like him before—not in Crossroads, Georgia. Who ever heard of letting children ask the teacher questions, and even disagree with the teacher sometimes? The other teachers wouldn't let you do doodly-squat. Spent most of the time telling you what you better not do. Can't do this—Can't do that. Mister Myles made you feel you had some sense in your head, and what you thought amounted to something; even though you were only a kid in school . . . He taught things that hadn't ever been taught before in Crossroads—And one of those things was Negro history—GreatGodAlmighty! All about things colored people had done. It was a whole lot better than a moving picture show. Made you feel like your folks amounted to something from way back yonder.[110]

Richard's pedagogical practice can be linked to the work of the Jefferson School, mainly the school's effort to collapse the space between the people and the scholar, as well as to foreground dialogue about cultural meaning-making. A document on improving instruction methods told faculty to "make it clear that all questions and difficulties should be expressed. Be especially alert to prevent sectarian approaches by more advanced students to those who have less knowledge of Marxism. Welcome divergent points of view, and deal with them seriously—to the end of conviction."[111] This pedagogical tactic was one of many recommended to achieve the Jefferson School's ultimate Marxist-Leninist purpose: to unite theory with practice to foster people's thirst for education and to encourage a student "to influence his associates in the shop and community."[112] Richard Myles's teaching in *Youngblood* does just that.

In a scene Keith Gilyard reads as having been inspired by Wilkerson and Du Bois, Richard Myles discusses with Rob Youngblood and his family the sorrow songs and their performance of collectivity, melancholy, and emancipation. In turn, Rob delivers his own interpretation of these songs at the annual Jubilee Pageant. This interpretive act challenges the standing function of the pageant, and brings the Black residents of Crossroads to a political catharsis. Rob "heard people crying in the audience, and over on the left he saw two men holding a shouting woman."[113] Jonathan Flatley argues that "for Du Bois the collective affect created in the singing of the [Sorrow] Songs holds onto and returns repeatedly to the problem of loss not in order that a therapeutic mourning can be accomplished, but in order to remain attuned to the unfinished work of the past, that is, to the problems of American racism."[114] The scene at the Jubilee Pageant heeds this lesson. The melancholy Rob invokes sparks political organizing among the Black residents of Crossroads.

Now older, Rob becomes involved in a union campaign at the hotel where he works. The campaign requires that Rob organize both white and Black workers, thus marking one of the many obstacles that racism played in trade union struggles in the first half of the twentieth century, not to mention a tactical reason why the Jefferson School sought to become a "fortress in Negro-White unity." Rob and the union organizer, Jim Collins, worry that no white workers at the hotel will be willing to go in with their Black colleagues. Rob remembers, however, that after the Jubilee Pageant years earlier, Oscar Jefferson, a member of the white union, had approached him, his father, and Richard Myles to tell them he had found the program "mighty nice."[115] Oscar had stood up for Rob's father on a number of occasions. On the strength of this dossier, Rob and Jim arrange for a meeting with Oscar and some Black workers interested in the union. There is plenty of initial skepticism among the assembled Black workers. One man states, "He was a cracker before he was a worker," articulating the logic that gives the white worker, according to Du Bois, a "public and psychological wage."[116] Another man worries that Jefferson's name signals historical allegiance to Jefferson Davis, the president of the Confederacy. Yet it soon becomes clear that Oscar Jefferson's name can be more aptly read as pointing beyond the novel to the Jefferson School. Rob certifies that Oscar is a willing collaborator by describing the multiple occasions when Oscar had stood up for his family and shown admiration for Black people, including at the Jubilee. After hearing these stories, another Black worker relents: "If we don't use the crackers against Mr. Ogle [the hotel boss], Mr. Ogle'll use them against us."[117] As the Jefferson School hoped to be, Oscar Jefferson is a key element toward the construction of a "fortress of Negro-white unity" throughout the novel.

These parts of *Youngblood* highlight what deploying culture as a weapon could do. It enables Black workers to "use the crackers" rather than being used themselves. This draws a line to the history of Black labor and civil organizing, as shown by Robin D. G. Kelley, Erik McDuffie, and Dayo Gore.[118] Killens's novel shows that a Jefferson School–style cultural education begets Black left organizing by providing racial and class consciousness for Black and white people. When these episodes are read in terms of Killens's admiration and participation in New York labor schools, they reveal what I have observed more broadly: that Black assembly in and through these institutions changed their offerings and operations, and thus provided a path toward generating inter- and intraracial solidarity. These institutions did not necessarily start as, or operate uniformly in, establishing an analysis of the intersecting operation of race, gender, and class. Instead, they provided space for Black radicals to develop these analyses, teach them in the classroom, and ultimately reconfigure the institution around them. Black women like Claudia Jones, but also like Gwendolyn Bennett and Rosalie Berry, were on the front lines of this work, and their ideas were adopted and implemented at the Jefferson School by Doxey Wilkerson. Jim Collins, the organizer in *Youngblood*, argues for the importance of women to the movement, seeing them as "the back-bone of the organization."[119] With *Youngblood*, John Killens suggests that a means for Black cultural interpretation forged out of the perspectives of Black people across class backgrounds could indeed spark a movement to combat racist institutions. In effect, *Youngblood* distills in literature the mission and history of Black radical efforts within and beyond the people's schools of the Communist Party in the late 1940s and '50s.

Killens does not idealize intra- and interracial organizing efforts in *Youngblood*. On the one hand, the writer's later commitment to Black nationalism suggests that he ultimately would find these energies best directed elsewhere. On the other hand, *Youngblood* reveals great hope for the pedagogical possibilities and field imaginaries afforded by the Jefferson School. Killens's faith in these possibilities aligns him with Du Bois, who argued that the Marxist education offered there laid the framework for a certain form of Black self-determination. While shaped by Communist Party interests, Du Bois identified that figures like Gwendolyn Bennett, Doxey Wilkerson, Lorraine Hansberry, and others were able to create space within people's schools to cultivate an argument for the weaponization of culture driven by and for the interests of Black radicals, among them Black women and Black working people. By positively situating the study of Black literature and Black culture in terms of a social and political struggle against racial capitalism and an imperial US state, affiliates of the Jefferson School avoided the turn to universalism that otherwise dominated the discussion of "Negro literature" in the period.

Black radicals in New York labor schools rejected the premise of a cultural universalism tout court. That rejection stemmed in part from the greater effect of the Black Belt thesis, but also came from a solidifying definition of Black culture that insisted on its social, political, and aesthetic functions within a struggle against white supremacy. Black radical writers in the midcentury saw the turn to "human nature" in some Black writing as being tied to the Agrarian New Critics and the American university system, which amplified these universalist ideas. In turn, the Jefferson School's pursuit of Black cultural study deliberately eluded and sought to dismantle the debates about universalism and integrationism that otherwise dominated the conversation about Black writing in the 1940s and 1950s. As outlined by scholars across the political spectrum, the midcentury critical discussions around Black literature were molded by Gunnar Myrdal's sense in *An American Dilemma* that "the Negro problem" was a moral issue and could be solved in part by the assimilation of Black people into the American grain.[120]

Members of the Jefferson School faculty and Jefferson School affiliates, like Oliver Cox, found this idea, which provided crucial support for federal racial liberalism, troubling and simply incorrect. In his book-length dismissal of the Myrdal thesis, for which Doxey Wilkerson composed the introduction, Herbert Aptheker anticipates Cox in arguing that "the Negro people are oppressed because the rulers of our society find it highly profitable to oppress them"—meaning that racism was a political and economic problem rather than a moral one.[121] Combined with the archive of the study of Black literature and culture at the Jefferson School, it becomes clear that the study of "Negro literature" in the labor school was not part of an argument that the work was worthy of inclusion on an American literature syllabus, but rather was a cultural project unto itself. Literature and culture could register political and economic contours while also providing a basis for social assemblies and forms of struggle and resistance. This argument was rooted in ideas about Black self-determination, and in a comprehensive analysis of the institutions of criticism that shaped the study of culture in the US academy.

The Jefferson School, the Carver School, the Douglass Center, and the broader national network of labor schools mark an effort to build the future world imagined by Du Bois. Yet these institutions were soon thwarted by the very forces they sought to dismantle. The dismantling occurred on a number of fronts. Myrdal's project, backed by the Carnegie Foundation, halted any funding available for Du Bois's proposed "Encyclopedia of the Negro" project, a massive study of Black life around the world. One reason the Swedish-born Myrdal was more appealing to funders than Du Bois was the fact that his distance from American racism gave him an objective advantage. Funders, using the rubric of objectivity, saw that Du Bois could not possibly be objective on the issue as a Black American man; and the same rubric made the Swedish-born Myrdal an attractive candidate. The American university system and the New Criticism employed objectivity, or autonomy from contemporary political "problems," as a means of disqualification from serious scholarly engagement. Of course, the federal government applied a similar rationale when it argued vociferously that the Jefferson School and its affiliates were not educational institutions but fronts for a subversive organization. Even after the school's official shuttering in 1956, the House Un-American Activities Committee called Doxey A. Wilkerson to Washington in July 1959 to question him on whether the institution had secretly reopened. Such actions can be deemed part of the broader red panic. But ultimately they were fueled by the publicly defined rationale that in order for education to be education, it must be impartial. The Jefferson School's partiality toward communism, Black people, women, working-class people, and other groups engaged in wider political struggles made it subversive, revealing objectivity's partial character toward the priorities of the Western liberal capitalist order. Drawing on this logic, the institutional forces of research foundations, the university system, and the US federal government temporarily eclipsed the horizon of possibility found within Black radical visions for interpretation, education, democracy, and socialism, the cultivation of which was the distinct mission of people's schools, in Du Bois's eyes. Simply put, without a concession to objectivity and certain modes of scientific thinking, these progressive people's schools could not operate or be an appropriate object for funding. While this led to their eventual closure, this positioning also made it possible for these institutions to develop a different approach to the study of Black life and culture.

Black radicals working in and through the people's schools of the Communist Party in this moment claimed that Black literature's entanglement with social and political organizing made that work more valuable toward realizing an imaginative future. The criticism Black radicals developed and taught in these schools as pedagogy and as social and political philosophy also shaped the institutions' larger practices. The Jefferson School actively recruited students and faculty of color; provided scholarships to students who otherwise could not afford to attend; enrolled all of its workers in a union; paid all faculty equally, including "stars" like Du Bois; and offered a full year of maternity leave for all women workers.[122] The school also stipulated that any "temporary" employees who worked there for a particular period of time—three months for office workers, six months for all other employees—would be converted to permanent employees. To be clear, the lesson here is not that doctrinaire Leninism is the answer to antiracism, or that the adoption of some or all of these institutional practices necessarily leads to a more egalitarian educational system. The development of a socially, politically, and materially attuned literary and cultural criticism—as practiced in New York's progressive people's schools—provided a significant material challenge to the racial and aesthetic order held up by New Critical principles in academe and by the US government's ostracization of the Black and red. One could argue that the continued marginalization of the histories of the Jefferson School and the Black-led Carver School and Douglass Center is evidence that this material challenge was ultimately ineffective. Yet the government's commitment to shuttering these institutions shows that to those in power, the work of these schools did indeed constitute a subversive threat to the Western liberal order—an order fueled, then as now, by racism, sexism, and imperialism.

Epilogue

In this book I have moved from identifying the logic of enclosure that structures the field of literary studies, the midcentury university, and the US state to examining increasingly public approaches to the study of literature, the building of educational institutions, and the imagining of a world beyond the confines of racial capitalism. This tactical work in the 1940s and '50s by Tolson, Hughes, Petry, Hansberry, and those affiliated with progressive people's schools in New York provides an argument for a socially and politically rooted method for studying literature. This method refuses to privilege the critic as separate and distinct from the work of literature, or from the people whom the critic addresses. Unlike the mainstream university system, which sought to organize people into the mold of the universal (white, liberal) individual, these Black radical methods and institutions pursued ways of knowing that attended to the differentiating cuts that emerged through race, class, and gender in a world defined by racial capitalism.

Certainly, the challenge to the US postsecondary education system and the political economy that supported it would become more widespread as the Black liberation movement reached the 1960s. The dynamic of struggle in the preceding decades inevitably shaped the approach to social and political change in postsecondary education. The persistence of the 1940s- and 1950s-era government crackdown on distinct "subversive" institutions led by communists and Black people did not end these interpretive and institution-building activities. Black and left activists shifted their attention to configuring the mainstream university system from within, rather than from without. Black and Third World movements in the late 1960s sought to change the char-

acter of the American university by demanding the radical reorgan-
ization of existing institutions. The state-university counterrevolution
redirected some of these political energies to serve its interests, even
when conceding to certain demands raised in protest. Organizers in
the Lumumba-Zapata movement at the University of California, San
Diego, for example, called for a new college that would stand, in the
words of Angela Davis, as a "place where our peoples could acquire the
knowledge and skills we needed in order to more effectively wage our
liberation struggles."[1] Just six years after Third College was established,
it was 60 percent white. For Roderick Ferguson, "what happened at
that university just above the sea is a microcosm of the chronicles of minority difference, a chronicle of how minority difference was deployed
against institutional hegemony and a report of how it was claimed by
and managed within the province of institutions and thereby alienated
from its originary mission."[2] The attempt to build something different
from the inside out, rather than from the outside in, revealed a marked
difference between the approach taken by midcentury Black writers
operating in, or in proximity to, communist labor schools and the Black
studies movement of the 1960s. As the scrutiny and coercive force of
the state was more fully applied, those who worked in, attended, and
were in solidarity with the labor schools sharpened their opposition to
the state-university consensus of racial liberalism.

I write at a different moment. The American university and its neoliberal presentation of racial capitalism have become so efficient at
incorporating minority difference that the university is now a nexus
for abolitionist demands to radically reimagine the planet's political
economy. To look again to California: when Third College was established in 1970, universities were funded with a greater share in the state's
budget than prisons; this situation would be sustainably and significantly flipped by 2003. The reasons are myriad, but it has not been lost
on critical observers that state university funding trended downward
and prison funding trended upward just as more racially marginalized
students in the state became eligible to enter the university system.[3]
This political-economic observation may seem distant from literary
studies, but the tactical critical acts of Black critics and the progressive
people's schools of midcentury suggest that a concern with literature
and culture's definition and interpretation is inextricable from institutional form and dimension. The forces of official state-university anti-

racism from the midcentury onward have newly articulated strategies for absorbing the movements that endeavored to make radical material changes to the operation of universities from within them. Because of this, it has become almost impossible to imagine that the university we currently have can be reformed to sufficiently redress that which these institutions have sought to ignore or contain.

Scholars and activists on the left have recently organized their critique of the university under the frame of abolitionism. As Abigail Boggs, Eli Meyerhoff, Nick Mitchell, and Zach Schwartz-Weinstein put it in their invitation to abolitionist university studies, "leftist abolitionisms have always been both destructive—dismantling racial capitalism—and constructive, building alternatives, from the 'abolition democracy' of Reconstruction to today's projects seeking to divert people's attachments to prisons and police into alternative practices of community accountability, safety, and transformative justice."[4] They term this approach "constructive abolitionism," and thus bring the pressure of a discourse largely shaped around slavery, prisons, and policing to the university. The university in this framework is not autonomous from the ills of the society of which it is a part. This means that to be against the university, as it means to be against the totalizing reality of racial capitalism, is to be *in but not of.* This positionality has been made known most recently by Harney and Moten's undercommons, though it is also shot through other Black and anticolonial critiques of the university, as well as a long tradition of Black and left thought. I am struck by how many readings of Harney and Moten's *in but not of* put too much emphasis on the *in,* or inside aspect, especially at a time when so many are actively being pushed outside the university through the shuttering of institutions, the withering of permanent faculty positions, and the crushing debt brought upon students. In 2020, Moten and Harney wrote against these readings and made the centrifugal dynamics explicit in a comment on their earlier essay: "The institution (the university, the prison, the hospital, the state) is regulatory; and regulation tends towards elimination."[5] The invocation of the university's tendency toward elimination raises an important question about the "maroon community of the university" referred to by Harney and Moten both historically and in the present. What has been built *outside* the university by those eliminated by these institutions, or by those who never entered them in the first place?

Harney and Moten speculate on the shape of what is built by the undercommons—what they reference once as the "internal outside"— and by those eliminated by the university's regulative tendency, in the final paragraph of their undercommons essay:

> Not so much the abolition of prisons but the abolition of a society that could have prisons, that could have slavery, that could have the wage, and therefore not abolition as the elimination of anything but abolition as the founding of a new society. The object of abolition then would have a resemblance to communism that would be, to return to Spivak, uncanny. The uncanny that disturbs the critical going on above it, the professional going on without it, the uncanny that one can sense in prophecy, the strangely known moment, the gathering content, of a cadence, and the uncanny that one can sense in cooperation, the secret once called solidarity. The uncanny feeling we are left with is that something else is there in the undercommons. It is the prophetic organization that works for the red and black abolition![6]

It is uncanny to me that what I have shown to have been rendered outside the university system as such at midcentury were in fact communist para-academic institutions for the red and Black, sites rendered as no-go zones or nonspaces by the state and by the era's academe. That is, tactical criticism and the progressive people's schools challenged fascism both at home and abroad, while being actively delegitimized by both the university and the state during the rise of the increasingly formalized university-state-military complex. The Carver School, the Douglass Education Center, and the Jefferson School relied either on faculty and students who were not allowed into the university system and thus were forced out, or on those who never deigned to be part of the university system in the first place. This is not to say that these institutions were outside the bounds of the world of racial capitalism, or were not at all in relation to the state university complex. Instead, these institutions and practices, though imperfect, were external sites built to create a world outside the one widely imagined in their present. Writers like Hughes, Tolson, Petry, and Hansberry thought up such material contexts in imagining certain assemblies and audiences as to render liberatory aspects of their work forcefully legible. These institutions, approaches, and methods offer not an answer to the overlapping crises of the present conjuncture, but at the very least a different means by which to reach for what has been, is now, and will be possible. They sought to build solidarity through education and interpretation where university and state styles of interpretation sought to make and enforce fracture. Part of that solidarity relies on deemphasizing the *in* of the university, and making available the rich contours of the outside. This perhaps has long been true of movements for abolition: their political and intellectual energies—if such energies can even be separated—have long been generated by those operating outside of the academic orbit.

As a final provocation, my hope is that this book offers a glimpse of possibility to the many who have been pushed outside the university or been rendered adjunct to it. This adjunctification has occurred through the stratification of academic labor, and by the white, Western assumptions about the appropriate subjects and objects of knowledge making. Overrepresented among these adjunct workers are people of color and women, especially Black women. The overrepresentation of people in positions that offer low wages, little to no job security, and no support for inquiry beyond teaching under a supposed meritocracy lends itself to yet another form of race- and gender-based material marginalization.[7] While adjunctification is not the same as attrition or departure from the university, it is nevertheless part of a process of elimination. The history I illuminate in this book suggests that those who are outside, as much as those who are in but not of, the state university system carry an essential analysis of the system's operation, and are in a unique position to create forceful knowledge, institutions, and interpretive practices that present a legitimate challenge to the existing political economic order. The progressive people's schools and the cultural-critical imaginings I describe were developed by those who were pushed outside the university system or never allowed near it, even if the anti-Black and anticommunist dimension of those midcentury exclusions was more explicit than today's rhetoric cast in the language of austerity and merit.

In offering an account of what is made possible in the racialized, gendered, and politicized outside, this book has highlighted other sites for historical inquiry and present strategy into the work of constructive abolitionism. It also encourages us to glimpse a university and a form of criticism unbound, even if just for a moment, of the strictures of liberalism and racial capitalism. Such a criticism would require the notion that literature, especially, must be seen as integral and connected to the political economy of the era. To think of how to engage literature, Black culture, and the university differently means challenging and imagining anew the material world by studying what is made possible in spite of the complex collisions of individuation and oppression that racial capitalism consistently reproduces. This is about organizing, as much as it is about method. It is about being a part of the wider world in which literature and institutions are situated, rather than being apart from what is studied. This book is a history, an analysis, and indeed an interpretation of the inevitably incomplete, and often invisible, but invaluable work of making such attempts.

Acknowledgments

Writing this book has taught me that it is people, not institutions, who make literature, criticism, and modes of coming together. Acknowledgments tend to mystify this observation, in that they offer a means to trace institutional histories, as well as economies of status, privilege, and prestige. I highlight the people who made this work with me through their support—a support that went beyond the labor an institution was paying them to perform. These acknowledgments are as much a reflection of what goes unrewarded and even exploited as they are of the possibility that people create within the existing formation of higher education.

This book has been over a decade in the making. Herman Beavers was there for my earliest thinking on this material, and has offered encouragement throughout. Michael Kreyling reliably, generously, and generatively read every word of this project, and modeled an open disposition toward critical possibility that endorsed an investigation of the full ramifications of the material at hand. Houston A. Baker Jr. has shown me the relation of theoretical consideration and institutional history in feedback and in anecdote. Through his mentorship, I find new modes of kinship. Jonathan Flatley also has been a consistent interlocutor; his encouragement of my work on communist labor schools truly opened up the project.

At one point while writing this book, I worked with non-tenure-track faculty at Vanderbilt University to form a union. Our election was ultimately thwarted by university legal challenges, which included the spurious claim that as an academic adviser I was a manager, and thus ineligible to vote in the election. These organizing efforts and the university's response to them completely changed my thinking about how colleges and universities operate. Solidarity to all of those who made this attempt with me, and to those who embark on similarly fraught paths in the present and the future.

I thank my students at Vanderbilt University, the University of Southern Indiana, and Franklin & Marshall College for learning with me.

The following people have written letters for me, provided words of support, or offered time and assurances that helped sustain me in this project materially, emotionally, or otherwise: Paul Saint-Amour, Jed Esty, Margreta de Grazia, Ben Wiebracht, Colin Dayan, Jen Fay, Scott Juengel, Dana D. Nelson, Charlotte Pierce-Baker, Hortense Spillers, Mark Wollaeger, Candice Amich, Pavneet Aulakh, Donna Caplan, Elizabeth Covington, Jessica Burch, Matt Congdon, Hubert Cook, Alex Dubilet, Lisa Guenther, Jessie Hock, Sheba Karim, Donika Kelly, Jonathan Leavitt, Ken MacLeish, Jesse Montgomery, Rachael Pomerantz, Petal Samuel, Anand Taneja, Claire Barber-Stetson, Ryan Carr, Ali Dean, Jeffrey Neilson, Cody Reis, Sakina Hughes, Julia Kiesel, Genevieve Abravanel, Patrick Bernard, Van Gosse, Judith Mueller, Kendra Dority, Rakia Faber, Stefano Harney, Laura Heffernan, Ben Glaser, Erin Greer, Meta DuEwa Jones, Evan Kindley, Anjuli Fatima Raza Kolb, John Marx, Fred Moten, Thomas Raines, Kathy Lou Schultz, Dorothy Wang, and Sa Whitley.

Matt Suazo has been in sustained dialogue with drafts of this project as part of our writing group. Stephen Pasqualina provided careful and generative feedback on several of the chapters at a late stage.

Tim Burke and Rachel Sagner Buurma saw value in the wider import of this book and offered me the space and time to finish it. My conversations with them about our work at the Aydelotte Foundation have sustained me and left an imprint on this book. Candy Roeder offered crucial support in my new role while my attention was in far too many places during the pandemic.

At the University of Chicago Press, I am grateful to Alan Thomas for his steadfast support and patience with the project, as well as to Randy Petilos, who assuaged my nerves at key moments. The feedback from the two anonymous reviewers helped me to clarify the stakes of the project, and made this a much better book.

My sincere gratitude to the tireless efforts of librarians and archivists, especially those affiliated with the following libraries: the Schomburg Center for Research in Black Culture; the Tamiment Library at New York University; the Beinecke Rare Book and Manuscript Library; the Library of Congress; the Wisconsin Historical Society; the Department of Rare Books and Special Collections at the Princeton University Library; the Special Collections Research Center at Syracuse University; the Special Collections and University Archives at the University of Massachusetts Amherst; the Swarthmore College Peace Collection; the Special Collections and Archives in the John Hope and Aurelia E. Franklin Library at Fisk University; the University of Pennsylvania Libraries; the Jean and Alexander Heard Libraries at Vanderbilt University; the David L. Rice Library at the University of Southern Indiana; the Albin O. Kuhn Library at the University of Maryland, Baltimore County; the Franklin & Marshall College Library; and Swarthmore College Libraries.

My parents, Marcy and Jack Hines, have supported me my entire life in all endeavors, and have been patient when so many things led me to call them less than I should. I am fortunate to have Jeanne Finberg and Bob Stalker as loving and interested parents-in-law. Olive Dog Finberg-Hines is the best dog, and has offered an incredible amount of affective labor when times were tough. Zev Finberg-Hines, my child, has reminded me to dance, to smile, and to smell flowers, all while somehow growing so big and developing a voracious love for taking books off the shelf. I am so glad you could be "een" this book.

Finally, this book would not exist without Keegan Cook Finberg, my wife and partner. She has read every word here (and the ones that have long been deleted), has offered the most munificent feedback, and has always seen that there was something in this work, even when I did not. When I was unemployed for a year, she subsidized the writing of this book with what we called a Finberg-Hines Fellowship; that is, she worked and supported us while I finished a draft of the manuscript. She has made time for me by taking Olive for walks and caring for Zev. She has supported me at my lowest moments and through hundreds of rejections; she has celebrated and toasted me and shown me the value in making space for joy and occasion. Together we have built a life while I have written this book, and I will be forever indebted to the ways I can trace the beauty of what we have made through and between the words on these pages. This book is dedicated to her.

Baltimore
March 2021

Earlier versions of portions of chapter 2 appeared previously under the title "Vehicles of Periodization: Melvin B. Tolson, Allen Tate, and the New Critical Police," in *Criticism* 59, no. 3 (Summer 2017): 417–39.

Notes

INTRODUCTION

1. "Draft Statement on the Position of the Jefferson School on Instruction in the Arts: Prepared as a Basis for Faculty Discussion." Doxey A. Wilkerson Papers, Schomburg Center for Research in Black Culture, New York Public Library, 2.

2. "Draft Statement," 2.

3. W. E. B. Du Bois, "Criteria of Negro Art," 776.

4. Du Bois, "Criteria of Negro Art," 772.

5. For more on the isolation and later reception of the midcentury Black left, see Gerald Horne, *Black and Red*; Mary Helen Washington, *The Other Blacklist*; Lawrence Jackson, *The Indignant Generation*; William Maxwell, *F.B. Eyes*; Michael C. Dawson, *Blacks in and out of the Left*; James Edward Smethurst, *The New Red Negro*.

6. The language of "overrepresentation" of white norms points to Sylvia Wynter's thinking on the overrepresentation of European modes at the exclusion of other genres of being human. See Wynter, "Unsettling the Coloniality of Being/Power/Truth/Freedom."

7. Melinda Cooper, *Family Values*, 229.

8. Jacquelyn Dowd Hall, "The Long Civil Rights Movement and the Political Uses of the Past." Martha Biondi has called this the "Black Popular Front," and Robert Korstad, "civil rights unionism." Martha Biondi, *To Stand and Fight the Struggle for Civil Rights in Postwar New York City*; Robert Rodgers Korstad, *Civil Rights Unionism*. Also see Manning Marable, *Race, Reform, and Rebellion*.

9. Katherine McKittrick, *Demonic Grounds*, xii–xiii.

10. McKittrick, *Demonic Grounds*, 18.

11. Cleanth Brooks, "The Formalist Critics," 72.

12. Katherine McKittrick, *Dear Science and Other Stories*, 36.

13. Jodi Melamed, *Represent and Destroy*, 18–26.

14. Lester K. Spence, *Knocking the Hustle*, 5.

15. Cedric J. Robinson, *Black Marxism*, 171.

16. Robinson, *Black Marxism*, 167.

17. Robinson, *Black Marxism*, 170.

18. Clyde Woods, *Development Arrested*, 16, 29.

19. See Robin D. G. Kelley, *Hammer and Hoe*; Kate A. Baldwin, *Beyond the Color Line and the Iron Curtain*; Steven S. Lee, *The Ethnic Avant-Garde*; Carole Boyce Davies, *Left of Karl Marx*; Michael Denning, *The Cultural Front*; Erik S. McDuffie, *Sojourning for Freedom*; Dayo F. Gore, *Radicalism at the Crossroads*; Brian Dolinar, *The Black Cultural Front*.

20. Richard Wright, *Black Boy*, 339.

21. Harold Cruse, letter to James T. Harris, 1959. Harold Cruse Papers, Tamiment Library. New York University.

22. Baldwin, *Beyond the Color Line*, 29–30.

23. McKay quoted in Baldwin, *Beyond the Color Line*, 72.

24. Kate Baldwin recounts the complex dance performed by the CPUSA to both discourage an international Negro conference while also including Black representatives among its delegation. She writes: "The CPUSA, McKay contended, had strategically selected [Otto] Huiswood as their Negro delegate because he was a light-skinned black" (54). For more on the formation of the Black Belt thesis and its relationship to earlier forms of Black nationalism, see Robinson, *Black Marxism*, 218–28.

25. See Keith Gilyard, *Louise Thompson Patterson*.

26. Washington, *The Other Blacklist*, 11.

27. Ann Rivington, "The George Washington Carver School," *Daily Worker*, October 26, 1943, 7.

28. Robin D. G. Kelley, *Freedom Dreams*, 8.

29. John Oliver Killens, *Youngblood*, 136.

30. Lorraine Hansberry, letter to Edith Cohen, 1951. Lorraine Hansberry Papers, Schomburg Center for Research in Black Culture, New York Public Library.

31. Jonathan Flatley argues that in the late 1960s, Black auto workers in Detroit were able to effectively establish what he calls a "revolutionary counter-mood" by passing mimeographed newspapers "from hand to hand, from worker to worker." These techniques were essential not only because the writers of the paper, who were workers themselves, could grasp the "moods, experiences, and situations" of their fellow workers, but also because the "mode of circulation . . . works against a feeling of isolation and establishes a way of being-with that contrasts to the institutional logic of the plant and the union." Jonathan Flatley, "How A Revolutionary Counter-Mood Is Made," 519.

32. In 1950, Blyden Jackson makes the following argument about the limitations for literary study in historically Black colleges and universities:

Perhaps it may be argued in extenuation of our inertia as productive scholar-critics that our teaching loads are too great and our facilities for research too meager to permit us to do those things which we are really chagrined to leave undone. The argument is objectively sufficient. It faithfully describes current conditions as they statistically are. It is subjectively specious. For it says nothing about our will to change those conditions. It says nothing about our determination to see that integration in American education shall mean not only simply the one-way traffic of Negroes going to white schools, but also the Americanizing in terms of budgets, curricula, physical plants, labor practices, administrative attitudes and scholarly proficiency of Negro schools so that we may reasonably cherish the hope of finding, in some not too far distant day, a fair amount of people who will want a two-way pattern of integration that will let them come to "Negro" schools.

Part of Jackson's wider argument is that Black colleges had yet to make significant room for the study of Black literature, a fact confirmed in the work of John S. Lash, who intimates that courses in "Negro Literature" are often "remedial," and that they are not contextualized in terms of the wider body of American literature. Blyden Jackson, "An Essay in Criticism," 342; John S. Lash, "Current Opinion on the Teaching of the Literature of the Negro," 25.

33. For the story of the suppression of Hansberry's remarks, see Washington, *The Other Blacklist*, 242–53. For AMSAC's connection to the CIA, see Hugh Wilford, *The Mighty Wurlitzer*, 197–224.

34. To speculate on the imagined operations of these partial and compromised documents, I draw on an approach to the archive that Saidiya Hartman has termed "critical fabulation." Hartman later writes of this method that "the endeavor is to recover the insurgent ground . . . to illuminate the radical imagination." Hartman's fabulations focus respectively on enslaved people and criminalized Black women in New York in the first half of the twentieth century. There is a necessary difference between those subjects and the documents available to Hartman in her work, and those I write about here. Even though I discuss somewhat prominent Black writers in the mid-twentieth century, the force of the law and of intellectual authority, and the related weights of racism, sexism, and homophobia, have made it difficult to recognize, recover, and illuminate what Black left critics imagined was possible for cultural criticism. See Hartman, "Venus in Two Acts," 11; and Hartman, *Wayward Lives, Beautiful Experiments*, 8. Also see Brent Hayes Edwards, "The Taste of the Archive."

35. See Gore, *Radicalism at the Crossroads*, 130–60; McDuffie, *Sojourning for Freedom*, 193–220.

36. For more on the development of the Black student movement, see Martha Biondi, *The Black Revolution on Campus*; Stefan M. Bradley, *Upending the Ivory Tower*; Ibram X. Kendi, *The Black Campus Movement*.

37. Robin D. G. Kelley, "Black Study, Black Struggle."

38. Addison Gayle Jr., *The Black Situation*, 177.

39. Gayle Jr., *The Black Situation*, 181.

40. For a thorough reading and critical review of Reed's novel, see Lavelle Porter, *The Blackademic Life*, 128–37.

41. Ishmael Reed, *Japanese by Spring*, 49.

42. One recent example of this phenomenon comes from the Pulitzer Prize–winning poet Jericho Brown, who writes:

> Dear Cleanth,
>
> I'm sorry, but seeing the poem as artifact without seeing the history and culture embedded in the poet suggests we read without any history at all. This may be a convenient way of reading for those who have a history they can't face.
>
> Good manners move beyond the professional into the reading of the work when writing the poem about race. Even Audre Lorde and Lucille Clifton wouldn't be poets we know and love if they treated black women badly.
>
> Missing you,
> Jericho

Jericho Brown, "You Can't Love Me If You Don't Love Politically," 232–33.

43. David E. Chinitz, *Which Sin to Bear?* 139.

44. Baldwin, *Beyond the Color Line*, 95.

45. Quoted in Biondi, *The Black Revolution on Campus*, 14.

46. Penny M. Von Eschen, *Race against Empire*; Mary L. Dudziak, *Cold War Civil Rights*; Nikhil Pal Singh, *Black Is a Country*.

47. Naomi Murakawa, *The First Civil Right*, 27.

48. Gunnar Myrdal, *American Dilemma*, xlvii. Murakawa, *The First Civil Right*, 27.

49. David Levering Lewis, *W. E. B. Du Bois*, 445–51.

50. Nick Mitchell, "(Critical Ethnic Studies) Intellectual"; Nick Mitchell, "Disciplinary Matters."

51. Myrdal, *American Dilemma*, 1021.

52. Myrdal, *American Dilemma*, 1021.

53. Keeanga-Yamahtta Taylor, *Race for Profit*, 175.

54. Denning, *The Cultural Front*, 46.

55. See Edward Humes, "How the GI Bill Shunted Blacks into Vocational Training"; Ira Katznelson, *When Affirmative Action Was White*, 113–41.

56. Jane Bond, letter to Lorraine Hansberry, December. 26, 1951. Lorraine Hansberry Papers, Schomburg Center for Research in Black Culture, New York Public Library.

57. For more history of Black students on campus in the mid-twentieth century, see Biondi, *The Black Revolution on Campus*, 16–37.

58. Sara Ahmed, *On Being Included*; Devon Carbado and Mitu Gulati, "Working Identity"; Roderick A. Ferguson, *The Reorder of Things*.

59. See, for example, Melamed, *Represent and Destroy*; Ferguson, *The Reorder of Things*; Abigail Boggs and Nick Mitchell, "Critical University Studies and the Crisis Consensus"; Tressie McMillan Cottom, *Lower Ed*; Ashon Crawley, "University."

60. Craig Steven Wilder, *Ebony & Ivy*, 11; Sharon Stein, "A Colonial History of the Higher Education Present: Rethinking Land-Grant Institutions through Processes of Accumulation and Relations of Conquest."

61. Abigail Boggs, Eli Meyerhoff, Nick Mitchell, and Zach Schwartz-Weinstein, "Abolitionist University Studies: An Invitation."

62. Christopher Newfield argues: "If the university could unify society, it would be at that society's center. If the humanities could offer a unified culture, it would put itself at the center of the university. If New Criticism could offer a means to this unity, English would lead the humanities. . . . If the humanities was to offer the university a way of unifying culture, New Criticism offered to the humanities the unifying methodology." Christopher Newfield, *Ivy and Industry*, 147.

63. John Guillory, *Cultural Capital*, xi.

64. Hershel Parker, *Flawed Texts and Verbal Icons*, 142. For an extended gloss on this passage, see Parker quoted in Gerald Graff, *Professing Literature*, 233.

65. Michael Kreyling, *Inventing Southern Literature*, 6. For more on the relationship between the Agrarian movement and the New Criticism, see Angie Maxwell, *The Indicted South*, 87–166.

66. Robert Penn Warren, "The Briar Patch," 264.

67. Thomas Jefferson, *Notes on the State of Virginia*, 150.

68. Jefferson, *Notes on the State of Virginia*, 151.

69. Lindon Barrett, *Blackness and Value*, 52.

70. Cooper, *Family Values*, 232–39; James M. Buchanan and Nicos E. Devletoglou, *Academia in Anarchy: An Economic Diagnosis*.

71. Nancy MacLean, *Democracy in Chains*, 32–34. For more on the impact of the Agrarians on US conservative thought and politics, see Paul V. Murphy, *The Rebuke of History*.

72. These notable exceptions include Terry Eagleton, *The Function of Criticism*; Evan Watkins, *Work Time*; Guillory, *Cultural Capital*.

73. Virginia Jackson, *Dickinson's Misery*, 93.

74. Marjorie Levinson, "What Is New Formalism?" 563.

75. I note here a long history of scholars commenting on the dead and alive dimension of the New Criticism. For example, Douglas Mao wrote in 1996: "It is presently a commonplace among scholars and teachers of literature that New Criticism is, and has been for decades now, both dead and alive." I invoke a weak association between the New Critical vampire-like grip on the discipline of literary studies to Marx's description of capital as "dead labour, that, vampire-like, only lives by sucking living labour, and lives the more, the more labour it sucks." For additional examples of the New Criticism's "dead and alive" status, see Richard Chase, "New vs. Ordealist," 12; David Hirsch, "Penelope's Web," 126; Douglas Mao, "The New Critics and the Text-Object," 227; Walter Kalaidjian, *The Edge of Modernism*, 128–56.

76. Evan Kindley, *Poet-Critics and the Administration of Culture*; Merve Emre, *Paraliterary*; Joseph North, *Literary Criticism*; Christopher Findeisen, "Injuries

of Class: Mass Education and the American Campus Novel"; Rachel Sagner Buurma and Laura Heffernan, *The Teaching Archive*.

77. Laura Heffernan, "New Disciplinary History."

78. Dorothy Wang, *Thinking Its Presence*; Sonya Posmentier, "Lyric Reading in the Black Ethnographic Archive"; Barrett, *Blackness and Value*.

79. Sarah Brouillette, *UNESCO and the Fate of the Literary*; Juliana Spahr, *Du Bois's Telegram*; Andrew Rubin, *Archives of Authority*; Maxwell, *F.B. Eyes*. Also see Frances Stonor Saunders, *The Cultural Cold War*.

80. La paperson, *A Third University Is Possible*, xxiii.

81. Sylvia Wynter, "On How We Mistook the Map for the Territory and Re-Imprisoned Ourselves in Our Unbearable Wrongness of Being, of Désêtre," 108.

82. Roderick A. Ferguson, *We Demand*, 14–34.

83. Stefano Harney and Fred Moten, *The Undercommons*, 42.

84. McKittrick, *Demonic Grounds*, 21.

85. US Department of Justice, "W. E. B. Du Bois," FBI Internal case file no. 100–99729.

86. Here echoes the question of Sylvia Wynter written to her Stanford colleagues in the wake of the 1992 Los Angeles uprising: "This is the point of my letter to you, why should the classifying acronym [No Humans Involved] with its reflex anti-Black male behaviour-prescriptions, have been so actively held and deployed by the judicial officers of Los Angeles, and therefore by 'the brightest and the best' graduates of both the professional and non-professional schools of the university system of the United States? By those whom we ourselves would have educated?" Sylvia Wynter, "No Humans Involved," 43.

CHAPTER 1

1. Cleanth Brooks and Robert Penn Warren, *Understanding Poetry*, iv.

2. Harvard Committee, *General Education In A Free Society*, 108. Also see Catherine Liu, *American Idyll*, 58–59; Mark Garrett Cooper and John Marx, *Media U*, 113.

3. Gerald Horne, *Black and Red*; Penny M. Von Eschen, *Race against Empire*; Mary L. Dudziak, *Cold War Civil Rights*; Carol Anderson, *Eyes off the Prize*; Nikhil Pal Singh, *Black Is a Country*; Erik S. McDuffie, "Black and Red: Black Liberation, the Cold War, and the Horne Thesis." For a further elaboration of these contradictions in "hot" deployments of US militarism in Asian geographies during the Cold War, see Christine Hong, *A Violent Peace*, 1–22.

4. John R. Thelin, *A History of American Higher Education*, 268.

5. David Caute quoted in Mary Helen Washington, *The Other Blacklist*, 3.

6. As Sarah Ehlers has established, Martha Millet, a CPUSA-affiliated literary critic who taught a workshop at the Jefferson School, would make a similar connection in the 1950s in an unpublished essay titled "Poets and Poverty." Of

the New Critics, Millet writes, "Capitalist values applied all along the line from the commodity market to the market of ideas which could be handled like commodities." Sarah Ehlers, *Left of Poetry*, 211.

7. Karl Marx, *Capital*, 165.

8. Arthur Ripstein, "Commodity Fetishism," 736; William Clare Roberts, *Marx's Inferno*, 83; Denise Ferreira da Silva, "Many Hundred Thousand Bodies Later: An Analysis of the 'Legacy' of the International Criminal Tribunal for Rwanda," 174. Also see Sara-Maria Sorentino, "The Abstract Slave: Anti-Blackness and Marx's Method."

9. Brooks and Warren, *Understanding Poetry*, 18–19.

10. Lisa Lowe, *The Intimacies of Four Continents*, 4.

11. Twelve Southerners, "Introduction: A Statement of Principles," li.

12. Paul Keith Conkin, *The Southern Agrarians*, 71.

13. Twelve Southerners, "Introduction: A Statement of Principles," xlv.

14. Twelve Southerners, "Introduction," xlv.

15. For more on the historical development of the plantocratic ruling class, especially in the South, see Clyde Woods, *Development Arrested*.

16. W. E. B. Du Bois, *Black Reconstruction in America*, 29.

17. For more on Warren's "directed amnesia" with regard to Du Bois, see Michael Kreyling, *The South That Wasn't There*, 54–64.

18. Michael Kreyling, *Inventing Southern Literature*; Paul V. Murphy, *The Rebuke of History*.

19. H. L. Mencken, *A Carnival of Buncombe*, 167.

20. For more on the Agrarians on Scopes and Mencken, see Mark Jancovich, *The Cultural Politics of the New Criticism*, 21–29; Edward S. Shapiro, "The Southern Agrarians, H. L. Mencken, and the Quest for Southern Identity."

21. Twelve Southerners, "Introduction: A Statement of Principles," xlviii. Paul V. Murphy points out that Ransom wrote the volume's introduction and the remaining contributors were asked to express their support. Murphy, *The Rebuke of History*, 17.

22. Denise Ferreira da Silva, *Toward a Global Idea of Race*, xiii.

23. Ferreira da Silva, *Toward a Global Idea of Race*, 52–53. Also see Alexander G. Weheliye, *Habeas Viscus*.

24. David Lloyd has suggested that "aesthetic philosophy has functioned as a regulative discourse of the human on which the modern conception of the political and racial order of modernity rests." David Lloyd, *Under Representation*, 3.

25. See Chandan Reddy, *Freedom with Violence*, 20–48.

26. Allen Tate, *Memoirs and Opinions: 1926–1974*, 28. See also Angie Maxwell, *The Indicted South*, 93.

27. Donald Davidson, "Regionalism and Education," 312.

28. Michael Bibby, "The Disinterested and Fine: New Negro Renaissance Poetry and the Racial Formation of Modernist Studies," 487.

29. Brooks and Warren, *Understanding Poetry*, 18, 9.

30. Lindon Barrett, *Blackness and Value*, 133–34.

31. Lisa Marie Cacho, *Social Death*, 13.

32. Barrett, *Blackness and Value*, 147; Also see Nahum Dimitri Chandler, *X: The Problem of the Negro as a Problem for Thought*; Ferreira da Silva, *Toward a Global Idea of Race*.

33. For me, this is not a general critique of poetic autonomy, but a claim about the particular Agrarian–New Critical version of the concept. Michael Szalay, *Hip Figures*, 12. Also see Paul Bové, who suggests that "one can trace how the Agrarian resistance to the terms offered by the core to the marginal South transformed itself into the literary critical institutions." Paul A. Bové, "Agriculture and Academe: America's Southern Question," 193.

34. Stanley Kunitz, "Bronze by Gold," 52.

35. Kunitz, "Bronze by Gold," 52. Emphasis mine.

36. Kunitz, "Bronze by Gold," 55.

37. Kunitz, "Bronze by Gold," 56.

38. William Jay Smith, "Performers and Poets," 534.

39. Also see Mary Helen Washington, who argues that Elizabeth Lawrence, Brooks's white editor of *Maud Martha*, "used the coded term 'universal' to warn Brooks against too much emphasis on racial issues and 'possible stereotyping of whites' in her future writing: She hoped that the poet's future work would have a universal perspective." Washington, *The Other Blacklist*, 189.

40. Hoyt W. Fuller, "Towards a Black Aesthetic," 152.

41. Brooks and Warren, *Understanding Poetry*, iv.

42. John Crowe Ransom, "Reconstructed but Unregenerate," 26–27.

43. Singh, *Black Is a Country*, 103.

44. Kate A. Baldwin, *Beyond the Color Line and the Iron Curtain*, 86–149. Lee, *The Ethnic Avant-Garde*, 119–49.

45. Jodi Melamed, *Represent and Destroy*, 19.

46. Melamed, *Represent and Destroy*, 13.

47. Melamed, *Represent and Destroy*, 18–26.

48. Howard Winant, *The World Is a Ghetto*, 160.

49. Du Bois, *Black Reconstruction in America*, 700.

50. David R. Roediger, *The Wages of Whiteness*.

51. Winant, *The World Is a Ghetto*, 161.

52. In *Eyes off the Prize*, Carol Anderson argues that Truman was "simply not philosophically or psychologically equipped to accept true black equality," and that "his disdain for social equality was a matter of public record." Groups on the left saw this disdain, despite some of Truman's action on civil rights, as explicitly aligning him with the Dixiecrats, to whom some historians claim he was opposed. For example, Naomi Murakawa cites "a 1951 political cartoon in the *Daily Worker* [that] depicted 'Dixiecrats,' the Supreme Court, and the Truman White House all together with their hands of 'white supremacy' flipping the switch to execute Willie McGee." Howard Winant also confirms this larger consolidation,

suggesting that the Dixiecrat revolt didn't divide the South as much as it reinforced the South's "solid" nature, meaning that the major parties had to remain
"moderate" on race in order to establish a ruling coalition. Anderson, *Eyes off
the Prize*, 155; Naomi Murakawa, *The First Civil Right*, 56; Winant, *The World Is a
Ghetto*, 161. Also see Szalay, *Hip Figures*, 5, 38.

53. Dudziak, *Cold War Civil Rights*, 6.

54. Washington, *The Other Blacklist*, 18.

55. United States, *Higher Education for American Democracy*, I.14.

56. Thelin, *A History of American Higher Education*, 268–70. Also see Julie A.
Reuben and Linda Perkins, "Introduction: Commemorating the Sixtieth Anniversary of the President's Commission Report, 'Higher Education for Democracy,'"; Claire Krendl Gilbert and Donald E. Heller, "Access, Equity, and
Community Colleges: The Truman Commission and Federal Higher Education
Policy from 1947 to 2011"; Nicholas M. Strohl, "The Truman Commission and
the Unfulfilled Promise of American Higher Education."

57. Strohl, "The Truman Commission and the Unfulfilled Promise of American Higher Education," 311.

58. United States, *Higher Education for American Democracy*, I.34–35, II.36.

59. Strohl, "The Truman Commission and the Unfulfilled Promise of American Higher Education," 348.

60. Edward Humes, "How the GI Bill Shunted Blacks into Vocational Training," 95.

61. Ira Katznelson, *When Affirmative Action Was White*, 132.

62. John Crowe Ransom, "Criticism as Pure Speculation," 108–9.

63. For the past-oriented perspective, see Robert H. Brinkmeyer, *The Fourth
Ghost*, 53; For the forward-looking perspective, see Tobin Siebers, *Cold War Crit-
icism and the Politics of Skepticism*, 31; and Deborah Nelson, *Pursuing Privacy in
Cold War America*, 108.

64. Ransom, "Reconstructed but Unregenerate," 14.

65. Evan Kindley, "Big Criticism." See also Evan Kindley, *Poet-Critics and the
Administration of Culture*.

66. Gerald Graff, *Professing Literature*, 173.

67. Graff, *Professing Literature*, 178.

68. United States, *Higher Education for American Democracy*, I.6. Emphasis
mine.

69. Ransom, "Reconstructed but Unregenerate," 25.

70. In 1978, Supreme Court Justice Lewis Powell would also draw on the idea
of white minoritarianism in his defining opinion in *Regents of the University of
California v. Bakke*. Powell's decision limited the implementation of affirmative
action by ruling unconstitutional a quota system for admissions, at the same
time as it codified diversity as a "compelling state interest" as long as diversity
reflected the fact that minority groups could not receive direct preferential
treatment. Roderick Ferguson suggests that this argument grew from Powell's

famous memorandum in which he implies that "social movements against racism, capitalism, patriarchy, and environmental abuse . . . had worsened the conditions of the real change agents and the most important people in society, one of society's most crucial minorities: corporations" (45). Ferguson points to the work of Anders Walker, who suggests that Powell's Southern background leads to the view that white people and corporations can be minorities. One essay that Walker points to in the development of his argument is the Agrarian Robert Penn Warren's "Briar Patch" in *I'll Take My Stand*, which again puts the Agrarian New Critics as a crucial forebear to the development of diversity logics even in the post-1960s era. See Ferguson, *We Demand*, 44–47; Anders Walker, "Diversity's Strange Career," 657–59.

71. Paul A. Bové, *Intellectuals in Power*, 54; Stephen Schryer, *Fantasies of the New Class*; Szalay, *Hip Figures*; Alan Liu, *The Laws of Cool*.

72. Christopher Newfield, *Ivy and Industry*, 146–47.

73. Lawrence H. Schwartz, *Creating Faulkner's Reputation*, 140.

74. Joseph North, *Literary Criticism*, 44.

75. Geoffrey Galt Harpham, *The Humanities and the Dream of America*, 161–62.

76. Harvard Committee, *General Education In A Free Society*, 108.

77. Cooper and Marx, *Media U*, 112.

78. Quoted in Murphy, *The Rebuke of History*, 89.

79. United States, *Higher Education for American Democracy*, I.65.

80. United States, I.55.

81. United States, *Higher Education for American Democracy*, I.55.

82. Bové, *Intellectuals in Power*, 76.

83. United States, *Higher Education for American Democracy*, I.103.

84. William Maxwell makes clear that the early readers of the FBI were not doctrinaire New Critics. In fact, he claims that "in logical distinction to the New Critical drift of CIA reading, FBI reading shares a fair bit with the most relevant academic criticism of its pre-New Critical origin," in that they selected "literary fact over value" (142–43). Yet he suggests that by the 1950s, "biohistorical and novice New Critical [language] would not seem exceptional in FBI reading," and therefore that "FBI ghostreaders joined their academic colleagues in serving as switch-hitting critic-scholars" (146–47). The fact that the 1950s mark the shift for Maxwell indicates how what had been first understood as a potentially elite, abstract method—which the CIA had happily embraced—had come to be perceived as democratic and in the national interest. See William J. Maxwell, *F.B. Eyes*, 127–74.

85. R. P. Blackmur, "A Burden for Critics," 179.

86. Blackmur, "A Burden for Critics," 178.

87. Blackmur, "A Burden for Critics," 175

88. Grant Webster, *The Republic of Letters*, 105.

89. Ehlers, *Left of Poetry*, 211.

90. Karl Shapiro, letter to the editor, *Baltimore Sun*, February 25, 1949. This letter is also cited in two comprehensive articles about the Bollingen controversy. See Karen Leick, "Ezra Pound v. 'The Saturday Review of Literature,'"; Thomas Daniel Young, "The Little Houses against the Great."

91. William Barrett, "A Prize for Ezra Pound," 345, 347.

92. This aligns with what Graff identifies as a reconciliation of the conflict between scholars and critics during the 1940s and 1950s. "More precisely," Graff writes, "criticism and history were but aspects of a total activity of literary understanding, so that potentially any professor was both critic and scholar, and the sense of a necessary antagonism between these functions began to wane." To discover something in the poem is to position criticism as a "fact-finding" mission as much as an evaluative one. Graff, *Professing Literature*, 183.

93. Quoted in Greg Barnhisel, *James Laughlin, New Directions, and the Remaking of Ezra Pound*, 120.

94. Lloyd, *Under Representation*, 3.

95. William E. Cain, "Notes toward a History of Anti-Criticism," 43.

96. Allen Tate, "A Note on Autotelism," 13; Cleanth Brooks, "List of 'Wicked Esthetes' Wanted," 24.

97. Austin Warren, "The Achievement of Some Recent Critics," 239.

98. Nancy MacLean, *Democracy in Chains*; Murphy, *The Rebuke of History*; Maxwell, *The Indicted South*; Newfield, *Ivy and Industry*, 147.

99. J. Saunders Redding, "Book Review: "Songs of Creations" Is a Refreshing Book of Poems," A5.

100. Redding, A5.

101. Langston Hughes, "World's Most Exciting Singer Poses Questions of Art, Politics, Race," 6.

102. Hughes, "World's Most Exciting Singer," 6.

103. Hughes, "World's Most Exciting Singer," 6.

104. Hughes, "World's Most Exciting Singer," 6.

105. Hughes seems to be invoking Pound in this column, in line with the wider discourse around the Bollingen Prize. That is, his grief is less with Pound himself and more with the entities—the New Criticism and the federal government, as well as white supremacist organizations—that endorse and authorize Pound. In these years, Hughes resumed a friendly correspondence with Pound for the first time since 1935. In fact, Hughes met with Pound for the first time in person while doing a reading at St. Elizabeth's at the invitation of Prentiss Taylor in 1950. Afterwards, both writers sent their work to each other. See David E. Roessel, "'A Racial Act': The Letters of Langston Hughes and Ezra Pound"; Arnold Rampersad, *The Life of Langston Hughes, Volume 2*, 184–85.

106. Shana L. Redmond, *Everything Man*, xiv.

CHAPTER 2

1. Melvin B. Tolson, *Harlem Gallery*, book 1, 336.
2. Tolson, *Harlem Gallery*, book 1, 335.
3. Tolson, *Harlem Gallery*, book 1, 335.
4. Tolson, *Harlem Gallery*, book 1, 337.
5. Dudley Randall, "Melvin B. Tolson: Portrait of a Poet as a Raconteur," 56.
6. Rampersad famously claimed that Tolson "gentrified his aesthetic into High Modernism" from a "militant pro-Marxism." Arnold Rampersad, *The Life of Langston Hughes, Volume II*, 193, 234. For more critical perspectives on Tolson, including those from Haki Madhubuti, see Gary Lenhart, "Caviar and Cabbage: The Voracious Appetite of Melvin Tolson," 79.
7. Melvin B. Tolson, letter to Allen Tate, March 15, 1950. Allen Tate Papers, Department of Rare Books and Special Collections, Princeton University Library (henceforth ATP).
8. Robert M. Farnsworth, *Melvin B. Tolson*, 139.
9. Robert M. Farnsworth, "Introduction," in *Caviar and Cabbage*, 4.
10. Michael Bérubé, *Marginal Forces / Cultural Centers*; Aldon L. Nielsen, "Melvin B. Tolson and the Deterritorialization of Modernism"; Kathy Lou Schultz, *The Afro-Modernist Epic and Literary History*.
11. Matthew Hart, *Nations of Nothing But Poetry*, 144.
12. Hart, *Nations of Nothing But Poetry*, 149.
13. W. E. B. Du Bois, *The Souls of Black Folk*, 5.
14. Du Bois, *The Souls of Black Folk*, 5.
15. Allen Tate, "Present Function of Literary Criticism," 203.
16. Tate, "Present Function of Literary Criticism," 202.
17. Melvin B. Tolson, letter to Allen Tate, March 15, 1950. ATP.
18. Aldon Nielsen has argued that the *Libretto* is a signal for "a decolonizing of American letters." See Nielsen, "Melvin B. Tolson and the Deterritorialization of Modernism," 244.
19. Robin D. G. Kelley, *Freedom Dreams*, 1–12.
20. Quoted in Farnsworth, *Melvin B. Tolson*, 214.
21. See Ferreira da Silva, *Toward a Global Idea of Race*, xvii–xli.
22. Melvin B. Tolson, "Libretto for the Republic of Liberia," l. 42.
23. Allen Tate, preface to *Libretto for the Republic of Liberia* by Melvin Tolson, ix.
24. Tate, preface, viii.
25. Melvin B. Tolson, letter to Allen Tate, February 19, 1949. ATP.
26. Tate, preface, viii.
27. Melvin B. Tolson, letter to Allen Tate, March 15, 1950. ATP.
28. Tolson, letter to Tate, March 15, 1950.
29. Du Bois, *The Souls of Black Folk*, 11.
30. See Nahum Dimitri Chandler, *X: The Problem of the Negro as a Problem for Thought*, 4.

31. Du Bois, *The Souls of Black Folk*, 11.

32. Melvin B. Tolson, letter to Allen Tate, March 4, 1950. Melvin Beaunorus Tolson Papers, Manuscript Division, Library of Congress (henceforth MTP).

33. Stoddard's biracialism sought to fully instantiate in the United States what Du Bois had decades earlier referred to as the "color line." Du Bois and Stoddard debated in person about precisely this issue on a number of occasions, the debate at the Chicago Coliseum on March 17, 1929, marking Du Bois's most sensational success. The headline in the *Chicago Defender* read, "Du Bois Shatters Stoddard's Cultural Theories." Tolson may be referencing this specifically, thus providing a clue as to the type of thinking he would target in his engagement with Tate's "sociologist." See Robert Vitalis, *White World Order, Black Power Politics*, 70; Matthew Pratt Guterl, *The Color of Race in America, 1900–1940*, 142–44.

34. Chandler, *X: The Problem of the Negro as a Problem for Thought*, 5.

35. Melvin B. Tolson, letter to Allen Tate, October 25, 1950. ATP.

36. Tate expressed "anxiety" and confusion about writing a preface for a poem that is a national celebration of Liberia. See Melvin B. Tolson, letter to Allen Tate, May 9, 1949. ATP.

37. Tate, preface, vii.

38. For more on Tate and Crane's attractive and repellant relationship, see Langdon Hammer, *Hart Crane and Allen Tate*, xiii.

39. Melvin B. Tolson, "Excerpts from a Letter to Allen Tate." Typescript. MTP.

40. Tolson, "Excerpts from a Letter to Allen Tate."

41. Gunnar Myrdal, *American Dilemma*, xlvii.

42. Oliver C. Cox, *Caste, Class, and Race*, 333, 332.

43. Bryan Wagner, *Disturbing the Peace*, 126.

44. Naomi Murakawa, *The First Civil Right*, 13–15.

45. W. E. B. Du Bois, *Black Reconstruction in America*, 55–84.

46. Allen Tate, "Narcissus as Narcissus," 595.

47. Tolson, "Excerpts from a Letter to Allen Tate."

48. Tolson, "Excerpts from a Letter to Allen Tate."

49. Tolson, "Excerpts from a Letter to Allen Tate."

50. Admittedly, the phrasing about the relation of the "for" to the pro and con is somewhat ambiguous. My reading that "for" is connected to positive definition is affirmed by a differently drafted version of Tolson's sentence. It reads: "<u>For</u> is always <u>pro</u> and never <u>con</u>, and this is the way to the <u>adola mentis</u>." Tolson, "Excerpts from a Letter to Allen Tate." Tolson may be quietly drawing on Cox's critique of Myrdal here. Cox argues that "attacking beliefs by negation," such as the morality of racism, "is obviously a negative procedure—sometimes even a futile one." Cox suggests instead, as Tolson does, that a "positive program . . . calls for an attack upon the source of the beliefs." See Cox, *Caste, Class, and Race*, 533–34.

51. Houston A. Baker Jr., *I Don't Hate the South*, 125.

52. Melvin Tolson, "E. & O. E.," 147.

53. Francis Bacon, *The New Organon*, book 1, section 38.

54. Melvin B. Tolson, letter to Allen Tate, November 28, 1950. MTP.

55. Tolson, "E. & O. E," ll. 25–44.

56. See Bacon, *The New Organon*, book 1, section 40.

57. Tolson, "Libretto for the Republic of Liberia," 205n619.

58. Tolson, "Libretto for the Republic of Liberia," 205n619.

59. Tolson, "Libretto for the Republic of Liberia," 205n619.

60. Tate, "Narcissus as Narcissus," 597.

61. Tolson, "Excerpts from a Letter to Allen Tate."

62. Tate, "Narcissus as Narcissus," 597.

63. Tolson, "Excerpts from a Letter to Allen Tate."

64. Tolson, "Excerpts from a Letter to Allen Tate."

65. On this historical point, see Du Bois, *Black Reconstruction*; and Clyde Woods, *Development Arrested*.

66. Tolson, *Libretto*, l. 198; Tolson, "Excerpts from a Letter to Allen Tate."

67. Tolson, "Excerpts from a Letter to Allen Tate."

68. Cox, *Caste, Class, and Race*, 519.

69. Melvin B. Tolson, letter to Allen Tate, November 18, 1950. MTP.

70. Joseph North argues that "Kant authorizes the famously radical New Critical attempt to secure the autonomy and self-sufficiency of the aesthetic object." Joseph North, *Literary Criticism*, 43. For more on the New Criticism's relation to Kant and its aesthetic holism, see René Wellek, "The New Criticism: Pro and Contra," 616–17; R. K. Meiners, "Marginal Men and Centers of Learning: New Critical Rhetoric and Critical Politics," 130; Nicholas Gaskill, "The Close and the Concrete: Aesthetic Formalism in Context."

71. Tolson, "Excerpts from a Letter to Allen Tate."

72. Dionne Brand, *A Map to the Door of No Return*, 2.

73. Tolson, "Libretto for the Republic of Liberia," ll. 2, 14.

74. Tolson, "Libretto," ll. 53–55.

75. Both Brent Edwards and Fred Moten have commented on the ways that Black writers' lyrical engagement with Black musical form presents a challenge to received lyric definitions. See Brent Hayes Edwards, *Epistrophies*; Fred Moten, *Black and Blur*, 1–27.

76. Tolson, "Libretto," ll. 520–24.

77. Peter Middleton, "Poetry, Physics, and the Scientific Attitude at Mid-Century," 151.

78. Tolson, "Libretto," ll. 149–52.

79. Cox, *Caste, Class, and Race*, 332.

80. Tolson, "Libretto," ll. 756–58.

81. This definition of abolition resonates with how Gaye Theresa Johnson and Alex Lubin have recently defined abolition:

Abolition—the destruction of racial regimes and racial capitalism—entails not only the end of racial slavery, racial segregation, and racism, but also the abolition of a capitalist order that has always been racial, and that not only extracts life from Black bodies, but dehumanizes all workers while colonizing indigenous lands and Incarcerating surplus bodies.

Gaye Theresa Johnson and Alex Lubin, "Introduction," 12.

82. Tolson, "Libretto," ll. 764–70.

83. Cedric J. Robinson, *Black Marxism*, 314.

84. See Bérubé, *Marginal Forces / Cultural Centers*, 181.

85. David Llorens, "Seeking a New Image: Writers Converge at Fisk University," 62.

86. Llorens, "Seeking a New Image," 62.

87. Llorens, "Seeking a New Image," 63.

88. Llorens, "Seeking a New Image," 63.

89. Quoted in Farnsworth, "Introduction," 4.

CHAPTER 3

1. Mozell E. Hill, letter to Langston Hughes, June 27, 1950. Langston Hughes Papers, 1862–1980. James Weldon Johnson Collection in the Yale Collection of American Literature, Beinecke Rare Book and Manuscript Library, Yale University (henceforth LHP). Mozell E. Hill, telegram to Langston Hughes, November 5, 1950. LHP.

2. Mozell E. Hill, letter to Langston Hughes, November 6, 1950. LHP.

3. Kenneth W. Warren, *What Was African American Literature?* 44–80.

4. Lawrence Jackson, *The Indignant Generation*, 331–33.

5. Mary Helen Washington, *The Other Blacklist*, 19.

6. Jackson, *The Indignant Generation*, 331.

7. Langston Hughes, "Some Practical Observations: A Colloquy," 309.

8. Hughes, "Some Practical Observations," 309. It is worth noting that the FBI would end up opening files on Frazier, Franklin, and Drake. That, in and of itself, is not evidence of subversive activity; as Mary Helen Washington notes in writing about the same issue of *Phylon*, "African Americans were, by virtue of their blackness, subversives in the Cold War." Mary Helen Washington, "Alice Childress, Lorraine Hansberry, and Claudia Jones: Black Women Write the Popular Front," 184.

9. Stefano Harney and Fred Moten, *The Undercommons*, 26.

10. The significant lack of access to the material and institutional realms of the literary world—publishing houses, universities, journals—was something that other Black midcentury observers identified as a major obstacle for establishing Black literature and Black literary critical culture. See, for instance, Zora Neale Hurston, "What White Publishers Won't Print"; John S. Lash, "What Is 'Negro Literature'?"

11. Blyden Jackson, "An Essay in Criticism," 338.

12. Jackson, "An Essay in Criticism," 342.

13. Quoted in Thomas A. Underwood, *Allen Tate*, 291. Tate oversells his tolerance for social exchanges between Black and white people in more cosmopolitan spaces, particularly when white women are present. Underwood mentions that Tate once refused to meet Countee Cullen in France because Tate would be with the poet Léonie Adams.

14. Though he situates Southern anxieties about communism and racism within a long history of Southern arguments about the threat of so-called outside agitators disrupting a white supremacist social order, Jeff Woods argues that Scottsboro both galvanized and was a catalyst for the particular dimensions of the Southern red scare. It is worth noting, however, that there were critiques from the left within the CPUSA regarding its openness to interracial marriage and relationships. Kate Weigand writes that in 1934 Black women requested that the party revise its policy on interracial relationships, because relationships between Black men and white women reflected larger patterns of "white chauvinism." There is a clear qualitative difference and political valence to these challenges—the former an instance of racism, the second a critique of its multiform instantiations. See Jeff R. Woods, *Black Struggle, Red Scare*, 19–21; Kate Weigand, *Red Feminism*, 99–100.

15. Michael Bibby, "The Disinterested and Fine: New Negro Renaissance Poetry and the Racial Formation of Modernist Studies," 486.

16. Bibby, "The Disinterested and Fine," 486.

17. Underwood, *Allen Tate*, 292. Also see Eugene D. Levy, *James Weldon Johnson, Black Leader, Black Voice*, 328.

18. Arnold Rampersad, *The Life of Langston Hughes: Volume I*, 231.

19. Langston Hughes, letter to Arna Bontemps, March 7, 1953. LHP.

20. Arnold Rampersad, *The Life of Langston Hughes, Volume II*, 206.

21. Jackson, *The Indignant Generation*, 288. For other accounts that suggest a resonance between Baldwin's "Everybody's Protest Novel" and the New Criticism, see Kevin Birmingham, "No Name in the South: James Baldwin and the Monuments of Identity"; Adam Hammond, "Through Fields of Cacophanous Modern Masters: James Baldwin and New Critical Modernism."

22. James Baldwin, "Everybody's Protest Novel," 33.

23. Langston Hughes, "The Negro Artist and the Racial Mountain," 1321.

24. Baldwin, "Everybody's Protest Novel," 29.

25. Langston Hughes, *Selected Letters of Langston Hughes*, 317.

26. Michel Fabre, *From Harlem to Paris*, 249. For his lengthy denial of CIA involvement, see Richard Gibson, "Richard Wright's 'Island of Hallucination' and the 'Gibson Affair.'" Charisse Burden-Stelly suggests, however, that "a multitude of documents are available that corroborate Gibson's involvement with the CIA." Charisse Burden-Stelly, "'Stoolpigeons' and the Treacherous Terrain of Freedom Fighting." It is worth noting that William Gardner Smith was a con-

tributor to the special issue of *Phylon*, and stood for the pursuit of universalism in Black writing. As an illustration of this point, his 1950 novel *Anger at Innocence* featured no Black characters.

27. Greg Barnhisel, "*Perspectives USA* and the Cultural Cold War: Modernism in Service of the State," 731.

28. Richard Gibson, "A No to Nothing," 255. For more on the institutionalization of academic creative writing, see Mark McGurl, *The Program Era*.

29. Gibson, "A No to Nothing," 254.

30. Arna Bontemps, letter to Langston Hughes, March 11, 1953. LHP.

31. Arna Bontemps, letter to Langston Hughes, July 15, 1954. LHP.

32. Arna Bontemps, "Recent Writings by Negroes," July 19, 1954. Typescript. Arna Bontemps Papers, Special Collections Research Center, Syracuse University, 14–15.

33. Bontemps, "Recent Writings by Negroes," 15.

34. Langston Hughes, "Recent American Anthologies Seem to Deliberately Omit Negro Poets."

35. Nikhil Pal Singh, *Black Is a Country*, 136.

36. Jackson, *The Indignant Generation*, 301.

37. Arnold Rampersad writes, "Hughes willingly became a figurehead for the general secretary, Harry Haywood, a communist. In a draft program published while Hughes was president, the League [of Struggle for Negro Rights] reaffirmed its old, controversial position calling for 'the confiscation without compensation of the land of the big landlords and capitalists in the South,' with the land to be given to black and white small farmers and sharecroppers, and for 'the complete right of self-determination for the Negro people in the Black Belt with full rights for the toiling white minority.'" Rampersad, *I, Too, Sing America*, 286.

38. Robin D. G. Kelley, *Race Rebels*, 121.

39. Langston Hughes, "Air Raid over Harlem."

40. Langston Hughes, "Goodbye Christ."

41. William J. Maxwell, *F.B. Eyes*, 166–67.

42. For more on AMSAC and the CIA, see Hugh Wilford, *The Mighty Wurlitzer*, 197–224.

43. Washington, *The Other Blacklist*, 242–49.

44. Washington, *The Other Blacklist*, 44.

45. Langston Hughes, "Writers: Black and White," 44.

46. Langston Hughes, "How to Be a Bad Writer (in Ten Easy Lessons)," 13.

47. Hughes had written in his 1956 autobiography, *I Wonder as I Wander*, that *Black and White*'s script was unrealistic. But the scholar Steven S. Lee has shown that Hughes exaggerated the inaccuracies of the original script. The movie was about a group of Southern Black workers who were rescued by Northern white workers, a plot Hughes described as "plausible enough, but almost *all* of its details were wrong and its accents misplaced." For Lee, Hughes's description of his time working on the film shows that the writer "sought to distance himself

from past leftist affinities, but in a way that preserved the USSR as a beacon of hope." In other words, Hughes's account "can be read as a reflectively nostalgic glimpse of the interwar, Soviet-centered avant-garde." Steven S. Lee, *The Ethnic Avant-Garde*, 123–24.

48. Hughes, "Writers: Black and White," 45.

49. Andrew Rubin argues that in the period after World War II, the United States recast British and French imperial strategies "against various 'communist' threats. Most of these methods of control and management were developed in their initial phase in the form of transatlantic and transnational relationships between critics and various organizations such as the Ford and Rockefeller Foundations." When reading Rubin's commentary beside Evan Kindley's account of the Rockefeller Foundation's role in the promotion and growth of the New Criticism, it becomes clear that the New Criticism was understood to be an essential part of a growing state-endorsed means of buoying the United States and the globe against communism. These insights support the idea that the ideological thicket of anticommunism, anti-Blackness, and the literary critical establishment came to create a forceful racist interpretation complex in this moment. Andrew Rubin, *Archives of Authority*, 50; Evan Kindley, "Big Criticism." Also see Greg Barnhisel, *Cold War Modernists*.

50. Langston Hughes, letter to Joseph McCarthy, March 22, 1953. LHP.

51. US Congress, Senate, Permanent Subcommittee on Investigations of the Committee on Government Operations, *Executive Sessions of the Senate Permanent Subcommittee on Investigations of the Committee on Government Operations*, 83rd Cong., 1st sess., 1953, 975.

52. US Congress, Senate, Permanent Subcommittee, *Executive Sessions*, 975.

53. Vera M. Kutzinski, *The Worlds of Langston Hughes*, 203.

54. Maxwell, *F. B. Eyes*, 167.

55. Rampersad, *I Dream a World*, 219.

56. US Congress, Senate, Permanent Subcommittee, *Executive Sessions*, 976.

57. Michel de Certeau, *The Practice of Everyday Life*, 37.

58. De Certeau, *The Practice of Everyday Life*, 39.

59. Robin D. G. Kelley, "'We Are Not What We Seem': Rethinking Black Working-Class Opposition in the Jim Crow South," 91.

60. Harney and Moten, *The Undercommons*, 75.

61. David Chinitz makes the claim that Hughes likely leaked details of his sealed testimony to the press, but he only reads this as a minor infraction against the committee. Like other Hughes scholars, Chinitz sees Hughes as making a "devil's bargain" with McCarthy in these hearings, which was sealed by a wink from McCarthy at the public hearing's closure. David E. Chinitz, *Which Sin to Bear?* 139–42.

62. US Congress, Senate, Permanent Subcommittee, *Executive Sessions*, 978.

63. US Congress, Senate, Permanent Subcommittee, *Executive Sessions*, 978.

64. US Congress, Senate, Permanent Subcommittee, *Executive Sessions*, 985.

65. US Congress, Senate, Permanent Subcommittee, *Executive Sessions*, 986.

66. US Congress, Senate, Permanent Subcommittee, *Executive Sessions*, 986.

67. Frederick Douglass, *Narrative of the Life of Frederick Douglass*, 72–73.

68. Fred Moten, *Stolen Life*, 57.

69. I recall here the opening paragraphs of Frantz Fanon's chapter "The Lived Experience of the Black Man." After describing being hailed as "A Negro!" he writes:

> I came into this world anxious to uncover the meaning of things, my soul desirous to be at the origin of the world, and here I am an object among other objects.
>
> Locked in this suffocating reification, I appealed to the Other so that his liberating gaze, gliding over my body suddenly smoothed of rough edges, would give me back the lightness of being I thought I had lost, and taking me out of the world put me back in the world. But just as I get to the other slop I stumble, and the Other fixes me with his gaze, his gestures and attitude, the same way you fix a preparation with a dye. I lose my temper, demand an explanation. . . . Nothing doing. I explode. Here are the fragments put together by another me.

Fanon's description of violent fragmentation and reconfiguration mirrors Hughes's attempts at narrating his description of being fitted into the shape of "the Negro" while being "fixed" by the committee's persistent effort to acknowledge his Blackness while moving past that very fact. Frantz Fanon, *Black Skin, White Masks*, 89.

70. US Congress, Senate, Permanent Subcommittee, *Executive Sessions*, 986.

71. US Congress, Senate, Permanent Subcommittee, *Executive Sessions*, 989.

72. US Congress, Senate, Permanent Subcommittee, *Executive Sessions*, 987.

73. Kate A. Baldwin, *Beyond the Color Line and the Iron Curtain*, 95.

74. Ralph Ellison, *Invisible Man*, 8.

75. Kenneth W. Warren, "Ralph Ellison and the Problem of Cultural Authority: The Lessons of Little Rock," 153.

76. Farah Jasmine Griffin, *Harlem Nocturne*, 87–88.

77. Alan Wald makes this connection in his thorough reading of *The Narrows* in *American Night*, 196.

78. Griffin, "Hunting Communists and Negroes in Ann Petry's *The Narrows*," 142. Wald suggests that there are different sources for Link: Petry's husband, George David Petry, and Carl Ruthven Offard, "two Black men who associated with the Left in the late 1930s and 1940s." Wald, *American Night*, 181.

79. Baldwin, *Beyond the Color Line*, 87.

80. Ann Petry, *The Narrows*, 378.

81. Petry, *The Narrows*, 372.

82. For the ongoing efforts of the press to shape Black people into the form of the "NEGRO CONVICT SHOT," see Maurice O. Wallace, *Constructing the Black Masculine*; Khalil Gibran Muhammad, *The Condemnation of Blackness*.

83. Petry, *The Narrows*, 370.

84. Petry, *The Narrows*, 386.

85. Petry, *The Narrows*, 388.

86. Petry, *The Narrows*, 402.

87. Lindon Barrett, *Blackness and Value*, 220. In his discussion of this scene, Keith Clark draws on Ann Petry's account of writing the episode: "The instant that he [Link] said to these people, 'We were in love,' it was a death sentence; and there was no way, logically, that he would not be killed." Keith Clark, *The Radical Fiction of Ann Petry*.

88. Ann Petry, "The Novel as Social Criticism," 33.

89. Wald, *American Night*, 190–91.

90. Lorraine Hansberry, "The Negro Writer and His Roots: Toward a New Romanticism," 11–12.

CHAPTER 4

1. Estel Ward, letter to Shirley Graham Du Bois, March 21, 1956. W. E. B. Du Bois Papers, Special Collections and University Archives, University of Massachusetts Amherst Libraries (henceforth WEBDBP).

2. US Department of Justice, "W. E. B. Du Bois," FBI Internal case file no. 100–99729.

3. W. E. B. Du Bois, *The Correspondence of W. E. B. Du Bois*, vol. 3, 371–72. Also see W. E. B. Du Bois, "[Memo on my teaching at the Jefferson School]," typescript, May 13, 1954. WEBDBP.

4. Steven Brint and Jerome Karabel, *Diverted Dream*, 72–73.

5. See Helen Fitzgerald, "Dr. Selsam Elated by Response to Jefferson School Program."

6. "Memorandum on the Jefferson School," 1956. Jefferson School of Social Science Records 1942–56, Wisconsin Historical Society (henceforth JSSW).

7. Du Bois had an intimate familiarity with the repressive dimension of the American education system and the US government's efforts to silence those it declared subversives. According to Eric Porter, the 1940s and 1950s are when Du Bois "moved from a socialist to communist political orientation and voiced an often uncompromising leftist and antiracist critique of the United States and its government's and corporate elite's actions." This alienated Du Bois from more moderate Black organizations like the NAACP, which in 1948 pushed him out of the group he had had a role in founding. Similarly, Du Bois's publicly stated political commitments drew increased scrutiny of his movements and affiliations from federal anti-Black and anticommunist surveillance arms. Eric Porter, *The Problem of the Future World*, 2. Also see David Levering Lewis, *W. E. B. Du Bois*, 496–553; Manning Marable, *W. E. B. Du Bois*, 166–89; Bill Mullen, *W. E. B. Du Bois*, 107–22.

8. W. E. B. Du Bois, "The Workers," typescript. March 1948, 16. WEBDBP.

9. Lisa Lowe, *The Intimacies of Four Continents*, 168.

10. W. E. B. Du Bois, *Black Reconstruction in America*, 634. Manning Marable, *Race, Reform, and Rebellion*.

11. Du Bois, *Black Reconstruction*, 632.

12. Du Bois, "The Workers," 20.

13. Recent work in Abolitionist university studies supports Du Bois's claim. See Craig Steven Wilder, *Ebony & Ivy*; Sharon Stein, "A Colonial History of the Higher Education Present: Rethinking Land-Grant Institutions through Processes of Accumulation and Relations of Conquest"; Abigail Boggs and Nick Mitchell, "Critical University Studies and the Crisis Consensus"; Abigail Boggs, Eli Meyerhoff, Nick Mitchell, and Zach Schwartz-Weinstein, "Abolitionist University Studies: An Invitation."

14. W. E. B. Du Bois, "The Future of the American Negro," typescript, February 4, 1954, 18. WEBDBP.

15. Roderick A. Ferguson, *The Reorder of Things*, 164.

16. Marvin Gettleman has been the most thorough chronicler of the Jefferson School and other midcentury labor schools in the United States. See Marvin E. Gettleman, "'No Varsity Teams': New York's Jefferson School of Social Science, 1943–1956"; Marvin E. Gettleman, "The Lost World of United States Labor Education: Curricula at East and West Coast Communist Schools, 1944–1957"; Marvin E. Gettleman, "Defending Left Pedagogy: U.S. Communist Schools Fight Back against the SACB (Subversive Activities Control Board) . . . and Lose (1953–1957)."

17. Nick Mitchell, "Disciplinary Matters," esp. 19–78. Juliana Spahr has made a similar argument about the disciplining function of philanthropy's entanglement with the racial liberal state on poetry. See Juliana Spahr, *Du Bois's Telegram*, 84–86.

18. "Former P. V. Editor Receives Appointment"; "Wilkerson Appointed."

19. Robert Vitalis, *White World Order, Black Power Politics*, 12.

20. W. E. B. Du Bois, "The Workers," 23.

21. Ellen Schrecker, *No Ivory Tower*, 10.

22. Schrecker, *No Ivory Tower*, 13.

23. Mary Helen Washington, "Alice Childress, Lorraine Hansberry, and Claudia Jones," 184.

24. [Advertisement for Jefferson School] *DW*, January 31, 1944, 4.

25. According to Mark McGurl, there were only eight creative writing programs in US universities at this time, none of which were located in New York. Mark McGurl, *The Program Era*, 25. Julia Mickenburg writes that a number of Jefferson School faculty and programs were important for developing and publishing radical children's literature in this period. Some of the influential people she mentions include Clara Ostrowsky and Betty Bacon. See Julia Mickenberg, *Learning from the Left*, 108, 134, 146, 251.

26. David Platt, "Jefferson School Opens Today."

27. Platt, "Jefferson School Opens Today."

28. "Annual Report for the School Year: 1945–1946," 2–3. JSSW.

29. "Newspapers and Periodicals Received Regularly, January 1954," Jefferson School of Social Science Records and Indexes, Tamiment Library, New York University (hereafter JSST).

30. [Henry Black], "What the Library Does," Communist Party of the United States of America Archives, Tamiment Library, New York University.

31. Lawrence Jackson, *The Indignant Generation*, 308.

32. Insert on classroom procedures in Howard Selsam, letter to W. E. B. Du Bois, September 15, 1953. WEBDBP.

33. "Report of the All School Self-Critical Conference," [1953], 4. JSST.

34. "Report of the All School Self-Critical Conference," [1953], 8.

35. "Report of the All School Self-Critical Conference," [1953], 8.

36. Craig Thompson, "Here's Where Our Young Commies Are Trained."

37. Quoted in Gerald Horne, *Black and Red*, 183.

38. Ramon Lowe, "Harlem's Carver School Draws Capacity Classrooms."

39. "Some Critical Observations on Our Work at the Jefferson School" [1950], 2. JSSW.

40. "Jefferson School Adopts Anonymity."

41. *How to Study: A Guide for Students* (New York: Jefferson School of Social Science, n.d.), 2. Communist Party of the United States of America Archives, Tamiment Library, New York University.

42. US Congress, House of Representatives, Committee on Un-American Activities, *Communist Training Operations*, 86th Cong., 1st sess., 1959, 1017.

43. Florence Van Swearengen, letter to Howard Selsam, March 1, 1955. JSSW.

44. George S. Schuyler, "Views and Reviews."

45. Thompson, "Commies," 150

46. Julian Nemeth, "Storming the Ivory Tower," 107.

47. Gettleman, "No Varsity Teams," 354.

48. Rebecca Hill, "Fosterites and Feminists, or 1950s Ultra-Leftists and the Invention of AmeriKKKa," 70.

49. Hill, "Fosterites and Feminists," 69.

50. Carole Boyce Davies, *Left of Karl Marx*, 51.

51. Erik S. McDuffie, *Sojourning for Freedom*, 164.

52. Kate Weigand, *Red Feminism*, 90–91.

53. "20 Week Seminar on the Negro Question." Curriculum. 4. JSST.

54. Quoted in Gettleman, "No Varsity Teams," 351.

55. Harold Cruse, *The Crisis of the Negro Intellectual*, 226-27.

56. Harold Cruse, "Education of a Rebel." Typescript. Harold Cruse Papers, Tamiment Library, New York University, 12; Also see Jackson, *The Indignant Generation*, 303.

57. Doxey Wilkerson, "The Negro and the American Nation," 653.

58. Cruse, "Education of a Rebel," 11.

59. Robin D. G. Kelley, *Hammer and Hoe*, 13.

60. "The Work of Our Cultural Departments at the Jefferson School: Some Critical Comments and Proposals" [1950], 2. JSST.

61. Karl Marx, *Critique of Hegel's Philosophy of Right*.

62. "Work of Our Cultural Departments," 3.

63. "Work of Our Cultural Departments," 5.

64. Cleanth Brooks, *The Well Wrought Urn*, 187.

65. "Draft Statement on the Position of the Jefferson School on Instruction in the Arts: Prepared as a Basis for Faculty Discussion." Doxey A. Wilkerson Papers, Schomburg Center for Research in Black Culture, New York Public Library, 1.

66. "Draft Statement on the Position of the Jefferson School on Instruction in the Arts," 1.

67. "Draft Statement on the Position of the Jefferson School on Instruction in the Arts," 2.

68. "[Student Evaluation of W. E. B. Du Bois's Course on Reconstruction]," November 17, 1954. WEBDBP.

69. Doxey A. Wilkerson, "Negro Culture: Heritage and Weapon," 3.

70. Wilkerson, "Negro Culture: Heritage and Weapon," 3.

71. Wilkerson, "Negro Culture: Heritage and Weapon," 3.

72. Wilkerson's essay is limited by its American scope, and by a racialization scheme that distinguishes American Black people from others in the African diaspora. This notion bedeviled Wilkerson when he employed it in a document on how the concept "Negro" should be defined at the Jefferson School. After an outcry from students and faculty, Wilkerson revised his position and acknowledged that his previous distinction, which resulted from a doctrinaire Marxist-Leninist interpretation of the "national question," was borne of a definition of race that reinforced "white chauvinism" and ran "counter . . . to the tactical line of the progressive movement." Doxey A. Wilkerson, memorandum, "On the Concept 'Negro,'" June 2, 1952, 1. JSST. Also see Doxey A. Wilkerson, memorandum, "On the Concept 'Negro,'" [September 1951]. JSST.

73. Wilkerson, "Negro Culture," 19.

74. Wilkerson, "Negro Culture," 19.

75. Wilkerson, "Negro Culture," 24.

76. Quoted in Melanie Herzog, *Elizabeth Catlett*, 37.

77. Quoted in Melanie Herzog, *Elizabeth Catlett*, 38.

78. Quoted in Melanie Herzog, *Elizabeth Catlett*, 66.

79. For more on the founding of the Carver School, see Brian Dolinar, *The Black Cultural Front*, 56–60.

80. "Six Directors Quit the Carver School."

81. See Erik S. McDuffie, *Sojourning for Freedom*, 112.

82. McGurl, *The Program Era*, 23.

83. *Journey's Start: Writing by Students of Poetry Course and the English Courses*

of the George Washington Carver School, Fall Term 1945. Gwendolyn Bennett Papers, Schomburg Center for Research in Black Culture, New York Public Library.

84. "Literature, Music, and Art of the Negro People," syllabus, [1942]. Gwendolyn Bennett Papers, Schomburg Center for Research in Black Culture, New York Public Library.

85. "Dinner to Discuss a People's Institute for Harlem, Held at Hotel Theresa, February 25, 1943." Gwendolyn Bennett Papers, Schomburg Center for Research in Black Culture, New York Public Library.

86. [George Washington Carver School Course Catalog], May and June 1945. Reference Center for Marxist Studies Collections, Tamiment Library, New York University, 10.

87. Lorraine Hansberry, handwritten note in her copy of W. E. B. Du Bois, *Black Folk: Then and Now,* May 18, 1953. Lorraine Hansberry Papers, Schomburg Center for Research in Black Culture, New York Public Library.

88. Wilkerson mandated the inclusion of at least a one-week unit on "the Negro Question" in the school's signature introductory course, "The Science of Society." See Gettleman, "The Lost World of United States Labor Education," 210.

89. *A Call to a Conference on a Proposed New People's School in Harlem,* January 12, 1952. Reference Center for Marxist Studies Collections, Tamiment Library, New York University.

90. *A Call to a Conference.*

91. Dolinar, *The Black Cultural Front,* 67.

92. Dayo F. Gore, *Radicalism at the Crossroads,* 74–99.

93. Frederick Douglass Educational Center course catalog, spring 1952. Print Ephemera Collection on Organization, Tamiment Library, New York University.

94. Doxey A. Wilkerson, "The Douglass Center."

95. John S. Lash, "Current Opinion on the Teaching of the Literature of the Negro," 18, 26.

96. Frederick Douglass Educational Center course catalog, fall 1952. Print Ephemera Collection on Organization, Tamiment Library, New York University.

97. For more on the entirety of Gregory's poem, see Gore, *Radicalism at the Crossroads,* 89–94.

98. Yvonne Gregory, "Long Distance to Life," 2.

99. A *DW* editorial of April 16, 1952, notes that the Jefferson School goal was achieved. This was an especially significant accomplishment because New York's nonwhite population in 1950 was approximately 10 percent. Preston Valien, "The Growth and Distribution of the Negro Population in the United States," 247.

100. Jefferson School of Social Science course catalog, winter 1953. Doxey A. Wilkerson Papers, Schomburg Center for Research in Black Culture, New York Public Library.

101. Keith Gilyard, *John Oliver Killens,* 85.

102. Cruse, *The Crisis of the Negro Intellectual*, 217.
103. Douglas Field, *All Those Strangers*, 26.
104. Gilyard, *John Oliver Killens*, 93–94.
105. Gilyard, *John Oliver Killens*, 94.
106. Alan M. Wald, *Trinity of Passion*, 63.
107. "Instruction in the Arts," 1.
108. John Oliver Killens, *Youngblood*, 135.
109. "20 Week Seminar on the Negro Question," 3.
110. Killens, *Youngblood*, 155.
111. "Some Observations on the Aim, Content and Methods of Teaching at the Jefferson School," September 23, 1954. Doxey A. Wilkerson Papers, Schomburg Center for Research in Black Culture, New York Public Library, 4.
112. "Some Observations," 1.
113. Killens, *Youngblood*, 279.
114. Jonathan Flatley, *Affective Mapping*, 107.
115. Killens, *Youngblood*, 285.
116. Killens, *Youngblood*, 404; Du Bois, *Black Reconstruction*, 700.
117. Killens, *Youngblood*, 404.
118. Kelley, *Hammer and Hoe*; McDuffie, *Sojourning for Freedom*; Gore, *Radicalism at the Crossroads*.
119. Killens, *Youngblood*, 403.
120. See Kenneth Warren, *What Was African American Literature*, 57–58; Jodi Melamed, *Represent and Destroy*, 56–63; Roderick Ferguson, *Aberrations in Black*, 82–110.
121. Herbert Aptheker, *The Negro People in America*, 8.
122. Memorandum on personnel practice, [1946]. JSSW.

EPILOGUE

1. Angela Y. Davis, *Angela Davis*, 196. For more, see Ferguson, *The Reorder of Things*, 42–44.
2. Ferguson, *The Reorder of Things*, 75.
3. Laura Hamilton and Kelly Nielsen argue: "As racially marginalized youth, often from low-income households, began to enter higher education in significant numbers, sentiment around government financing soured. Although causation is difficult to prove, the timing is striking. For most of the twentieth century, families of color as part of the tax base were paying for wealthy white students to attend universities where their own offspring were not welcome. Everything changed as marginalized populations gained more access to historically white organizations." *Broke*, 11–14. Nick Mitchell has observed that, beginning in the 1970s, universities began to devote more significant shares of their policing budget than they had prior to that moment—a shift Mitchell attributes to the

overall increase in students of color matriculated. See Mitchell, interview with Adrian Daub and Laura Goode.

4. Abigail Boggs, Eli Meyerhoff, Nick Mitchell, and Zach Schwartz-Weinstein, "Abolitionist University Studies: An Invitation."

5. Stefano Harney and Fred Moten, "The University: Last Words," 2.

6. Harney and Moten, *The Undercommons*, 42–43.

7. See Martin Finkelstein, Valerie Martin Conley, and Jack H. Schuster, "Taking the Measure of Faculty Diversity."

Archives and Collections Consulted

Gwendolyn Bennett Papers, Schomburg Center for Research in Black Culture, New York Public Library

Arna Bontemps Papers, Special Collections Research Center, Syracuse University

Communist Party of the United States of America Archives, Tamiment Library, New York University

Harold Cruse Papers, Tamiment Library, New York University

W. E. B. Du Bois Papers, Special Collections and University Archives, University of Massachusetts Amherst Libraries

Lorraine Hansberry Papers, Schomburg Center for Research in Black Culture, New York Public Library

Langston Hughes Papers, James Weldon Johnson Collection in the Yale Collection of American Literature, Beinecke Rare Book and Manuscript Library, Yale University

Jefferson School of Social Science Records, 1942–56, Wisconsin Historical Society

Jefferson School of Social Science Records and Indexes, Tamiment Library, New York University

Print Ephemera Collection on Organization, Tamiment Library, New York University

Reference Center for Marxist Studies Collections, Tamiment Library, New York University

Allen Tate Papers, Department of Rare Books and Special Collections, Princeton University Library

Melvin Beaunorus Tolson Papers, Manuscript Division, Library of Congress

Doxey A. Wilkerson Papers, Schomburg Center for Research in Black Culture, New York Public Library

Bibliography

Advertisement for Jefferson School, *Daily Worker* (New York). January 31, 1944.

Ahmed, Sara. *On Being Included: Racism and Diversity in Institutional Life.* Durham, NC: Duke University Press, 2012.

Anderson, Carol. *Eyes off the Prize: The United Nations and the African American Struggle for Human Rights, 1944–1955.* Cambridge: Cambridge University Press, 2003.

Aptheker, Herbert. *The Negro People in America.* New York: International Publishers, 1946.

Bacon, Francis. *The New Organon; or, True Directions Concerning the Interpretation of Nature.* Translated and self-published by Jonathan Bennett, 2017. https://www.earlymoderntexts.com/assets/pdfs/bacon1620part2.pdf.

Baker, Houston A., Jr. *I Don't Hate the South: Reflections on Faulkner, Family, and the South.* Oxford: Oxford University Press, 2007.

Baldwin, James. "Everybody's Protest Novel." In *The Price of the Ticket*, 27–33. New York: St. Martin's Press, 1985.

Baldwin, Kate A. *Beyond the Color Line and the Iron Curtain: Reading Encounters between Black and Red, 1922–1963.* Durham, NC: Duke University Press, 2002.

Barnhisel, Greg. *Cold War Modernists: Art, Literature, and American Cultural Diplomacy.* New York: Columbia University Press, 2015.

———. *James Laughlin, New Directions, and the Remaking of Ezra Pound.* Amherst: University of Massachusetts Press, 2005.

———. "Perspectives USA and the Cultural Cold War: Modernism in Service of the State." *Modernism/Modernity* 14, no. 4 (2007): 729–54.

Barrett, Lindon. *Blackness and Value: Seeing Double.* Cambridge: Cambridge University Press, 1999.

Barrett, William. "A Prize for Ezra Pound." *Partisan Review* 16, no. 4 (April 1949): 344–347.

Bérubé, Michael. *Marginal Forces / Cultural Centers: Tolson, Pynchon, and the Politics of the Canon*. Ithaca, NY: Cornell University Press, 1992.

Bibby, Michael. "The Disinterested and Fine: New Negro Renaissance Poetry and the Racial Formation of Modernist Studies." *Modernism/Modernity* 20, no. 3 (September 2013): 485–501.

Biondi, Martha. *The Black Revolution on Campus*. Berkeley: University of California Press, 2014.

———. *To Stand and Fight: The Struggle for Civil Rights in Postwar New York City*. Cambridge, MA: Harvard University Press, 2003.

Birmingham, Kevin. "No Name in the South: James Baldwin and the Monuments of Identity." *African American Review* 44, no. 1–2 (2011): 221–34.

Blackmur, R. P. "A Burden for Critics." *Hudson Review* 1, no. 2 (July 1948): 170–85.

Boggs, Abigail, Eli Meyerhoff, Nick Mitchell, and Zach Schwartz-Weinstein. "Abolitionist University Studies: An Invitation." *Abolition*, August 28, 2019. https://abolitionjournal.org/abolitionist-university-studies-an-invitation.

Boggs, Abigail, and Nick Mitchell. "Critical University Studies and the Crisis Consensus." *Feminist Studies* 44, no. 2 (2018): 432–63.

Bové, Paul A. "Agriculture and Academe: America's Southern Question." *boundary 2* 14, no. 3 (April 1986): 169–96.

———. *Intellectuals in Power: A Genealogy of Critical Humanism*. New York: Columbia University Press, 1986.

Boyce Davies, Carole. *Left of Karl Marx: The Political Life of Black Communist Claudia Jones*. Durham, NC: Duke University Press, 2007.

Bradley, Stefan M. *Upending the Ivory Tower: Civil Rights, Black Power, and the Ivy League*. New York: New York University Press, 2018.

Brand, Dionne. *A Map to the Door of No Return: Notes to Belonging*. Toronto: Vintage Canada, 2001.

Brinkmeyer, Robert H. *The Fourth Ghost: White Southern Writers and European Fascism, 1930–1950*. Baton Rouge: Louisiana State University Press, 2009.

Brint, Steven, and Jerome Karabel. *Diverted Dream: Community Colleges and the Promise of Educational Opportunity in America, 1900–1985*. New York: Oxford University Press, 1986.

Brooks, Cleanth. "The Formalist Critics." *Kenyon Review* 13, no. 1 (January 1951): 72–81.

———. "List of 'Wicked Esthetes' Wanted." *Saturday Review of Literature*, October 29, 1949, 24.

———. *The Well Wrought Urn: Studies in the Structure of Poetry*. New York: Houghton Mifflin Harcourt, 1947.

Brooks, Cleanth, and Robert Penn Warren, eds. *Understanding Poetry: An Anthology for College Students*. New York: Henry Holt, 1938.

Brouillette, Sarah. *UNESCO and the Fate of the Literary*. Stanford, CA: Stanford University Press, 2019.

Brown, Jericho. "You Can't Love Me if You Don't Love Politically." In *The Racial Imaginary: Writers on Race in the Life of the Mind*, edited by Claudia Rankine, Beth Loffreda, and Max King Cap, 232–33. Albany, NY: Fence Books, 2016.

Buchanan, James M., and Nicos E. Devletoglou. *Academia in Anarchy: An Economic Diagnosis*. New York: Basic Books, 1970.

Burden-Stelly, Charisse. "'Stoolpigeons' and the Treacherous Terrain of Freedom Fighting." *AAIHS* (blog), September 13, 2018. https://www.aaihs.org /stoolpigeons-and-the-treacherous-terrain-of-freedom-fighting/.

Buurma, Rachel Sagner, and Laura Heffernan. *The Teaching Archive: A New History for Literary Study*. Chicago: University of Chicago Press, 2021.

Cacho, Lisa Marie. *Social Death: Racialized Rightlessness and the Criminalization of the Unprotected*. New York: New York University Press, 2012.

Cain, William E. "Notes toward a History of Anti-Criticism." *New Literary History* 20, no. 1 (Autumn 1988): 33–48.

Carbado, Devon, and Mitu Gulati. "Working Identity." *Cornell Law Review* 85, no. 5 (July 2000): 1259–1308.

Chandler, Nahum Dimitri. *X: The Problem of the Negro as a Problem for Thought*. New York: Fordham University Press, 2014.

Chase, Richard. "New vs. Ordealist." *Kenyon Review* 11, no. 1 (January 1949): 11–13.

Chinitz, David E. *Which Sin to Bear? Authenticity and Compromise in Langston Hughes*. Oxford: Oxford University Press, 2013.

Clark, Keith. *The Radical Fiction of Ann Petry*. Baton Rouge: Louisiana State University Press, 2013.

Conkin, Paul Keith. *The Southern Agrarians*. Knoxville: University of Tennessee Press, 1988.

Cooper, Mark Garrett, and John Marx. *Media U: How the Need to Win Audiences Has Shaped Higher Education*. New York: Columbia University Press, 2018.

Cooper, Melinda. *Family Values: Between Neoliberalism and the New Social Conservatism*. New York: Zone Books, 2017.

Cottom, Tressie McMillan. *Lower Ed: The Troubling Rise of for-Profit Colleges in the New Economy*. New York: New Press, 2017.

Cox, Oliver C. *Caste, Class, and Race: A Study in Social Dynamics*. New York: Monthly Review Press, 1959.

Crawley, Ashon. "University." In *Keywords for African American Studies*, edited by Erica R. Edwards, Roderick A. Ferguson, and Jeffrey O. G. Ogbar, 213–16. New York: New York University Press, 2018.

Cruse, Harold. *The Crisis of the Negro Intellectual: A Historical Analysis of the Failure of Black Leadership*. New York: New York Review of Books, 2005.

Davidson, Donald. "Regionalism and Education." *American Review* 4, no. 3 (January 1935): 310–25.

Davis, Angela Y. *Angela Davis: An Autobiography*. New York: International Publishers, 2008.

Dawson, Michael C. *Blacks in and out of the Left*. Cambridge, MA: Harvard University Press, 2013.

De Certeau, Michel. *The Practice of Everyday Life*. Translated by Steven Rendall. Berkeley: University of California Press, 2002.

Denning, Michael. *The Cultural Front: The Laboring of American Culture in the Twentieth Century*. New York: Verso, 1998.

Dolinar, Brian. *The Black Cultural Front: Black Writers and Artists of the Depression Generation*. Jackson: University Press of Mississippi, 2012.

Douglass, Frederick. *Narrative of the Life of Frederick Douglass, an American Slave: Written By Himself*. Documenting the American South. University Library, University of North Carolina at Chapel Hill, 1999 [1845]. https://docsouth.unc.edu/neh/douglass/douglass.html.

Du Bois, W. E. B. *Black Reconstruction in America: 1860–1880*. New York: The Free Press, 1998.

————. *The Correspondence of W. E. B. Du Bois*. Vol. 3. Edited by Herbert Aptheker. Amherst: University of Massachusetts Press, 1973.

————. "Criteria of Negro Art." In *The Norton Anthology of African American Literature*, Third Edition, Vol. 1, edited by Henry Louis Gates Jr. and Valerie Smith, 771–78. New York: W. W. Norton, 2014.

————. *The Souls of Black Folk*. Edited by Henry Louis Gates Jr. and Terri Hume Oliver. New York: . W. W. Norton, 1999.

Dudziak, Mary L. *Cold War Civil Rights: Race and the Image of American Democracy*. Princeton, NJ: Princeton University Press, 2001.

Eagleton, Terry. *The Function of Criticism: From the Spectator to Post-Structuralism*. London: Verso, 1984.

Edwards, Brent Hayes. *Epistrophies: Jazz and the Literary Imagination*. Cambridge, MA: Harvard University Press, 2017.

————. "The Taste of the Archive." *Callaloo* 35, no. 4 (2012): 944–72.

Ehlers, Sarah. *Left of Poetry: Depression America and the Formation of Modern Poetics*. Chapel Hill: University of North Carolina Press, 2019.

Ellison, Ralph. *Invisible Man*. New York: Vintage, 1995.

Emre, Merve. *Paraliterary: The Making of Bad Readers in Postwar America*. Chicago: University of Chicago Press, 2017.

Fabre, Michel. *From Harlem to Paris: Black American Writers in France, 1840–1980*. Urbana: University of Illinois Press, 1991.

Fanon, Frantz. *Black Skin, White Masks*. Translated by Richard Philcox. New York: Grove Press, 2008.

Farnsworth, Robert M. Introduction to Melvin B. Tolson, *Caviar and Cabbage: Selected Columns by Melvin B. Tolson from the Washington Tribune, 1937–1944*, edited by Robert M. Farnsworth, 1–25. Columbia: University of Missouri Press, 1982.

————. *Melvin B. Tolson: 1898–1966, Plain Talk and Poetic Prophecy.* Columbia: University of Missouri Press, 1984.

Ferguson, Roderick A. *Aberrations in Black: Toward a Queer of Color Critique.* Minneapolis: University of Minnesota Press, 2004.

————. *The Reorder of Things: The University and Its Pedagogies of Minority Difference.* Minneapolis: University of Minnesota Press, 2012.

————. *We Demand: The University and Student Protests.* Oakland: University of California Press, 2017.

Ferreira da Silva, Denise. "Many Hundred Thousand Bodies Later: An Analysis of the 'Legacy' of the International Criminal Tribunal for Rwanda." In *Events: The Force of International Law*, edited by Fleur Johns, Richard John Joyce, and Sundhya Pahuja, 165–76. Abingdon, UK: Routledge, 2011.

————. *Toward a Global Idea of Race.* Minneapolis: University of Minnesota Press, 2007.

Field, Douglas. *All Those Strangers: The Art and Lives of James Baldwin.* Oxford: Oxford University Press, 2015.

Findeisen, Christopher. "Injuries of Class: Mass Education and the American Campus Novel." *PMLA* 130, no. 2 (March 2015): 284–98.

Finkelstein, Martin, Valerie Martin Conley, and Jack H. Schuster. "Taking the Measure of Faculty Diversity." TIAA Institute, April 2016. https://www .tiaainstitute.org/sites/default/files/presentations/2017-02/taking_the _measure_of_faculty_diversity.pdf.

Fitzgerald, Helen. "Dr. Selsam Elated by Response to Jefferson School Program." *Daily Worker* (New York), February 13, 1944.

Flatley, Jonathan. *Affective Mapping Melancholia and the Politics of Modernism.* Cambridge, MA: Harvard University Press, 2008.

————. "How a Revolutionary Counter-Mood Is Made." *New Literary History* 43, no. 3 (2012): 503–25.

"Former P. V. Editor Receives Appointment." *Philadelphia Tribune*, February 3, 1948.

Fuller, Hoyt W. "Towards a Black Aesthetic." In *SOS—Calling All Black People: A Black Arts Movement Reader*, edited by John H. Bracey Jr., Sonia Sanchez, and James Smethurst, 151–57. Amherst: University of Massachusetts Press, 2014.

Gaskill, Nicholas. "The Close and the Concrete: Aesthetic Formalism in Context." *New Literary History* 47, no. 4 (2016): 505–24.

Gayle, Addison, Jr. *The Black Situation.* New York: Horizon Press, 1970.

Gettleman, Marvin E. "Defending Left Pedagogy: U.S. Communist Schools Fight Back against the SACB (Subversive Activities Control Board) . . . and Lose (1953–1957)." *Convergence* 41, no. 2–3 (2008): 193–209.

————. "The Lost World of United States Labor Education: Curricula at East and West Coast Communist Schools, 1944–1957." In *American Labor and the Cold War: Grassroots Politics and Postwar Political Culture*, edited by Robert

Cherny and William Issel, 205–15. New Brunswick, NJ: Rutgers University Press, 2004.

———. "'No Varsity Teams': New York's Jefferson School of Social Science, 1943–1956." *Science & Society* 66, no. 3 (Fall 2002): 336–59.

Gibson, Richard. "A No to Nothing." *Kenyon Review* 13, no. 2 (Spring 1951): 252–55.

———. "Richard Wright's 'Island of Hallucination' and the 'Gibson Affair.'" *MFS Modern Fiction Studies* 51, no. 4 (2005): 896–920.

Gilbert, Claire Krendl, and Donald E. Heller. "Access, Equity, and Community Colleges: The Truman Commission and Federal Higher Education Policy from 1947 to 2011." *Journal of Higher Education* 84, no. 3 (2013): 417–43.

Gilyard, Keith. *John Oliver Killens: A Life of Black Literary Activism*. Athens: University of Georgia Press, 2011.

———. *Louise Thompson Patterson: A Life of Struggle for Justice*. Durham, NC: Duke University Press, 2017.

Gore, Dayo F. *Radicalism at the Crossroads: African American Women Activists in the Cold War*. New York: New York University Press, 2011.

Graff, Gerald. *Professing Literature: An Institutional History*. Chicago: University of Chicago Press, 2007.

Gregory, Yvonne. "Long Distance to Life." *Freedom* 1, no. 2 (February 1951): 2.

Griffin, Farah Jasmine. *Harlem Nocturne: Women Artists & Progressive Politics during World War II*. New York: Basic Civitas, 2013.

———. "Hunting Communists and Negroes in Ann Petry's *The Narrows*." In *Revising the Blueprint: Ann Petry and the Literary Left*, edited by Alex Lubin, 137–49. Jackson: University Press of Mississippi, 2007.

Guillory, John. *Cultural Capital: The Problem of Literary Canon Formation*. Chicago: University of Chicago Press, 1993.

Guterl, Matthew Pratt. *The Color of Race in America, 1900–1940*. Cambridge, MA: Harvard University Press, 2002.

Hall, Jacquelyn Dowd. "The Long Civil Rights Movement and the Political Uses of the Past." *Journal of American History* 91, no. 4 (March 2005): 1233–63.

Hamilton, Laura T., and Kelly Nielsen. *Broke: The Racial Consequences of Underfunding Public Universities*. Chicago: University of Chicago Press, 2021.

Hammer, Langdon. *Hart Crane and Allen Tate: Janus-Faced Modernism*. Princeton, NJ: Princeton University Press, 1993.

Hammond, Adam. "Through Fields of Cacophonous Modern Master: James Baldwin and New Critical Modernism." In *Rereading the New Criticism*, edited by Miranda B. Hickman and John D. McIntyre, 151–70. Columbus: Ohio State University Press, 2012.

Hansberry, Lorraine. "The Negro Writer and His Roots: Toward a New Romanticism." *The Black Scholar* 12, no. 2 (April 1981): 2–12.

Harney, Stefano, and Fred Moten. *The Undercommons: Fugitive Planning & Black Study*. Wivenhoe, UK: Minor Compositions, 2013.

———. "The University: Last Words." Paper circulated for FUC 012, Zoom, July 9, 2020. https://www.fuc-series.org/#PastEvents.

Harpham, Geoffrey Galt. *The Humanities and the Dream of America*. Chicago: University of Chicago Press, 2011.

Hart, Matthew. *Nations of Nothing But Poetry: Modernism, Transnationalism, and Synthetic Vernacular Writing*. Oxford: Oxford University Press, 2010.

Hartman, Saidiya. "Venus in Two Acts." *Small Axe* 12, no. 2 (June 2008): 1–14.

———. *Wayward Lives, Beautiful Experiments: Intimate Histories of Social Upheaval*. New York: W. W. Norton, 2019.

Harvard Committee. *General Education in a Free Society*. Cambridge, MA: Harvard University Press., 1945.

Heffernan, Laura. "New Disciplinary History." *Modernism/Modernity* 1, no. 1 (March 2016). https://modernismmodernity.org/forums/posts/new-disciplinary-history.

Herzog, Melanie. *Elizabeth Catlett: An American Artist in Mexico*. Seattle: University of Washington Press, 2000.

Hill, Rebecca. "Fosterites and Feminists, or 1950s Ultra-Leftists and the Invention of AmeriKKKa." *New Left Review* 228 (April 1998): 67–90.

Hirsch, David. "Penelope's Web." *Sewanee Review* 90, no. 1 (Winter 1982): 119–31.

Hong, Christine. *A Violent Peace: Race, U.S. Militarism, and Cultures of Democratization in Cold War Asia and the Pacific*. Stanford, CA: Stanford University Press, 2020.

Horne, Gerald. *Black and Red: W. E. B. Du Bois and the Afro-American Response to the Cold War, 1944–1963*. Albany: State University of New York Press, 1986.

Hughes, Langston. "Air Raid over Harlem." In *The Collected Poems of Langston Hughes*, edited by Arnold Rampersad, 185–88. New York: Vintage, 1994.

———. "Goodbye Christ." In *The Collected Poems of Langston Hughes*, edited by Arnold Rampersad, 166–67. New York: Vintage, 1994.

———. "How to Be a Bad Writer (In Ten Easy Lessons)." *Harlem Quarterly* 1, no. 2 (Spring 1950): 13–14.

———. "The Negro Artist and the Racial Mountain." In *The Norton Anthology of African American Literature*, Third Edition, Vol. 1, edited by Henry Louis Gates Jr. and Valerie Smith, 1320–24. New York: Norton, 2014.

———. "Recent American Anthologies Seem to Deliberately Omit Negro Poets." *Chicago Defender*, National Edition, January 12, 1952.

———. *Selected Letters of Langston Hughes*. Edited by Arnold Rampersad and David E. Roessel. New York: Alfred A. Knopf, 2015.

———. "Some Practical Observations: A Colloquy." *Phylon* 11, no. 4 (December 1950): 307–11.

———. "World's Most Exciting Singer Poses Questions of Art, Politics, Race." *Chicago Defender*, September 24, 1949.

———. "Writers: Black and White." In *The American Negro Writer and His Roots: Selected Papers from the First Conference of Negro Writers, March 1959*. New York: American Society of African Culture, 1960.

Humes, Edward. "How the GI Bill Shunted Blacks into Vocational Training." *Journal of Blacks in Higher Education*, no. 53 (2006): 92–104.

Hurston, Zora Neale. "What White Publishers Won't Print." *Negro Digest* 8 (April 1950): 85–89.

Jackson, Blyden. "An Essay in Criticism." *Phylon* 11, no. 4 (December 1950): 338–43.

Jackson, Lawrence Patrick. *The Indignant Generation: A Narrative History of African American Writers and Critics, 1934–1960*. Princeton, NJ: Princeton University Press, 2011.

Jackson, Virginia Walker. *Dickinson's Misery: A Theory of Lyric Reading*. Princeton, NJ: Princeton University Press, 2005.

Jancovich, Mark. *The Cultural Politics of the New Criticism*. Cambridge: Cambridge University Press, 1993.

"Jefferson School Adopts Anonymity." *New York Times*, October 3, 1950.

Jefferson, Thomas. *Notes on the State of Virginia*. Documenting the American South. University Library, University of North Carolina at Chapel Hill, 2006 [1788]. https://docsouth.unc.edu/southlit/jefferson/jefferson.html.

Johnson, Gaye Theresa, and Alex Lubin. Introduction to *Futures of Black Radicalism*, edited by Gaye Theresa Johnson and Alex Lubin, 9–18. London: Verso, 2017.

Kalaidjian, Walter. *The Edge of Modernism: American Poetry and the Traumatic Past*. Baltimore: Johns Hopkins University Press, 2005.

Katznelson, Ira. *When Affirmative Action Was White: An Untold History of Racial Inequality in Twentieth-Century America*. New York: W. W. Norton, 2005.

Kelley, Robin D. G. "Black Study, Black Struggle." *Boston Review*, March 7, 2016. http://bostonreview.net/forum/robin-d-g-kelley-black-study-black-struggle.

———. *Freedom Dreams: The Black Radical Imagination*. Boston: Beacon Press, 2003.

———. *Hammer and Hoe: Alabama Communists during the Great Depression*. Chapel Hill: University of North Carolina Press, 2015.

———. *Race Rebels: Culture, Politics, and the Black Working Class*. New York: Free Press, 1996.

———. "'We Are Not What We Seem': Rethinking Black Working-Class Opposition in the Jim Crow South." *Journal of American History* 80, no. 1 (June 1993): 75–112.

Kendi, Ibram X. *The Black Campus Movement: Black Students and the Racial*

Reconstitution of Higher Education, 1965–1972. New York: Palgrave Macmillan, 2012.

Killens, John Oliver. *Youngblood*. New York: Trident Press, 1966.

Kindley, Evan. "Big Criticism." *Critical Inquiry* 38, no. 1 (2011): 71–95.

———. *Poet-Critics and the Administration of Culture*. Cambridge, MA: Harvard University Press, 2017.

Korstad, Robert Rodgers. *Civil Rights Unionism: Tobacco Workers and the Struggle for Democracy in the Mid-Twentieth-Century South*. Chapel Hill: University of North Carolina Press, 2003.

Kreyling, Michael. *Inventing Southern Literature*. Jackson: University Press of Mississippi, 1998.

———. *The South That Wasn't There: Postsouthern Memory and History*. Baton Rouge: Louisiana State University Press, 2010.

Kunitz, Stanley. "Bronze by Gold." *Poetry*, April 1950, 52–56.

Kutzinski, Vera M. *The Worlds of Langston Hughes: Modernism and Translation in the Americas*. Ithaca, NY: Cornell University Press, 2012.

Lash, John S. "Current Opinion on the Teaching of the Literature of the Negro." *Journal of Negro Education* 14, no. 1 (1945): 18–27.

———. "What Is 'Negro Literature'?" *College English* 9, no. 1 (October 1947): 37–42.

Lee, Steven S. *The Ethnic Avant-Garde: Minority Cultures and World Revolution*. New York: Columbia University Press, 2015.

Leick, Karen. "Ezra Pound v. 'The Saturday Review of Literature.'" *Journal of Modern Literature* 25, no. 2 (Winter 2001/2002): 19–37.

Lenhart, Gary. "Caviar and Cabbage: The Voracious Appetite of Melvin Tolson." In *The Stamp of Class*, 64–84. Ann Arbor: University of Michigan Press, 2006.

Levinson, Marjorie. "What Is New Formalism?" *PMLA* 122, no. 2 (March 2007): 558–69.

Levy, Eugene D. *James Weldon Johnson, Black Leader, Black Voice*. Chicago: University of Chicago Press, 1973.

Lewis, David Levering. *W. E. B. Du Bois: The Fight for Equality and the American Century, 1919–1963*. New York: Henry Holt, 1993.

Liu, Alan. *The Laws of Cool: Knowledge Work and the Culture of Information*. Chicago: University of Chicago Press, 2004.

Liu, Catherine. *American Idyll: Academic Antielitism as Cultural Critique*. Iowa City: University of Iowa Press, 2011.

Llorens, David. "Seeking a New Image: Writers Converge at Fisk University." *Negro Digest* 15, no. 8 (June 1966): 54–68.

Lloyd, David. *Under Representation: The Racial Regime of Aesthetics*. New York: Fordham University Press, 2018.

Lowe, Lisa. *The Intimacies of Four Continents*. Durham, NC: Duke University Press, 2015.

Lowe, Ramon. "Harlem's Carver School Draws Capacity Classrooms." *Chicago Defender*, February 5, 1944.

MacLean, Nancy. *Democracy in Chains: The Deep History of the Radical Right's Stealth Plan for America*. New York: Penguin, 2018.

Mao, Douglas. "The New Critics and the Text-Object." *ELH* 63, no. 1 (April 1996): 227–54.

Marable, Manning. *Race, Reform, and Rebellion: The Second Reconstruction and Beyond in Black America, 1945–2006*. Jackson: University Press of Mississippi, 2007.

———. *W. E. B. Du Bois: Black Radical Democrat*. Boulder, CO: Paradigm Publishers, 2005.

Marx, Karl. *Capital: A Critique of Political Economy*. Translated by Ben Fowkes. V. 1. London: Penguin, 1981.

———. *Critique of Hegel's Philosophy of Right*. Translated by Annette Jolin and Joseph O'Malley. Marxists.org, 2000.

Maxwell, Angie. *The Indicted South: Public Criticism, Southern Inferiority, and the Politics of Whiteness*. Chapel Hill: University of North Carolina Press, 2014.

Maxwell, William J. *F.B. Eyes: How J. Edgar Hoover's Ghostreaders Framed African American Literature*. Princeton, NJ: Princeton University Press, 2015.

McDuffie, Erik S. "Black and Red: Black Liberation, the Cold War, and the Horne Thesis." *Journal of African American History* 96, no. 2 (2011): 236–47.

———. *Sojourning for Freedom: Black Women, American Communism, and the Making of Black Left Feminism*. Durham, NC: Duke University Press, 2011.

McGurl, Mark. *The Program Era: Postwar Fiction and the Rise of Creative Writing*. Cambridge, MA: Harvard University Press, 2009.

McKittrick, Katherine. *Dear Science and Other Stories*. Durham, NC: Duke University Press, 2021.

———. *Demonic Grounds: Black Women and the Cartographies of Struggle*. Minneapolis: University of Minnesota Press, 2006.

Meiners, R. K. "Marginal Men and Centers of Learning: New Critical Rhetoric and Critical Politics." *New Literary History* 18, no. 1 (1986): 129–50.

Melamed, Jodi. *Represent and Destroy: Rationalizing Violence in the New Racial Capitalism*. Minneapolis: University of Minnesota Press, 2011.

Mencken, H. L. *A Carnival of Buncombe*, edited by Malcolm Moos. Baltimore: Johns Hopkins University Press, 1956.

Mickenberg, Julia. *Learning from the Left: Children's Literature, the Cold War and Radical Politics in the United States*. Oxford: Oxford University Press, 2005.

Middleton, Peter. "Poetry, Physics, and the Scientific Attitude at Mid-Century." *Modernism/Modernity* 21, no. 1 (January 2014): 147–68.

Mitchell, Nick. "(Critical Ethnic Studies) Intellectual." *Critical Ethnic Studies* 1, no. 1 (2015): 86–94.

———. "Disciplinary Matters: Black Studies and the Politics of Institutionalization." PhD dissertation, University of California, Santa Cruz, 2011.

———. Interview with Adrian Daub and Laura Goode. *The Feminist Present.* Podcast audio. November 18, 2020. https://gender.stanford.edu/podcast.

Moten, Fred. *Black and Blur. Consent Not to Be a Single Being*, vol. 1. Durham, NC: Duke University Press, 2017.

———. *Stolen Life. Consent Not to Be a Single Being*, vol. 2. Durham, NC: Duke University Press, 2018.

Muhammad, Khalil Gibran. *The Condemnation of Blackness: Race, Crime, and the Making of Modern Urban America.* Cambridge, MA: Harvard University Press, 2010.

Mullen, Bill. *W. E. B. Du Bois: Revolutionary across the Color Line.* London: Pluto Press, 2016.

Murakawa, Naomi. *The First Civil Right: How Liberals Built Prison America.* Oxford: Oxford University Press, 2014.

Murphy, Paul V. *The Rebuke of History: The Southern Agrarians and American Conservative Thought.* Chapel Hill: University of North Carolina Press, 2001.

Myrdal, Gunnar. *American Dilemma: The Negro Problem and Modern Democracy.* New York: Harper & Brothers, 1944.

Nelson, Deborah. *Pursuing Privacy in Cold War America.* New York: Columbia University Press, 2002.

Nemeth, Julian. "Storming the Ivory Tower: The Politics of Academic Freedom in the Twentieth Century United States." PhD dissertation, Brandeis University, 2014.

Newfield, Christopher. *Ivy and Industry: Business and the Making of the American University, 1880–1980.* Durham, NC: Duke University Press, 2003.

Nielsen, Aldon L. "Melvin B. Tolson and the Deterritorialization of Modernism." *African American Review* 26, no. 2 (July 1992): 241–55.

North, Joseph. *Literary Criticism: A Concise Political History.* Cambridge, MA: Harvard University Press, 2017.

paperson, la. *A Third University Is Possible.* Minneapolis: University of Minnesota Press, 2017.

Parker, Hershel. *Flawed Texts and Verbal Icons: Literary Authority in American Fiction.* Evanston, IL: Northwestern University Press, 1984.

Petry, Ann. *The Narrows.* Boston: Beacon Press, 1988.

———. "The Novel as Social Criticism." In *The Writer's Book*, edited by Helen Hull, 31–39. New York: Harper & Brothers, 1950.

Platt, David. "Jefferson School Opens Today." *Daily Worker* (New York). February 14, 1944.

Porter, Eric. *The Problem of the Future World: W. E. B. Du Bois and the Race Concept at Midcentury.* Durham, NC: Duke University Press, 2010.

Porter, Lavelle. *The Blackademic Life: Academic Fiction, Higher Education, and the Black Intellectual.* Evanston, IL: Northwestern University Press, 2019.

Posmentier, Sonya. "Lyric Reading in the Black Ethnographic Archive." *American Literary History* 30, no. 1 (January 2018): 55–84.

Rampersad, Arnold. *The Life of Langston Hughes, Volume I: 1902–1941; I, Too, Sing America.* Oxford: Oxford University Press, 2002.

———. *The Life of Langston Hughes, Volume II: 1941–1967; I Dream a World.* Oxford: Oxford University Press, 2002.

Randall, Dudley. "Melvin B. Tolson: Portrait of a Poet as a Raconteur." *Negro Digest* 15, no. 3 (January 1966): 54–57.

Ransom, John Crowe. "Criticism as Pure Speculation." In *The Intent of the Critic*, edited by Donald Stauffer, 89–124. Princeton, NJ: Princeton University Press, 1941.

———. "Reconstructed but Unregenerate." In *I'll Take My Stand: The South and the Agrarian Tradition*, 1–27. Baton Rouge: Louisiana State University Press, 2006.

Redding, J. Saunders. "Book Review: "Songs of Creations" Is a Refreshing Book of Poems." *Afro-American* (Baltimore), December 17, 1949.

Reddy, Chandan. *Freedom with Violence: Race, Sexuality, and the US State.* Durham, NC: Duke University Press, 2011.

Redmond, Shana L. *Everything Man: The Form and Function of Paul Robeson.* Durham, NC: Duke University Press, 2020.

Reed, Ishmael. *Japanese by Spring.* New York: Penguin Books, 1996.

Reuben, Julie A., and Linda Perkins. "Introduction: Commemorating the Sixtieth Anniversary of the President's Commission Report, 'Higher Education for Democracy.'" *History of Education Quarterly* 47, no. 3 (2007): 265–76.

Ripstein, Arthur. "Commodity Fetishism." *Canadian Journal of Philosophy* 17, no. 4 (1987): 733–48.

Rivington, Ann. "The George Washington Carver School." *Daily Worker* (New York), October 26, 1943.

Roberts, William Clare. *Marx's Inferno: The Political Theory of Capital.* Princeton, NJ: Princeton University Press, 2018.

Robinson, Cedric J. *Black Marxism: The Making of the Black Radical Tradition.* Chapel Hill, NC: University of North Carolina Press, 2000.

Roediger, David R. *The Wages of Whiteness: Race and the Making of the American Working Class.* London: Verso, 2007.

Roessel, David E. "'A Racial Act': The Letters of Langston Hughes and Ezra Pound." *Paideuma* 29, no. 1/2 (2000): 207–42.

Rubin, Andrew. *Archives of Authority: Empire, Culture, and the Cold War.* Princeton, NC: Princeton University Press, 2012.

Saunders, Frances Stonor. *The Cultural Cold War: The CIA and the World of Arts and Letters*. New York: New Press, 2001.

Schrecker, Ellen. *No Ivory Tower: McCarthyism and the Universities*. New York: Oxford University Press, 1986.

Schryer, Stephen. *Fantasies of the New Class: Ideologies of Professionalism in Post–World War II American Fiction*. New York: Columbia University Press, 2011.

Schultz, Kathy Lou. *The Afro-Modernist Epic and Literary History: Tolson, Hughes, Baraka*. New York: Palgrave Macmillan, 2013.

Schuyler, George S. "Views and Reviews." *Pittsburgh Courier*, March 29, 1952.

Schwartz, Lawrence H. *Creating Faulkner's Reputation: The Politics of Modern Literary Criticism*. Knoxville: University of Tennessee Press, 1988.

Shapiro, Edward S. "The Southern Agrarians, H. L. Mencken, and the Quest for Southern Identity." *American Studies* 13, no. 2 (1972): 75–92.

Siebers, Tobin. *Cold War Criticism and the Politics of Skepticism*. New York: Oxford University Press, 1993.

Singh, Nikhil Pal. *Black Is a Country: Race and the Unfinished Struggle for Democracy*. Cambridge, MA: Harvard University Press, 2004.

"Six Directors Quit the Carver School." *New York Times*, December 18, 1943.

Smethurst, James Edward. *The New Red Negro*. New York: Oxford University Press, 1999.

Smith, William Jay. "Performers and Poets." *Sewanee Review* 58, no. 3 (July 1950): 527–38.

Sorentino, Sara-Maria. "The Abstract Slave: Anti-Blackness and Marx's Method." *International Labor and Working-Class History* 96 (2019): 17–37.

Spahr, Juliana. *Du Bois's Telegram: Literary Resistance and State Containment*. Cambridge, MA: Harvard University Press, 2018.

Spence, Lester K. *Knocking the Hustle: Against the Neoliberal Turn in Black Politics*. Brooklyn, NY: Punctum Books, 2015.

Stein, Sharon. "A Colonial History of the Higher Education Present: Rethinking Land-Grant Institutions through Processes of Accumulation and Relations of Conquest." *Critical Studies in Education*, 2017, 1–17.

Strohl, Nicholas M. "The Truman Commission and the Unfulfilled Promise of American Higher Education." PhD dissertation, University of Wisconsin–Madison, 2018.

Szalay, Michael. *Hip Figures: A Literary History of the Democratic Party*. Stanford, CA: Stanford University Press, 2012.

Tate, Allen. *Memoirs and Opinions: 1926–1974*. Chicago: Swallow Press, 1975.

———. "Narcissus as Narcissus." In *Essays of Four Decades*, 593–607. Wilmington, DE: ISI Books, 1999.

———. "A Note on Autotelism." *Kenyon Review* 11, no. 1 (January 1949): 13–16.

———. Preface to *Libretto for the Republic of Liberia*, by Melvin B. Tolson. New York: Twayne Press, 1953.

———. "Present Function of Literary Criticism." In *Essays of Four Decades*, 197–210. Wilmington, DE: ISI Books, 1999.

Taylor, Keeanga-Yamahtta. *Race for Profit: How Banks and the Real Estate Industry Undermined Black Homeownership*. Chapel Hill: University of North Carolina Press, 2019.

Thelin, John R. *A History of American Higher Education*. Baltimore: Johns Hopkins University Press, 2004.

Thompson, Craig. "Here's Where Our Young Commies Are Trained." *Saturday Evening Post*, March 12, 1949.

Tolson, Melvin B. "E. & O. E." In *"Harlem Gallery" and Other Poems of Melvin B. Tolson*, edited by Raymond Nelson, 134–49. Charlottesville: University Press of Virginia, 1999.

———. "Harlem Gallery: Book I, The Curator." In *"Harlem Gallery" and Other Poems of Melvin B. Tolson*, edited by Raymond Nelson, 207–363. Charlottesville: University Press of Virginia, 1999.

———. "Libretto for the Republic of Liberia." In *"Harlem Gallery" and Other Poems of Melvin B. Tolson*, edited by Raymond Nelson, 158–206. Charlottesville: University Press of Virginia, 1999.

Twelve Southerners. "Introduction: A Statement of Principles." In *I'll Take My Stand*, xli–lii. Baton Rouge: Louisiana State University Press, 2005.

Underwood, Thomas A. *Allen Tate: Orphan of the South*. Princeton, NJ: Princeton University Press, 2003.

United States. *Higher Education for American Democracy: A Report of the President's Commission on Higher Education, Washington, December 1947*. Washington: Government Printing Office, 1947.

US Congress. House of Representatives. Committee on Un-American Activities. *Communist Training Operations*. 86th Cong., 1st. sess., 1959. H. Rep, 965–1068.

US Congress. Senate. Permanent Subcommittee on Investigations of the Committee on Government Operations. *Executive Sessions of the Senate Permanent Subcommittee on Investigations of the Committee on Government Operations*, 83rd Cong., 1st sess., March 24, 1953.

Valien, Preston. "The Growth and Distribution of the Negro Population in the United States." *Journal of Negro Education* 22, no. 3 (1953): 242–49.

Vitalis, Robert. *White World Order, Black Power Politics: The Birth of American International Relations*. Ithaca, NY: Cornell University Press, 2017.

Von Eschen, Penny M. *Race against Empire: Black Americans and Anticolonialism, 1937–1957*. Ithaca, NY: Cornell University Press, 1997.

Wagner, Bryan. *Disturbing the Peace: Black Culture and the Police Power after Slavery*. Cambridge, MA: Harvard University Press, 2009.

Wald, Alan M. *American Night: The Literary Left in the Era of the Cold War*. Chapel Hill: University of North Carolina Press, 2014.

————. *Trinity of Passion: The Literary Left and the Antifascist Crusade.* Chapel Hill: University of North Carolina Press, 2014.

Walker, Anders. "Diversity's Strange Career: Recovering the Racial Pluralism of Lewis F. Powell Jr." *Santa Clara Law Review* 50, no. 3 (2010): 647–80.

Wallace, Maurice O. *Constructing the Black Masculine: Identity and Ideality in African American Men's Literature and Culture, 1775–1995.* Durham, NC: Duke University Press, 2002.

Wang, Dorothy J. *Thinking Its Presence: Form, Race, and Subjectivity in Contemporary Asian American Poetry.* Stanford, CA: Stanford University Press, 2015.

Warren, Austin. "The Achievement of Some Recent Critics." *Poetry* 77, no. 4 (January 1951): 239–43, 245.

Warren, Kenneth W. "Ralph Ellison and the Problem of Cultural Authority: The Lessons of Little Rock." In *Ralph Ellison and the Raft of Hope*, edited by Lucas E. Morel, 142–57. Lexington: University Press of Kentucky, 2004.

————. *What Was African American Literature?* Cambridge, MA: Harvard University Press, 2011.

Warren, Robert Penn. "The Briar Patch." In *I'll Take My Stand: The South and the Agrarian Tradition*, 246–64. Baton Rouge: Louisiana State University Press, 2006.

Washington, Mary Helen. "Alice Childress, Lorraine Hansberry, and Claudia Jones: Black Women Write the Popular Front." In *Left of the Color Line: Race, Radicalism, and Twentieth-Century Literature of the United States*, edited by Bill V. Mullen and James Smethurst, 183–204. Chapel Hill: University of North Carolina Press, 2003.

————. *The Other Blacklist: The African American Literary and Cultural Left of the 1950s.* New York: Columbia University Press, 2014.

Watkins, Evan. *Work Time: English Departments and the Circulation of Cultural Value.* Stanford, CA: Stanford University Press, 1989.

Webster, Grant. *The Republic of Letters: A History of Postwar American Literary Opinion.* Baltimore: Johns Hopkins University Press, 1979.

Weheliye, Alexander G. *Habeas Viscus: Racializing Assemblages, Biopolitics, and Black Feminist Theories of the Human.* Durham, NC: Duke University Press, 2014.

Weigand, Kate. *Red Feminism: American Communism and the Making of Women's Liberation.* Baltimore: Johns Hopkins University Press, 2001.

Wellek, René. "The New Criticism: Pro and Contra." *Critical Inquiry* 4, no. 4 (July 1978): 611–24.

Wilder, Craig Steven. *Ebony & Ivy: Race, Slavery, and the Troubled History of America's Universities.* New York: Bloomsbury Press, 2013.

Wilford, Hugh. *The Mighty Wurlitzer: How the CIA Played America.* Cambridge, MA: Harvard University Press, 2009.

"Wilkerson Appointed." *Afro-American* (Baltimore). January 31, 1948.

Wilkerson, Doxey A. "The Douglass Center." *Daily Worker* (New York). March 23, 1953.

———. "The Negro and the American Nation." *Political Affairs* 25 (July 1946): 652–68.

———. "Negro Culture: Heritage and Weapon." *Masses & Mainstream* 2, no. 8 (August 1949): 3–24.

Winant, Howard. *The World Is a Ghetto: Race and Democracy since World War II*. New York: Basic Books, 2001.

Woods, Clyde Adrian. *Development Arrested: The Blues and Plantation Power in the Mississippi Delta*. London: Verso, 2000.

Woods, Jeff R. *Black Struggle, Red Scare: Segregation and Anti-Communism in the South, 1948–1968*. Baton Rouge: Louisiana State University Press, 2003.

Wright, Richard. *Black Boy: (American Hunger): A Record of Childhood and Youth*. New York: HarperPerennial, 2006.

Wynter, Sylvia. "No Humans Involved: An Open Letter to My Colleagues." *Forum N.H.I.: Knowledge for the 21st Century* 1, no. 1 (Fall 1994): 42–74.

———. "On How We Mistook the Map for the Territory and Re-Imprisoned Ourselves in Our Unbearable Wrongness of Being, of Désêtre: Black Studies toward the Human Project." In *Not Only the Master's Tools: African-American Studies in Theory and Practice*, edited by Lewis R. Gordon and Jane Anna Gordon, 107–69. Boulder, CO: Paradigm Publishers, 2006.

———. "Unsettling the Coloniality of Being/Power/Truth/Freedom: Towards the Human, after Man, Its Overrepresentation; An Argument." *CR: The New Centennial Review* 3, no. 3 (2003): 257–337.

Young, Thomas Daniel. "The Little Houses against the Great." *Sewanee Review* 88, no. 2 (1980): 320–30.

Index

Civil Rights Congress, 19

civil rights movement, 4, 113, 114, 152, 162

Civil War, 35, 74, 76, 81

Clark, Tom H., 139

close reading, 32, 33, 48, 52, 77

Cohn, Roy, 108, 109, 111–15

Cold War, 44, 47, 53, 54, 61, 97, 124; and "Cultural Cold War," 32, 99

Colon, Jesus, 157

Columbia University, 64, 134

Combahee River Collective, 16

Committee for the Negro in the Arts (CNA), 157

commodity fetish, 33

communism: Agrarians and fear of, 4, 24, 35, 46; and Black scholars, 93, 143; and Black writers, 9, 60, 102–3, 117; and the Cold War, 32, 42, 44, 52; Robin D. G. Kelley and historiography of, 10; and labor schools, 153, 161, 169; and McCarthyism, 108, 109; and *The Narrows* (Petry), 116–18, 121; and the university, 134, 174; and *Youngblood* (Killens), 162. *See also* anticommunism; Communist Party USA (CPUSA)

Communist Party USA (CPUSA): and Black intellectual life, 12, 29; historiography of, 9; and interracial solidarity, 117, 196n14; and the labor schools, 56, 129, 134, 135, 140; and the "Negro Question," 10, 11; and the Popular Front, 127, 141; and the Scottsboro Boys case, 96, 158; and the Second Red Scare, 103

Conant, James Bryant, 50

concrete universal, 46–48, 52

context (in literary criticism), 98, 112

Cooper, Mark Garrett, 50, 51

Cooper, Melinda, 3

Council on African Affairs, 137, 157

Cox, Oliver Cromwell, 137, 168; and *Caste, Class, and Race,* 74, 75, 87; and *The Foundations of Capitalism,* 67, 68,

73; and Melvin B. Tolson, 7, 80, 82, 89, 193n50

Crane, Hart, 72

creative writing, 100, 135, 154

criminalization, 24, 75, 118–20, 122

Crosscup, Richard, 153

Cruse, Harold: and anticommunism, 9, 10, 142–44, 161–62; and *Harlem Quarterly,* 103; and the suppression of Black radical critique, 15, 104

Cullen, Countee, 64, 90, 154, 160

cultural unification, 32, 49, 50, 53, 128

Daily Worker (newspaper), 112, 135, 138, 159, 160

Davidson, Donald, 25, 38

Davis, Angela, 15, 172

Davis, Ben, 2, 137

Delany, Hubert, 11

Democratic Party, 42, 43

Denning, Michael, 21

Detroit (Michigan), 74, 76, 77, 79, 80, 81, 157, 182n31

Dirksen, Everett, 107, 108, 115

diversity, 11, 22, 48–50, 53, 86, 138, 189n70

"Dixie" (song), 35

Dixiecrats, 43, 45

double consciousness, 70–72, 82

Douglas, Aaron, 154, 155

Douglass, Frederick, 12, 113, 114, 130, 146, 163

Douglass Educational Center, 132, 140, 144, 157–59, 168, 170, 174

Drake, St. Clair, 93

Du Bois, W. E. B., 132; and the Agrarians, 36; on art, 1, 123; and the Black radical tradition, 7, 8, 13, 89, 91, 150; and *Black Reconstruction,* 35, 73, 128, 163; and the Civil War, 74, 76; and the "color line," 65, 86, 193n33; and the Council on African Affairs, 137; and decolonial movements, 82, 85; and double consciousness, 66, 70–73; government persecution of,

Murphy, Paul V., 36

music: and blues epistemologies, 9, 194n75; and Ralph Ellison, 117; and people's schools, 135, 137, 151, 154; and Paul Robeson, 60, 61; and Melvin B. Tolson, 85–87

Myrdal, Gunnar, 19, 20, 74, 75, 82, 87, 144, 167, 168

NAACP, 153, 200n7

narcissism, 1, 77

Nashville (Tennessee), 118, 119; and the Agrarians, 35, 37, 39, 41, 100, 119; and Langston Hughes, 96, 97, 116, 118; and Vanderbilt University, 25, 101

National Negro Congress (NNC), 11, 131, 152

National United Committee to Free Angela Davis, 15

Native Son (Wright), 155

"Negro Question, the," 10, 131, 137, 142, 156, 164, 204n88

Negro Woman, The (Catlett), 151, 152

Negro Women Incorporated, 13, 117

Negro Writers Conference of the American Society of African Culture (AMSAC), 103

Nemeth, Julian, 140

New Criticism, 103, 105; and the Agrarians, 36, 38; and anticommunism, 53, 198n49; and Black critique of, 7, 14, 16, 17; and the Bollingen Prize controversy, 54–61; and the Cold War US state, 18, 29, 32, 42, 43; and commodity fetishism, 33, 34, 54; death of, 185n75; and democracy, 48; and Lorraine Hansberry, 123; and the Harvard Redbook, 51; and the history of literary studies, 26, 27, 31; and Langston Hughes, 30, 92–101, 103–6, 108, 110, 191n105; and institutional context of, 13; and isolation of literary object from social context, 3; and the management of difference, 49, 50; and "objectivity,"

168; and the postwar university, 22, 23, 25, 185n68; and racial liberalism, 6, 104, 116, 125, 129, 130; and racism, 2, 4; resistance to in labor schools, 1, 132, 144, 147; and suppression of Black critique of, 15; and Melvin B. Tolson, 63–65, 68, 69, 78, 79, 80, 82, 83, 85

Newfield, Christopher, 50, 185n62

New Masses (magazine), 96, 103

New Negro, The (anthology), 152

New York Intellectuals, 50

New York University, 153

Nielsen, Aldon, 64

North, Joseph, 26, 50

"Ode to the Confederate Dead" (Tate), 74, 76, 77, 81, 82

Office of Strategic Services, 53

Page, Myra, 137

Panther and the Lash, The (Hughes), 105, 114

Parker, Dorothy, 137

Parker, Hershel, 23

Partisan Review (literary magazine), 56, 58, 97

Patterson, Frederick Douglass, 45, 137

Patterson, Louise Thompson, 10, 15, 130, 141, 153, 157

Payne, E. George, 153

Peabody College, 101, 122

pedagogy, 17, 128, 130, 131, 148, 154, 155, 161, 169

People's Voice, 117

Perry, Pettis, 137

Perspectives USA (magazine), 97, 98, 99, 100

Petry, Ann, 2, 3, 13, 117, 118, 120, 122–25, 171, 174

philanthropy, 130, 131, 201n17

Phylon (journal), 91–94, 101–6, 117

Pisan Cantos (Pound), 54

Pittsburgh Courier (newspaper), 140

Play School Association Project, 13

Tolson, Melvin B. (*cont.*)
79, 80; and W. E. B. Du Bois, 66, 70,
71; and the Fisk University Black
writers' conference of 1966, 90;
and *Harlem Gallery*, 62, 64, 67; and
Libretto for the Republic of Liberia,
63, 72, 80, 83–88; and "Ode to the
Confederate Dead" (Tate), 81, 82;
relationship with Allen Tate, 65, 68,
69; and unpublished essay "Excerpts
from a Letter to Allen Tate," 73, 74,
76–78, 83
Trilling, Lionel, 97–99
triple exploitation, 15, 141, 153
Trotskyism, 140, 162
Truman, Harry, 43, 44, 139
Truman Commission, 45, 50–52, 127,
129
Tubman, William, 83
Tuskegee Institute, 45

Uncle Remus, 74–76
undercommons, 27–28, 93–94, 110,
173–74
Understanding Poetry (Brooks and
Warren), 31, 38, 41
universalism, 41, 53, 68, 69; and Black
literary debates, 41, 91, 92, 102, 124;
and the "concrete universal," 46, 47,
49, 52; and Langston Hughes, 93–
95, 104–6, 119, 120; and the "Negro
problem," 20; and New Criticism, 3,
46, 147; and Ann Petry, 122, 123; and
"race-neutrality," 21, 40; and radical
pedagogy, 147–50, 167, 171; and Western philosophical tradition, 37; and
Melvin B. Tolson, 85, 86; and Western historiography, 89
university, the, 3–8, 11, 14, 16, 17, 19,
21–28, 33, 38, 43; and abolitionist
university studies, 173, 175, 176; and
anticommunism, 131, 133, 134, 139,
140, 153; and Black studies, 130, 157,
159; and creative writing pedagogy,
145; formation of, 58; and labor

schools, 2, 126, 132, 135, 145, 169, 171;
and legitimation, 86; and the management of difference, 50; and New
Criticism, 47, 48, 95, 101, 167, 168;
and racial capitalism, 128, 129, 171;
and radical campus movements,
172; and racial liberalism, 93; and
the undercommons, 93, 110, 174
University of California, San Diego,
172
University of Virginia, 25
US Department of Education, 127

Vanderbilt University, 25, 96, 97, 101
Vitalis, Robert, 132
Voläpuk, 85, 86

Wagner, Bryan, 75
Wald, Alan, 11
Walker, Margaret, 90
Warren, Austin, 58
Warren, Kenneth, 91, 92, 117
Warren, Robert Penn, 147; and *I'll
Take My Stand*, 24, 35, 36; and the
Library of Congress, 48, 55; and
New Criticism, 1, 23; racism of,
97, 147; and *Understanding Poetry*,
31, 33, 38; and *Who Speaks for the
Negro?*, 78
Washington, Booker T., 24, 160, 163
Washington, DC, 55, 72, 73, 97, 107, 162,
163, 169
Washington, George, 81
Washington, Mary Helen, 11, 44, 91,
92, 104, 134
Webster, Grant, 55
Welles, Orson, 155
Wheatley, Phyllis, 24, 159, 161
White, Charles, 2, 136, 137, 150
White, Walter, 153
white chauvinism, 164, 203n72
whiteness, 120; and anticommunism,
5; and Black criticism, 17; and liter-
ary studies, 29; and New Criticism,
36, 63, 69, 119; and personhood, 122;